ISBN 978-1-333-31791-1
PIBN 10489156

# 1 MONTH OF
# FREE
# READING

## at

## www.ForgottenBooks.com

By purchasing this book you are eligible for one month membership to ForgottenBooks.com, giving you unlimited access to our entire collection of over 700,000 titles via our web site and mobile apps.

To claim your free month visit: www.forgottenbooks.com/free489156

English
Français
Deutsche
Italiano
Español
Português

# www.forgottenbooks.com

**Mythology** Photography **Fiction**
Fishing Christianity **Art** Cooking
Essays Buddhism Freemasonry
Medicine **Biology** Music **Ancient**
**Egypt** Evolution Carpentry Physics
Dance Geology **Mathematics** Fitness
Shakespeare **Folklore** Yoga Marketing
**Confidence** Immortality Biographies
Poetry **Psychology** Witchcraft
Electronics Chemistry History **Law**
Accounting **Philosophy** Anthropology
Alchemy Drama Quantum Mechanics
Atheism Sexual Health **Ancient History**
**Entrepreneurship** Languages Sport
Paleontology Needlework Islam
**Metaphysics** Investment Archaeology
Parenting Statistics Criminology
**Motivational**

# THE GAME
# OF LIFE

## REAL-IZED BY

## TIMOTHY LEARY, Ph.D.

Starring
The 24 Stages of Your Neurological Tarot

Directed by Covert Activities/Robert Clark
Written by Timothy Leary
Historical and Scholarly Scripts by Robert Anton Wilson
Edited by Arel Lucas
Adapted from a Musical Comedy by Barbara Leary
Special Video Effects by George Di Caprio and Peter Von Sholly
Graphics by Robert Clark

Volume V of the FUTURE HISTORY SERIES

1993
NEW FALCON PUBLICATIONS
PHOENIX, ARIZONA U.S.A.

International Standard Book Number: 1-58184-050-5

Library of Congress Catalog Card Number: 79-02283


First Edition (Peace Press) 1979
Second Edition (New Falcon) 1993


NEW FALCON PUBLICATIONS
655 East Thunderbird
Phoenix, Arizona 85022 U.S.A.

# EDITORIAL

This is an important book to those of us who wish to understand and participate in the acceleration of our own evolution and that of our divergent human family.

The science of exo-psychology, which analyzes human affairs from an extraterrestrial (future) viewpoint, here links up with ancient, pre-scientific psychologies which were so futique that they all but disappeared into the occult (meaning "hidden") traditions, and have suffered distortions and loss to the scientific community until now.

Before you read how Dr. Leary relates the 22 trumps of the Medieval Tarot deck, the 12 "sun signs" of astrology and the 8 trigrams of the Chinese Book of Changes (*I Ching*) to the evolving periodic table (here spiral) of elements, the ethological concept of castes, and, most important, to the next quantum leap in human consciousness (as well as the next several down the line), I want to back up a bit and reiterate two basic principles of exo-psychology.

*Recapitulation*—that ontogeny repeats phylogeny. This concept is easily demonstrated in the development of the human embryo (which at various times has gills and a tail), but seldom extended to the whole lifespan of the individual as here. You will find in *Game of Life*, as in *Intelligence Agents* and *Exo-psychology*, not only the idea that evolution is proceeding into pre-programmed post-human stages which will carry us off this planet, but also that some human beings are (have always been) literally ahead of their times in having activated what Dr. Leary calls "circuits" of their nervous systems years or even centuries ahead of general human development. Recapitulation is thus only a part of a genetic process which throws ("castes") out tutique as well as antique forms. This would explain the development pre-scientifically of concepts now being explored in such modern sciences as human ethology (sociobiology) and quantum physics.

*Imprinting*—The idea that during preprogrammed periods in an individual's development the organism is open to fixating on certain behaviors is still mainly confined to animal psychology (Konrad Lorenz). That this might extend to human behaviors is only now being investigated by such researchers as Dr. Marshall Klaus of Cleveland and psychologist Donna Kontos of Toronto, who appear to be amassing evidence that human infants (and mothers) experience a period of heightened suggestibility following birth in which both baby and mother will imprint each other as love/care objects—or in which both gain the impression, through hospital procedures, that the other is not really there for hir.

If you put these two ideas together, you can see the possibility that, from a genetic point of view, a whole species might experience periods of great suggestibility during which it might make great leaps ahead in intelligence—learn to make fire, develop a planetary perspective.

The timeliness of this book is in the context of the dominance in Southern California—the last terrestrial frontier—of what Dr. Leary once called "suntanned, graceful, sensory-equipped, yogic" Fifth Circuit (see Part III) individuals. As a result of his insight that this flowering of beauty and self-actualization is not the end of human evolution (nor a mere sign of Western decadence), Dr. Leary points to the next step—a fusion of human energies to lift life off the planet and thus open up the ecological and economic system of Sol 3. The human species is accelerating to escape velocity.

What kind of transmission would be most helpful in facilitating the exploration of human communities tolerant and knowledgeable enough to withstand the accleration/radiation of post-terrestrial individuals? One answer lies in human ethology: in the exo-psychological concept of seasonally varied genetic differences in human nervous systems. Exo-psychology's success in prediction is backed by Dr. Leary's career of anticipating the movements of human consciousness.

And your success in surfing the evolutionary waves to come may be dependent on the extent to which you understand the concepts presented here. As for comprehending Dr. Leary's work, I'll give you George Koopman's advice: read each sentence as though it were a paragraph.

Now: surf's up! (Serfs are down! T.L.)

—Arel Lucas

# THE GAME OF LIFE
## By Timothy Leary

## INDEX OF TRANSMISSIONS

THIS BOOK, THE GAME OF LIFE

AIMS TO ACTIVATE THE BRAIN CIRCUITS

WHICH ARE ENGAGED BY THE <u>NATIONAL ENQUIRER</u>

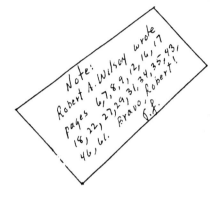

The <u>National Enquirer</u>
is the largest publication
in the world.

It combines shocking-scandal
with a vulgar, teasing appeal
to those genetic solutions
which the American gene-pool
expects science to provide·

contact with Post-terrestrial
Intelligence (U.F.O.s)

rejuvenation, life-extension,
aids to health and beauty

genetic control (cloning)

The <u>National Enquirer</u> is low-down
and far out.  Imprecise and tacky

THIS BOOK ALSO ATTEMPTS TO BE

SHOCKING, LOW-DOWN AND FAR-OUT

WITH SCIENTIFIC PRECISION AND PHILOSOPHIC ELEGANCE

THE MARGINAL INSERTS AND CARTOON ASIDES

REPRESENT A VALIANT ATTEMPT TO WRENCH THE "FINAL CUT"

AWAY FROM THE PRINTER'S CONTROL

TO ALLOW THE AUTHORS AND AVAILABLE CRITICS

TO HAVE THE LAST WORD BEFORE THE BOOK IS PRESSED FROZEN.

WE HOPE THAT THE AESTHETIC COMPLICATIONS

DO NOT HIDE THE FACT THAT

THIS IS THE MOST IMPORTANT COMMUNICATION OF INFORMATION

EVER PUBLISHED.

SOME APOLOGETIC FORE-WORDS ABOUT PUBLICATION AND PUBLISHERS

> Publication: The communication of information
> to the public. (Public means gene-pool.)  Good
> publication, i.e. the accuracy and scope of the
> information provided a gene-pool, is thus of
> crucial survival importance.

HERE'S A TASTY PARADOX FOR STARTERS.

THIS BOOK,

(WHICH ASSERTS THAT NATURAL ELECTION,

I.E. AESTHETIC-EROTIC CHOICE,

IS THE KEY STRATEGY OF EVOLUTION...)

> Natural Election occurs at every
> level of energy exchange.
> Aesthetic choice determines who
> bonds with whom.
> For example, which, of many free
> electrons is invited (chosen) to
> enter into an atomic bond
>
> Aesdhetic choice determines the
> bondings involved in the evolution
> of the species and the individual.

IS AN ARTISTIC SHAMBLES.

WHY?

BUREAUCRATIC INERTIA
> It is the genetic function of
> bureaucracies to maintáin social
> control by limiting free erotic-
> aesthetic choice.

EACH VOLUME IN THIS FUTURE HISTORY SERIES:

> What Does WoMan Want?
> Exo —Psychology
> Neuropolitics
> The Intelligence Agents
> Game of Life

HAS ATTEMPTED TO BREAK THE "GUTENBERG LOCK"

> Control by printers of artist's
> singularity.

# PART I

*IT'S NOT A TABLE IT'S AN EXPANDING SPIRAL*

# THE PERIODIC TABLE IS THE SYSTEMATIC MODEL AND THE NERVOUS SYSTEM IS THE BASIC INSTRUMENT FOR STUDYING ENERGY AT ALL LEVELS OF EVOLUTION

| | | | | | | | | |
|---|---|---|---|---|---|---|---|---|
| Group 8: | Noble Gases | Ne | Ar | Kr | Xe | Rn | | |
| Group 7: | Halogen Gases | F | Cl | Br | I | At | | |
| Group 6: | Oxygen Family | O | S | Se | Te | Po | | |
| Group 5: | Nitrogen Family | N | P | As | Sb | Bi | | |
| Group 4: | Carbon Family | C | Si | Ge | Sn | Pb | | |
| Group 3: | Boron Family | B | Al | Ga | In | Tl | | |
| | | | | (Transition Metals) | | | | |
| Group 2: | Earth Metals | Be | Mg | Ca | Sr | Ba | Ra | |
| Group 1: | Alkali Metals | Li | Na | K | Rb | Cs | Fr | |

Post-terrestrial gases

Earth metals

*THIS ALL BECOMES CLEAR IN PART III*

# "BRAIN DID IT" SAYS INFORMER

*All events in nature, including human behavior, exist for us only as registered, recorded and mediated by the Brain.*

**THE NERVOUS SYSTEM IS THE INSTRUMENT FOR RECEIVING, INTEGRATING AND TRANSMITTING KNOWLEDGE. THE BRAIN IS THE CENTER, SOURCE AND SOLE TRANSCEIVING INSTRUMENT OF CONSCIOUSNESS, LEARNING, MEMORY, BEHAVIOR, INTELLIGENCE AND PLEASURE**

ITS THE STATE NOT THE BRAIN THAT DOES ALL THIS

WE AGREE LEONID, DONT WORRY WE'LL QUASH THESE IDEAS

There is only one field of science and knowledge and that is Neurologic: the signals received, integrated-stored and transmitted by the nervous system.

All events in nature, including human behavior, exist for us only as registered, recorded and mediated by the Brain. The dimensions, variables, divisions, groupings, lawful relations defined by the sciences and all other fields of human endeavor are based on, filtered through, determined by the receptive, integrating and transmitting characteristics of the Brain.

EVERY BUREAUCRAT IS GONNA HATE THIS!

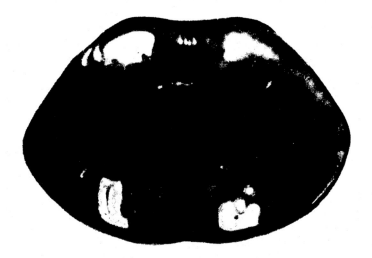

*Just as every natural science and every branch of
engineering has been revised, expanded and redefined in
the light of nuclear physics, so is it necessary to expand
and redefine every branch of human knowledge in the light
of the transmutational relativity and the re-imprint
capacities of the post-hive nervous system.*

Let us speak of the Einsteinianization of human knowledge by Neurologic.

One might object that this concept of the nervous system as relativistic center of sensation, perception, consciousness and intelligence is not new. Again we shall make the comparison with atomic physics. Democritus pointed out over two thousand years ago that all matter was composed of atoms, but in spite of this clue, Newtonian physics, which is neuro-muscular, disregarded the elemental energy-structure of matter. Assume that the larval symbolic mind, using the lower circuits of the nervous system, has, in exactly the same fashion, produced magnificent and complex systems of muscular thought in ignorance of the electro-chemical neural structure of con_sciousness and intelligence.

The Einsteinian formulae demonstrated the metamorphic relativity of energy, time and matter and made possible the transmutation of elements and the release of enormous energy by means of fission and fusion.

Symbols are Newtonian representations of reality created by laryngeal muscles (words) or by manual muscles (artifacts).

Neurologic studies the fluid, metamorphic, transmutational relativity of evolution, as experienced by those who have activated post-terrestrial brain circuits which fission and fuse symbols in new combinations.

WHO ME ??
A ROBOT ?!

YES, BUT
THATS IN-
APPROPRIATE
TO SAY TILL
AFTER NEW
HAMPSHIRE

# EVERYTHING EXISTS AS A NERVOUS SYSTEM

*Human beings are robots operationally programmed by*
*(1) neurogenetic templates, (2) neural imprints,*
*(3) social conditioning*

*Neuro-Ecology*, the study of the nervous system in relation to the environment, might be considered a basic science of which every other science is a sub-division.

Let *Neuro-Geology* be, for example, the study of how our knowledge of geological processes is limited and directed by the capacities of the evolving nervous system and how the nervous system is formed and influenced by geological forces.

Let *Neuro-Physics* be the study of how our knowledge of atomic and nuclear processes is limited and guided by the capacities of the evolving nervous system, by the genetic templating, by the neural imprinting and conditioning of the scientists who study these processes; and how the nervous system is formed and influenced by physical forces.

This list defining hyphenated sciences could continue for pages. *We are attempting to illustrate the fact that the basic instrument for receiving, observing, recording, storing, synthesizing and transmitting information about all fields of knowledge and branches of human activity is the nervous system, along with the extensions of the nervous system which have been designed by the nervous system, e.g., computers, electronics, etc.*

It is obligatory in every scientific report to describe in great precision the instruments used to obtain the data and the methods used to analyze the data. Science has operated with inefficiency and shortsightedness because of ignorance about the instrument used, i.e., the nervous system. Human beings (including scientists) are larval robots operationally programmed by 1) genetic templates, 2) neural imprints, and 3) social conditionings of which they have little knowledge.

# TIMOTHY LEARY

# EXO-PSYCHOLOGY

## A MANUAL ON THE USE OF THE HUMAN NERVOUS SYSTEM ACCORDING TO THE INSTRUCTIONS OF THE MANUFACTURERS

A description of the neuro-genetic blueprints which program and direct evolution, and the circuits of the nervous system, their function and the sequential nature of their emergence in the individual (and the species) is presented in the book *Exo-Psychology: Manual for the Use of the Nervous System According to the Instructions of the Manufacturers.*[1]

# INTELLIGENCE CLUES SOUGHT

## *Human beings come in very different models, wired with different brain circuits.*

*Exo-Psychology* suggests that a rudimentary understanding of the operation and management of the nervous system would clarify and enlighten every aspect of life—allowing human beings to decode the answers to the basic genetic questions:

> why are we here?
> where are we going?
> how do we get there?

It is time we had some answers to these riddles beyond the pompous (and unproven) dogmas of larval religion, the bland no-answer of Zen, or the humorous resignation of the wit who wrote:

> We're here because we're here
> because we're here
> because we're here.

And our answer must begin with examination of the instrument of investigation itself: the human brain.

Let us review our neurological ABC's. Nobody but the most naive would claim that a dog perceives the same room as his human companion. We know, for instance, that human beings differ from other animals in using vision more than smell to orient themselves; we use the vision circuitry of our brain as much as those quite distant relatives, the birds. The dog (like the wolf, tiger, hamster and other mammals) marks his territory by smell, identifies friend and foe by odor, lives in what would appear to us an incredibly rich and subtle olfactory continuum, and sees perhaps only two basic colors to our eight. The dog's nervous system, lacking the symbolic-linguistic circuits of ours, codes these mostly-olfactory signals into pre-linguistic categories, mostly keyed to immediate glandular-emotional response.

The mosquito flying in through the window has a very different brain circuitry and realizes a room different from that of either dog or WoMan.

Finally, since no two humans are alike in 1. genetic wiring 2. neural imprinting 3. social conditioning and learning, no two people ever "see" (smell, hear, taste, integrate) the "same" room. The Sufi parable of the twenty-four blind men and the elephant remains the paradigm of neurologic, reminding us that human beings come in very different models, wired with different brain circuits.

Now, this is more or less understood in optics, in general neurology, in semantics, etc., but we still tend to attribute a kind of universal reality to our very unique neural abstractions.

THIS IS GENETIC ELITISM!

In the terminology of Carlos Castaneda's books on Mexican shamanism, we live inside a "bubble" of concretized, extrojected abstractions and we mistake the "bubble" for consensual reality. Or, as Alan Watts said so charmingly, we are a weird bunch who can't tell the menu from the meal.

We do not regard our impressions as "part of ME," my creation, my logical-artistic map of the world with my thoughts and aesthetics woven into its very fabric. We can be shown, with optical and neurological diagrams, how the signal from the space-time event travels to our receptors and is transmitted through the unique circuitry of our nervous system, but we still retain the paradoxical feeling that the final sensory abstraction (our "perception" of the event) is more "real" than the energy-signals themselves.

We fear that accepting the proven scientific facts and redefining our concept of reality will plunge us into subjectivism, hippie Zen, agnosticism, loss of all standards, moral impotence, confusion. Or, if we can conquer this fear (which basically exists in confronting every new discovery) we still can't see the need for re-programming our circuits to remember, moment-by-moment, what is actually happening as we receive, code, classify, integrate energy signals. Thus, we voluntarily retain the lazy, inaccurate, unscientific assumption that it is reasonable and safe to continue acting as if the world were no more than our private map of it.

*Each human dyad is Robinson Crusoe and Friday,*
*two alien intelligences, groping for signals that can*
*transmit experiences across space-time.*

In a deeper sense, each DNA-robot abstracts via its unique nervous system a *seemingly* complete model of the universe. This model *seems* complete in that it is "whole," integrated, harmonious, includes all data consciously apprehended by the organism, meshes with continuous sensory input (or is rapidly revised), and is regarded as "real." The habit of treating this private model as if it were the universe is called *identification* by both Korzybski, the semanticist, and Gurdjieff, the "mystic." This habit produces reality dogmatism, reality intolerance, reality fanaticism.

Exo-psychology assumes. in evolutionary sequence, 8 circuits or 24 stages of neural integration. At each stage, the nervous system responds to different signals, recognizes different levels of energy and meaning, integrates a *new model of the universe*. On the primitive levels of development there is an inescapable tendency to make the identification: my model = universe. The primitive nervous system has no way of becoming "conscious of abstracting," no method of learning that the private model is not the universe. At later stages of neural evolution, this tendency still has to be battled, but is no longer irresistible. Yogis, shamans, alchemists, using primitive but direct reimprinting techniques, and modern scientists working in such diverse fields as optics, neurology, neurologic, semantics, relativity physics, bio-psychology, psychology, etc., can gradually become conscious of their own abstracting processes, recognize the relativity of nervous systems, and begin consciously evolving toward ever-higher modes of knowing and being.

We may write the equations

$R_1 = F$ (Stage 1)

$R_2 = F$ (Stage 2)
   etc.

$R_{24} = F$ (Stage 24)

where $R_1$, $R_2$, etc., to $R_{24}$ are the various Reality Models (or "maps" as the semanticists say), F as usual means "a function of" and Stage 1, Stage 2 . .  to Stage 24 are the evolutionary stages of the neurogenetic array. Each evolutionary stage produces its own functional model of the universe, according to the signals received, integrated and transmitted by the circuitry. Slot 3 (Taurus) cannot "share" the universe of Slot 12 (Aquarius) because the Caste 3 brain is wired differently from the Caste 14.

This theory is entirely general. My Stage 10 is never your Stage 10. We always have differences in genetic templating, neural imprinting, social conditioning and life experience. Learning, then, is endless. Each new nervous system with which we interlock, however briefly, can be a whole new learning-teaching experience. Each dyad is Robinson Crusoe and Friday, two Alien Intelligences, groping for signals that can transmit experiences across space-time.

*We search everywhere for it and all the while it is
carrying us about. It is our nervous system.*

PETE VON SHOLLY

This is the point of the old Sufi parable in which Mullah Nasrudin, the sage who always pretends to be a clown, races through town on his donkey. "Where are you going in such a hurry, Nasrudin?" the neighbors ask.

"I'm looking for my donkey!" he replies.

Like other Sufi jokes, this is intended to amuse the general population, receive wide circulation among both adults and children, and be in the memory-banks of any robot who turns up at a Sufi school seeking re-wiring. At some point in Hir training, then, the candidate will be told the joke-within-the-joke. The donkey represents the "magical technique," the "hidden knowledge," the "alchemical Elixir," the great "Philosopher's Stone" which gives wisdom to the adept. We search everywhere for It and all the while It is carrying us about. It is our nervous system.

The same epistemological hot-foot is contained in the Zen riddle, "Who is the movie Director who makes the grass green?"

# Chessboard
# of
# Evolution

| Group 8:<br>Noble Gases | | Ar | | Xe | | | | |
| Group 7:<br>Halogen<br>Gases | F | | Br | | At | | | |
| Group 6:<br>Oxygen<br>family | | S | | Te | | | | |
| Group 5:<br>Nitrogen<br>family | N | | As | | Bi | | | |
| Group 4:<br>Carbon<br>family | | Si | | Sn | | | | |
| Group 3:<br>Boron family | B | | Ga | | Tl | | TRANSITION METALS | |
| Group 2:<br>Earth Metals | | Mg | | Sr | | Ra | | |
| Group 1:<br>Alkali<br>Metals | Li | | K | | Cs | | | |

I THOUGHT CHESS WAS A WAR GAME!

10

ROOKS AND CROOKS EH HANK?

# THE PERIODIC TABLE OF ELEMENTS IS A TAROT ARRAY WHICH ARRANGES THE CHEMICAL ELEMENTS IN ORDER OF ATOMIC NUMBERS THUS REVEALING A SYSTEMATIC VARIATION IN THEIR PROPERTIES

The Periodic Table of Chemical Elements was first described in 1868 by the Russian, Dmitri Mendeleyev.*

Before Mendeleyev the elements and compounds of inorganic chemistry were disorganized and chemical theory was based on diffuse, unsystematic experimentation.

All matter "however dissimilar in shape, look or purpose—[is] made up, in one compound or another, of only 88 natural elements . . . This limited larder of materials has produced the infinite variety of things by which man lives in much the same way a 26-letter alphabet has provided the enormous array of words by which he communicates: through differing combinations, arrangements, and juxtapositions. . . ."[2]

A great scientific achievement of the mid 18th century was the classification of biological families by Carolus Linnaeus. Taxonomy always precedes evolutionary revelation at any level of energy. Thus we see how the conscientious species classification of Linnaeus provided Darwin with the raw material from which he deduced the evolution of genetic families interacting with each other.

A great achievement of the mid 19th century was the classification of chemical elements by Mendeleyev. Like Linnaeus, Dimitri discovered that each element is a species grouped into families, division and classes. Each element being defined by its interpersonal interactions with members of other species.

The taxonomy of Mendeleyev made possible the insights of the 20th century physicists that chemical elements evolve and mutate.

We now understand that each of the natural and each of the experimentally produced elements is a species and belongs to a family. The octave arrangement of the Periodic Table goes from the down-to-earth metals up to the "noble" gases.

When Mendeleyev began his task of classification 65 elements had been defined. But the elements were a jungle of disorder and no taxonomic principles existed for relating and predicting elements and their familial interaction. Chemistry was in the position of biology before Linnaeus and psychology today. What was needed was an ordering principle, a taxonomic system which would logically and empirically relate the bewildering diversity.

The Periodic Table of Elements which is known to every school child is the result of Mendeleyev's intuitive genius. The realization that this periodic ordering of elements in terms of their atomic weight is also a description of the evolution of matter and corresponds in an uncanny way with the periodic rhythm of the evolution of biological species.

The central thesis of this manual is that the classic alchemical-philosophic systems (including I Ching, Tarot, Zodiac, Chess) are expressions of the ordinal-sequence of energy-matter as codified in the Periodic Table of Elements.

*Actually, the basic structure of the Periodic Table was announced by the English chemist, J.A.R. Newland, 4 years earlier. He was laughed at in a public meeting of the Royal Society and roundly rejected, evidently because the eight-part division of the table recalled the attempt of Pythagoras to relate all physical laws to the 8 notes (octave) of the musical scale and thereby suggested "mysticism."

Dmitri all smiles as he receives prize for neuro-cryptography

# MENDELEYEV GIVES KEY TO LIFE PLAN

A grab-bag of unrelated facts does not define a science any more than a heap of bricks and lumber constitutes a house. It is the artistic achievement of the scientific de-coder to sift the facts into coherence, order, *structure;* just as it is the scientific discipline of the architect to let his building materials fuse into a dwelling machine. Many theoretical structures are possible, but only a few mesh with the actual energy-structure of the universe. If the scientist's map is as bizarre as Korzybski's hypothetical Dresden-Paris-Warsaw example, future researchers will find it misleading and wasteful of effort. If the architect's structure falls to harmonize with the Laws of Energy, the house will fall down.

The search for coherent order in the energy sciences, like the pursuit of harmony in art, is neuro-cryptography. Decoding the grand strategy of the Game of Life.

# THE EIGHT FAMILIES OF
# ELEMENTS ARE ARRANGED IN A RHYTHMIC, DIRECTIONAL SEQUENCE

So let us review, in personal, interpersonal and evolutionary terms, the Mendeleyev table.

Group 1: *The alkali metals.* The elements in this unstable family have only one electron in their outer shell. The one electron is easily lost, zapping off to fuse with other species. This family of metals is easily bound into molecules, heavy, terrestrial and is not found in the air or in space.

Group 2: *The alkaline earth metals.* The species in this family are "down-to earth." They are found in rocks, indeed, they are basic to geological formations—and are not found as frequently in the airy atmosphere.

Group 3: *The Boron family.* Here we deal with species which make up much of the earth's crust. They are trivalent (having three electrons in the outer layer) and thus combine easily with other species. We are again reminded of the defeotional tendency of the families of elements—they move from earth upward to the gaseous atmosphere.

Group 4: *The Carbon family.* With four electrons in the outer shell these elements combine wildly in a wide diversity of compounds. The carbons form organic molecules—almost twice as many compounds as all the other inorganic species. All living matter is organic, i.e. carbon derived. All living matter lives on the surface of the planet, which, as we have seen is formed of the alkaline, earth and boron families. The scum of film which covers the planet is carbon-based. The movement upward away from the earth's core is the direction of the periodic rhythm of matter.

Group 5: *The Nitrogen family.* Nitrogen is a gas and makes up 78% of our atmosphere. This family exists in many forms in nature—gaseous and solid. The movement upward-outward is thus continued. From the lightest (nitrogen) to the heaviest (bismuth) this family moves from non-metallic to metallic. We deal here with a group which is transitional from earth to heaven.

Group 6: *The Oxygen family.* These elements possess six electrons in their outer shells. They are both gaseous and solid—again representing the transition from earth-core to space.

Group 7: *The Halogens.* Fluorine and chlorine are gases. Bromine is a liquid at room temperature. We deal here with fast-moving species, spacey, super-terrestrial.

Group 8: *The Noble Gases.* Here is an aloof, haughty, aristocratic, "high" family that disdains to descend to form compounds with the earthy folk. The outer shell of these species are completely filled with electrons—so that they have no earthly needs to combine with other elements. Here the evolutionary trip—from earth core, to earth crust, to atmosphere to post-terrestrial status is completed.

THE BORONS SOUND JEWISH TO ME!

# HE LISTED ON CARDS ALL HE KNEW ABOUT EACH ELEMENT

We are, of course, interested in the psychology of Mendeleyev because it was his nervous system which first translated, integrated and transmitted the numerical key. Mendeleyev, we are told, arrived at his insight in the most "get-down," personal manner. He became friends with the elements whose nature he sought to understand. He studied their personality characteristics, literally psychoanalyzed their interactive tendencies, traced their "family" relations, probed the vicissitudes of their development. He experienced them!

It takes an unusually open, confident, we might even say *loving* person, to get synergistically involved with the external world in this fashion. To personalize, we are not surprised to learn that Dmitri Mendeleyev was, apparently, this sort of human—a lover, an active, sharing person, a committed participant in the risky libertarian events of his time. As is the case with almost every monumental alchemist-philosopher in history, he was in trouble with the law and risked imprisonment because of his liberal political and cultural lifestyle.

Most relevant to the theme of this book is the technique used by the Russian sage to organize his knowledge. *He listed on separate cards everything he knew about each element.* He carried the cards with him, continually sorting them in various arrangements, seeking the rhythmic sequence of relationship. He was often teased by his friends for centering his scientific activities on the game of "Patience," i.e., "Solitaire."

This book is an attempt to relate the *cards* of Mendeleyev to the cards of the Tarot.

---

*This book is an attempt to relate the cards of Mendeleyev to the cards of the Tarot.*

---

A sixteen month search leads Mendeieyev to a Swiss ski resort where he discovers Carbon and Chlorine.

The key to scientific understanding of natural laws—at every level of complexity—is to personalize the events; to experience them, to empathize with them.

The nervous system is the instrument for experiencing.

Neurons are composed of atoms and RNA-constructed organic molecules. The nervous system, thus has within its own structure, the elemental and molecular events which scientists study in the outside world.

Humans whose 5th, 6th, 7th and 8th circuits have been activated are able to directly experience

somatic
neurological
molecular
atomic-nuclear
} events.

The unfolding, evolving sequence of the chemical elements sets up an ordinal rhythm which must be related to cycles of evolution at more macroscopic levels.

If we can personalize, experience the elements as they evolve and as they interact with each other, we may understand not only chemistry but also the periodicity at the molecular-genetic and the neurogenetic levels.

Popularizers of modern science, in dramatizing the high velocities of the modern metamorphic-evolutionary view (in contrast to the ancient Aristotelian-Euclidean model of a static, rigid world) often refer to the "mad dance of atoms." This is inept semantic fumbling. The metamorphic dance of energy, as revealed in the 8 pirouettes of the Periodic Table, is elegant as any ballet. *Swan Lake* itself may look quite "mad" to a naive observer, before the rules, rhythms and periodicities are recognized.

15

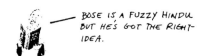

# MINERALS, PLANTS, ANIMALS, HUMANS, POST-HUMANS ALL DANCE TO THE SAME TUNE

As Korzybski notes in *Science and Sanity:*

> One of the most baffling problems has been the peculiar periodicity or rhythmicity which we find in life. Lately, Lillie and others have shown that this rhythmicity could not be explained by purely physical nor purely chemical means, but that it is satisfactorily explained when treated as a *physico-electro-chemical structural occurrence.* The famous experiments of Lillie, who used an iron wire immersed in nitric acid and reproduced, experimentally, a beautiful periodicity resembling closely some of the activities of *protoplasm and the nervous system,* show conclusively that both living and the non-living systems depend for their rhythmic behaviour on the chemically alterable film, which divides the electrically conducting phases. . . . In both systems, the electromotive characteristics of the surfaces are determined by the character of the film. . . .[3]

In his seminars, Korzybski stressed again and again that, if we are going to talk sense about human behavior, we must give up words like "mind" and "soul," which were borrowed from philosophers (who, being bankrupt, are in no position to loan anything); we must talk scientifically of the chemical, electrical and structural properties of the brain and of DNA which designed and constructed the brain.

In this connection, consider the long-neglected researches of Sir J.G. Bose, who demonstrated around the turn of the century that *reaction curves* in metals and living systems are often *mathematically identical.* "Further work began to convince Bose that the boundary line between so-called 'nonliving' metals and 'living' organisms was tenuous indeed. . . . When he chloroformed plants, Bose discovered that they were as successfully anesthetized as animals, and that when the narcotic vapor was blown away by fresh air like animals they revived." Bose also got similar curves on muscles and metals responding to the effects of fatigue or of stimulating, depressing and poisoning drugs.[4]

Sir Robert Austen, leading authority on metallurgy, also believed metals are "alive" and hinted at this before the Royal Society, but was rebuffed. He later defended Bose's researches vigorously.

Said Dr. Bose himself: "It was when I came upon the mute witness of these self-made records"—of metal, plant and animal response-patterns—"that I understood for the first time a little of that message proclaimed by my ancestors on the banks of the Ganges thirty centuries ago: 'They who see but one in all the changing manifold-ness of this universe, unto them belongs Eternal Truth—unto none else, unto none else!' "

DON'T WORRY ...
NO ONE WILL
UNDERSTAND THIS
BOOK.

THIS GUY WILL
PUT US
MONOTHEISTS
OUT OF BUSINESS!!

# ORDERED VARIETY AND
# SEQUENTIAL UNITY
# REPLACE BLAND HINDU
# "ALL IS ONE"

The danger of such pantheistic insights about the unity of nature is that they often freeze thought precisely where it is most illuminating and amusing to enquire further. *One* is a good place to start a number system, but an idiot-lazy place to stop. "All is One" has become such a platitude among the intellectually lethargic that it is necessary, today, to emphasize that the Game of Life involves both sequential unity *and* plurality, both binding serial coherence *and* infinite diversity, both eternal Law and eternal Play. intoning "All is One" adds nothing new to the human information pool and merely demonstrates that the intoner has taken the first and simplest step beyond conditioned consciousness (or else that SHe has learned to *parrot* a popular transmission from those who *have* taken the first post-larval step).[*]

YOU CAN'T
INSULT BABA RAM
DASS LIKE THAT!

[*]MYSTICISM. A systematic philosophy of anti-philosophy developed by premature post-larvale on backward planets. The science of mysticism always consists of some abnormal physiological stress leading to bio-chemical alteration of the nervous system and reception of signals usually screened out by social conditioning. However meager or incoherent the new data so received, primitives always over-estimate it as "Enlightenment," "Pure Mind," "Absolute Truth" or some such self-congratulatory and grandiose achievement. They then typically become aloof, condescending, dogmatic and fanatical, in various degrees. Mysticism did not begin to disappear until the early post-larval ages when systematic scientific study of neural function made all possible neurogenetic circuits available for systematic comparison and evaluation. See "Transcendental Masturbation," "Dogma," "Primate Psychology."

WEBSTER'S GALACTIC DICTIONARY
23rd Edition

17

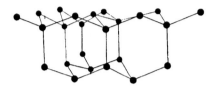

This metamorphic octave apparently defines the rhythm of all matter—on Earth and throughout the galaxies. If there is any code, any basic pattern to life it must surely be based on or relate to this eightfold sequence.

This book explores the possibility that the eightfold rhythm of the Periodic Table defines the metamorphic course of neurogenetic evolution—earthly and post-terrestrial. And, the possibility that the Periodic Table is the basis for the great systems of neurogenetic philosophy which have been passed on from antiquity in the code-form of:

> *The Tri-Octave Systems* (24)
> The Tarot
> The Greco-Roman Pantheon
> The Hebrew Alphabet
> The Zodiac (Zodiac I + Zodiac II)
> The Backgammon Board
> The Playing Card Deck

> *The Octave Systems* (64)
> The I Ching
> The Chess Board

We recall that the Periodic Table is not a static system. The elements evolve through the atomic numbers. They decay, fission, fuse, link-up. The Periodic Table is an evolutionary, metamorphic array.

Using this clue we shall study the alchemical-philosophic system of Tarot to see if it expresses a metamorphic system, an evolutionary code.

A second clue is provided by the February 19, 1979, issue of *Brain/Mind Bulletin,* in which the question is raised, "Why are all the elements involved in biological systems—calcium, magnesium, potassium, for example—adjacent in the periodic table of elements?" Quoting recent research by Louis Kevran, Histoki Komaki and Frederic Jueneman, the article suggests that these elements "may have been transmuted from one another" and that "Such a transmutation obviously would have great significance for evolutionary theory," since it implies a derivation of organic chemicals from metallic chemicals—much as we would expect from the research of Bose and Lillie already mentioned.

Another line of investigation, by such physicists as Dr. Nick Herbert, Dr. Jack Sarfatti and Saul Paul Sirag, suggests a similar continuity between the sub-microscopic quantum jumping of the inner-atomic world and "macroscopic quantum behavior" of living systems—e.g. the rhythmic staccato of crickets' chirping, the migratory habits of various species, the mutational cycles of insects and of nervous systems, etc. In all of these periodicities we see *structure* as a basic fact not in space but in space-time.

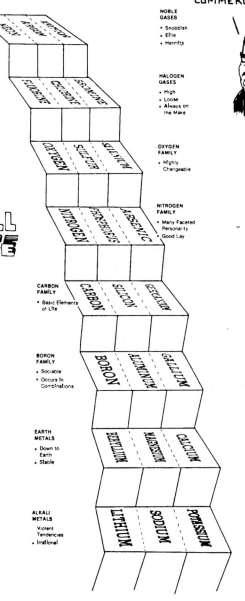

**KAΓ××!!** IS THIS AN <u>ARTHUR MURRAY</u> COMMERCIAL?!

THIS IS THE STAIRWAY OF EVOLUTION UP WHICH WE ALL DANCE

**NOBLE GASES**
- Snobbish
- Elite
- Hermits

**HALOGEN GASES**
- High
- Loose
- Always on the Make

**OXYGEN FAMILY**
- Highly Changeable

**NITROGEN FAMILY**
- Many Faceted Personality
- Good Lay

**CARBON FAMILY**
- Basic Elements of Life

**BORON FAMILY**
- Sociable
- Occurs in Combinations

**EARTH METALS**
- Down to Earth
- Stable

**ALKALI METALS**
- Violent Tendencies
- Irrational

NEON ARGON KRYPTON

FLUORINE CHLORINE BROMINE

OXYGEN SULFUR SELENIUM

NITROGEN PHOSPHORUS ARSENIC

CARBON SILICON GERMANIUM

BORON ALUMINUM GALLIUM

BERYLLIUM MAGNESIUM CALCIUM

LITHIUM SODIUM POTASSIUM

YEAH!!

# THE GAME OF LIFE HAS BEEN DECODED SLOWLY, SERENDIPITOUSLY AND MOSTLY BY PERSONS UNAWARE OF WHAT THEY WERE SAYING

While Mendeleyev was bringing order into the busy, buzzing world of molecular metamorphoses, a shy, timid hypochondriac, biased by a dozen varieties of racism, sexism and monotheistic chauvinism but gifted with a 21st century-model brain—by name Charles Darwin—was performing a like service for the bloody, brawling world of animal life.

Darwin was a chronic user, perhaps an abuser, of the wide variety of opiate drugs prescribed by English physicians in his time. These eased the agonies of his many inexplicable illnesses, which modern biographers tend to regard as psychosomatic. It is usual to explain that Darwin was so often ill because of the psychological stress of his extreme sexual timidity and social shyness. Kenneth Burke, more incisively, has suggested that the great evolutionist, who was the son of a clergyman and the husband of a pious Methodist lady, knew all-too-well the pain, rage and fury his scientific work would cause in Christian nervous systems. His illnesses, then, were both a self-punishment for his "blasphemy" and a bio-neural dramatization of his self-doubt.

Opium and opium derivatives produce "little death" experiences and suck the user into fibrous, coiling vegetative realities. It is part of the junky mystique that each "hit"

20

# ASSIGNMENT—DESTROY JUDEO-CHRISTIAN THEORY OF CREATION —LIQUIDATE MONOTHEISTIC ARCHITECT-GOD

Charles Darwin

is an overdose gamble. The Game of Addiction is to come as close as possible to the botanical one-way Exit.

Darwin's insight into the deep-dark regions of vegetative consciousness was due to the fact that he was a confirmed opium addict. Most of the great Victorian poets used opiates and their verse is haunted with the same vegetative death-rebirth-metamorphoses imagery, the same Gothic horror, that Darwin organized so brilliantly and painstakingly into the Theory of Evolution by Natural Selection.

Charles Darwin was also an obsessively dedicated scientist, a hard worker of heroic endurance. It is recorded that when dissatisfied with some details in his interpretation of barnacle evolution, he laid aside all other work and remorselessly concentrated on barnacles for nearly seven years. His youngest son, assuming this was the normal adult male role, once asked a neighbor's child, "What sort of barnacles does your father work on?"

At the point of death, or near-death, or in the opiate quasi-death, vast evolutionary perspectives often appear. We define this as the seventh circuit of the nervous system. Darwin has been proven right on many points where his actual scientific evidence was wrong or inadequate. We suggest that his seventh circuit neurogenetic visions guided him almost as well as his careful scientific research. Most biographers stress his love for and empathy with all forms of life. His book on worms, behind its objective style, has all the tenderness of a popular dog story for children.

# PLANT KINGDOM
# SENDS NEURO-CHEMICAL
# INVITATION TO APES

James Joyce                    George Gurdjieff

The synergetic combination of pain-and-dope will prove to have much explanatory value to future exo-psychólogical historians and biographers. In addition to Darwin, we think of Nietzsche, who battled his chronic migraine headaches with so many patent medicines that Stefan Zweig described the philosopher's tiny room as looking like "a pharmacist's shop"; Gurdjieff, whose Nietzsche-old visions of evolution from mechanistic robotry to Cosmic Consciousness were all written while suffering acute pain from war-wounds and dosing himself with cocaine and hashish; James Joyce, whose painful eye problems, leading eventually to blindness, were treated with cocaine, and who created his own hilariously non-Euclidean "in risible universe" as normal vision faded and "it darkled (tinct! tinct!) all this our funnanimal world."[5] In the repeated cycle of pain-bliss-pain-bliss some especially gifted individuals can obtain neurological vistas far beyond the reflex robotry of yokel terrestrial life.

Of course, it soon emerged that Darwin's English-Imperialist view of evolution in terms of merciless competition did not explain all, or even most, of the facts. It had to wait half-a-century for the rediscovery of the works of an equally shy and timid individual, the monk Gregor Mendel, before the genetic mechanism itself was understood. Modern geneticists have noted that there is something rather implausible about Mendel's luck in picking for his experiments just those species of peas which were capable of producing genetic patterns expressible in simple arithmetic. In fact, the odds against such "luck" are astronomical. Some have even proposed that Mendel "fudged" his results a little. Others, unwilling to cast such suspicions on a great scientist, propose that one of Mendel's assistants did the "fudging." The stark truth is that, according to probability, Mendel should have chosen any of thousands of other species which would have yielded results not capable of expression in any mathematics known to his time; not expressible at all until the invention of the genetic

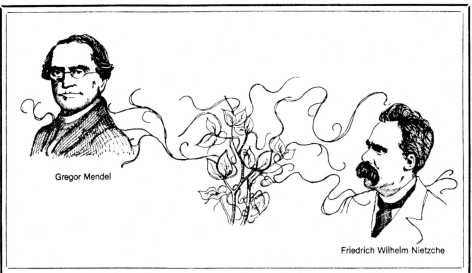

Gregor Mendel

Friedrich Wilhelm Nietzche

calculus by English mathematician-biologist J. B. S. Haldane in our own time. Where and how did Mendel receive this revelation from Egg Intelligence?

It must be remembered that Gregor Mendel was a monk in an ascetic order. He was trained in the Catholic form of yogic meditation, which consists (in vernacular terms) of monotony and isolation from hive pressure. Modern researchers call this "sensory or social deprivation" and have noted that it produces neurological effects similar to various neurotransmitter drugs, e.g. LSD and mescaline. (The interested reader can pursue this subject in the works of John Lilly, M.D., who has conducted extensive and courageous self-experiments with both LSD and social deprivation, as recounted in his *Programming and Metaprogramming in the Human Biocomputer, The Center of the Cyclone* and *Simulations of God.*) Mendel, it is possible, had passed through a neurological "little death" in which hive imprints and conditioning are suspended via meditation and social deprivation, and was able to receive signals from the neurogenetic archives (Seventh Circuit).

The philosophical meaning of the discoveries of Darwin and Mendel were not understood in 1979, even by the "intellectual" classes.

When Watson, Crick and Franklin discovered the double-helix of the DNA molecule, the energy laws underlying Darwinism and Mendelism became clearer.

Despite the mathematical beauty of Mendel's (and, later, Haldane's) genetic laws, despite the increasing revelation of beauty and harmony throughout the energy sciences, the power of Darwin's grim, prim vision hooked biologists (outside Soviet Russia, where Marxist dogma ironically led toward a Lamarkian approximation of the now-emerging true picture). Darwinian "blind mechanism" allegedly explained everything, even the facts it most glaringly didn't explain.

We know that DNA pre-programs evolution in much the same sense that a human operator programs a computer. The DNA code is the tape-loop of the Game of Life.

# GENES CAN BE TURNED ON AND OFF!!!

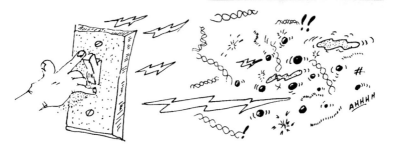

---

*The half of the DNA code blocked by histones may be
the future-blueprinting sections of the code which
are not to be manifested until further stages of evolution.*

---

IS THE TAROT A GENERAL, DIRECTION SUMMARY OF THE NEUROGENETIC CODE?
The genetic code is an amino-acid blueprint which preprograms the course of evolution. The DNA of any living creature carries the design of all the preceding forms and the forms to come. Each human being starts as a one-celled organism (at the moment of conception) and recapitulates the earlier forms of evolution during the embryonic period (gills, etc.). Recent evidence suggests that part of the DNA code is blocked by chemical masks called *histones*. According to Paul of Glasgow, the half of the DNA code blocked by histones may be the future-blueprinting sections of the code which are not to be manifested until later stages of evolution.

The most recent summary of what is perhaps the most important area of contemporary scientific research—the suppression and activation of genetic information—was published in the February 1975 issue of *Scientific American*. The title of this monumental article is: *Chromosomal Proteins and Gene Regulation*. The authors are Gary S. Stein, Janet Swinehart Stein and Lewis J. Kleinsmith.

The editorial headline for this article dramatically states the importance of the subject:

**"THE ROLE OF THE PROTEINS ASSOCIATED WITH DNA IN THE NUCLEUS OF HIGHER ORGANISMS IS BEGINNING TO BE UNDERSTOOD. APPARENTLY THE HISTONES KEEP GENES TURNED OFF AND THE NONHISTONE PROTEINS SELECTIVELY TURN THEM ON"**[6]

---

*The control of gene activity resides in the selectivity of transcription in both time and place." . . .*

---

The article begins with a concise summary of the situation:

"As is now well known, the genes, which transmit the hereditary information from one generation to the next and direct the function of every living cell, are made of DNA. In the cells of higher organisms, however, the genes are arranged on chromosomes, and chromosomes and nucleoproteins: complexes of nucleic acids and proteins. If the DNA is the genetic material, what is the function of the chromosomal proteins? Apparently they play a major role in maintaining the structure of the genetic material and in regulating the activity of the genes, that is, in determining which genes in each cell are turned on, and when. The control of genes is central to such fundamental processes as differentiation, embryonic development and hormone action, and to such abnormal processes as cancer, metabolic diseases and those birth defects that are related to the expression of genetic information."

### "Gene Regulation

A cell's genetic information is encoded in the sequences of nucleotides that constitute its DNA. To utilize this information the cell transcribes nucleotide sequences into the complementary strands of RNA that are translated into chains of amino acids to form proteins. The control of gene activity resides in the selectivity of transcription in both time and place."

### "The Histones . . .

Histones [chromosomal proteins] . . . are regulatory molecules involved in the control of gene transcription, but they must be regulatory in a nonspecific sense."

Whereas histone proteins seem to be fixed parts of the chromosomal structure, the nonhistone proteins seem to be in a "dynamic flux" and there is strong evidence that they are involved in modifying genes in very specific ways:

### "Nonhistone Proteins . . .

. . . Certainly the histone and nonhistone proteins play important roles in determining the structural and functional properties of the genome. Where histones are involved in the maintenance of chromatin structure and in the nonspecific repression of genetic sequences, nonhistone chromosomal proteins appear to recognize defined gene loci and thereby regulate the transcription of specific genetic information.

It may not be long before proteins that regulate the expression of specific genes are isolated, introducing the possibility of a certain kind of genetic engineering: the proteins might be inserted into cells in order to modify abnormalities in gene transcription associated with development, differentiation and a broad spectrum of diseases, including cancer." [6]

# FUTURE IS
# CODED IN DNA

Even the restrained scholarly prose of these sober scientists resonates with the staggering genetic implications of the "turn-on" role of nonhistone proteins. But when we consider the neurogenetic implications and the metamorphic suggestions these findings become even more important. We know that the DNA of the baby contains the coded instructions for manufacturing 14 years in the future (!) a sexually equipped adult. Adolescence begins when the appropriate nonhistone proteins (NHP's) selectively turn on the generative (sperm-egg) section of the DNA code. Aging begins when the selective NHP turns on the menopausal section of the DNA. The DNA of the caterpillar contains the instructions for building a butterfly. The DNA of the four-brained Domesticated Ape (homo sapiens) contains the blueprint for the next mutational stages—post-human, i.e., post hive.*

The DNA of the baby contains the coded instructions for manufacturing 14 years in the future (!) a sexually equipped adult.

*The reader is invited to consider the specifics of research on Chromosomal Proteins and Gene Regulation by consulting the following articles:

The Structure and Biological Function of Histones, L.S. Hnilice, CRC Press, 1972.

Nonhistone Chromosomal Proteins and Gene Regulation T.C.

Spelsberg and L.J. Kleinsmith in Science, March 1, 1974.

Chromosomal Proteins and their role in the Regulation of Gene Expression. Edited by G.S. Stein, J.S. Stein, and L.J. Kleinsmith, Academic Press, 1975.

# PYNCHON JOINS DANTE JOYCE CLASS

## GRAVITY'S RAINBOW CITED AS ENCYCLOPEDIC NOVEL OF AMERICAN CULTURE—DOPE AND TECHNOLOGY

Thomas Pynchon had dramatized this intricacy in the micro-miniaturized details of the Game of Life by comparing the most unconscious and automated (in the Fuller sense) design of a typical human hive to a printed circuit.

*The Tarot is the hieroglyphic key to stages of evolution.*

At the present time the scientific status of biology, neurology, psychology, philosophy is similar to that of chemistry before Mendeleyev. The life sciences and the human sciences have amassed an enormous collection of facts but there is no model for systematically inter-relating the facts. Some of the mechanisms of genetics have been discovered, but the overall strategy and direction of the evolutionary process is unclear. Psychology and neurology, in particular, are fragmented and ineffective because there are no systematic guideposts or basic structural explanations.

THIS IS THE STAIRWAY OF EVOLUTION UP WHICH WE ALL DANCE

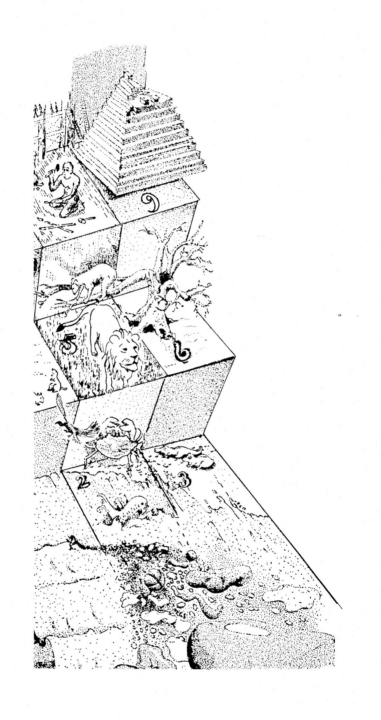

# JUDEO-CHRISTIAN PLOT TO DENY EVOLUTION

These rascals assume that there is no pattern or meaning in the Game of Life. They sententiously intone the neolithic nihilism of *Ecclesiastes:*

Vanity of vanities, saith the Preacher, vanity of vanities; all is vanity.

One generation passeth away, and another generation cometh; but the earth abideth for ever.

The sun also riseth, and the sun goeth down, and hasteth to the place where he arose.

The thing that hath been, it is that which shall be; and that which is done is that which shall be done: and there is no new thing under the sun.

*Popes, Rabbis, Mullahs are richly rewarded by their Hives for producing such sedative drivel.*

# HINDU-VICO CULT
# GETS NOWHERE

## THEY COULDN'T
## KEEP EVOLUTION
## A SECRET
## ANY MORE!

Swami Makananda and his "current"
mate fleeing Calcutta en route to
Swiss ski resort

Joyce put it more jovially in his Punch-and-Judy version of history, *Finnegans Wake,* where "It is the same told of all. Many. Miscegenations on miscegenations. Tieckle. They lived und laughed ant loved end left. Forsin. Thy thingdome is given to the Meades and Porsons* . . . In the ignorance that implies impression that knits knowledge that finds the nameform that whets the wits that convey contacts that sweeten sensation that drives desire that adheres to attachment that dogs death that bitches birth that entails the ensuance of existentiality." The robot-hero peddles along pointlessly, "a human pest cycling past and recycling (post) and there he is (pist!) again." This is, of course, the orthodox Hindu view of the four larval circuits (called *yuga*s in Sanskrit) repeating endlessly for no purpose. The Game of Life, from this earthbound perspective based on the Historistics of Vico has no goal, no point, no winners. (Joyce, as we shall see, knew better. The cycle in *Finnegans Wake* is actually an upward DNA spiral rising to the stars.)

*"Many . . . Tickle . . . Forsin" puns (among other things) on "Mene Mene Teeckle Upharsen," the Caballstic cryptogram announcing the Fall of one civilization, the Rise of another.

31

# EVOLUTION
# MOVES DNA UP

In this book we shall suggest that the Periodic Table of Elements is not just a model of the systematic variation in the properties of atoms, but is also a system for arranging the metamorphic stages of biological and neurological evolution. *Thus we can speak of the Periodic Table of Energy as the blueprint of evolution.*

Specifically, we suggest that the eight families of elements define eight metamorphic periods of evolution and that the properties of the eight groups predict the characteristics of the eight phases of evolution.

The general direction of the Periodic Table from Group 1 to Group 8 is from Earth to atmosphere, from Earth metals to gases. The general trend is clear—the more electrons in the outer shell, the more likely the element is to be escaping from the Earth's gravity. Metals tend to fall downward toward the center of the Earth; gases tend to move upward away from the center of Earth gravity and into extra-terrestrial atmosphere.

The direction of the Periodic Table of Elements is from terrestrial to extra-terrestrial.

**Group 8:** Noble gases
**Group 7:** Halogen gases
**Group 6:** Oxygen family
**Group 5:** Nitrogen family

**Group 4:** Carbon family
**Group 3:** Boron family
**Group 2:** Earth metals
Group 1: Alkali metals

The first four families are metallic, solid, electropositive and terrestrial.

The last four families are acidic, electronegative, gaseous or, if solid, easily sublimated. They are thus extra-terrestrial.

# THE PRE-SCIENTIFIC "MYSTICISM" OF PYTHAGORAS APPLIED THIS OCTAVE RHYTHM TO ALL NATURAL PROCESSES

Taking this cue from the Periodic Table of Elements we shall examine other post-Pythagorean systems of energy classification to see if they follow the eightfold trend from terrestrial to extra-terrestrial, from Euclidean earthiness to Fullerian ephemeralization.

The first such correlation to leap to the mind, as already mentioned, is the 8 notes of the (Western) musical scale. Sing them aloud and *hear* the progression from the grave and heavy to the High and light.

Do, re, mi, fa, sol, la, ti, do!

The pre-scientific "mysticism" of Pythagoras applied this octave rhythm to all natural processes and, 2500 years later, inspired the ridicule heaped on chemist J. A. R. Newlands when he announced a pre-Mendeleyevian grouping of the 8 families of elements. (Then again, the rejection of the Newlands discovery may just have been the Semmelweis Reflex again.) See p. 43.

According to Graves' *The White Goddess*, Egyptian priests once greeted the rising sun each morning by singing this octave aloud. That this may have been part of a neurological training system is indicated by the attempts of some modern "occult" schools (of allegedly Egyptian origin) to relate the eight octave notes to the eight "chakras" of the kundalini yoga system. The alleged locations of the chakras, and the corresponding notes, are as follows:

| CHAKRA | NOTE |
|---|---|
| above the head | high do |
| crown of head | ti |
| center of forehead | la |
| throat | sol |
| chest | fa |
| abdomen | mi |
| behind genital | re |
| base of spine | low do |

The Egyptian doctrine that we each contain seven souls may also have been a pre-scientific intuition of the first seven neurological circuits. (We can hardly be said to "contain" the 8th circuit, since the spatial metaphor of inside and outside does not apply there.)

# YOGIS PLAY ON NEUROLOGICAL OCTAVE

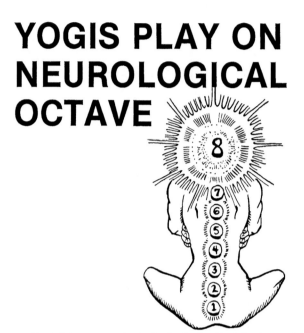

Kundalini yoga operates by "activating" each chakra in turn, from the bottom up. Activation is accomplished by steady concentration* on the chakra until its alleged energy is experienced and new perceptions appear. Many claim that if the musical notes are struck on an instrument before and repeatedly during such meditation-activation, the effect emerges faster. Medical and physiological science has not found any physical basis for these alleged chakras because these events are neurological not anatomical.

Kundalini yoga does produce effects that are measureable on an electro-encephalogram. The yogi is obviously doing something real to hir nervous system while concentrating on these imaginary chakras. Since we propose that there are eight potential circuits in the human nervous system, it is possible that kundalini yoga is a primitive system for reception, integration, transmission, programming, re-programming and meta-programming on these circuits.

Other primitive neurogeneticists have also discovered various properties of these eight circuits—the neurological octave—and have sent us transmissions, in the mythic-poetic language available in their historical epochs. Decoding such transmissions is the historical side of exo-psychology.

---

*Steady concentration in this sense is not likely to be understood by larval readers. Any "break"—intrusion of a word or image *not* the object of the concentration exercise—is a failure ruining the whole experiment. Here are some typical entries from the diary of a brave, persistent, highly motivated but pre-technological neuro-explorer: "After 3 weeks of daily practice, 59 minutes concentration with 25 breaks." "After 60 days, 23 minutes with 9 breaks." "After 70 days, 32 minutes with 10 breaks." A few days later, real concentration, without breaks, was finally achieved. (From the diaries of Aleister Crowley, quoted in Israel Regardie, *The Eye in the Triangle*.) This arduous traditional system of yoga can now be accelerated and vastly simplified by bio-feedback machines. See the works of Dr. Barbara Brown, Dr. Jean Mayo, Margery King.

34

YES... WELL, I JUST HATE ALL OF THIS STUFF!!

# LIFE

Schrödinger's famous phrase, "Life feeds on negative entropy," expresses in vivid metaphor the perpetual creation of order, system, intelligence—information—in all those enclaves where life flourishes. Paul Segal, UC-Berkeley biologist, offers another illuminating metaphor: "The DNA is pure information." Self-organizing systems, information-forming systems, are a mathematical reciprocal of the entropy process. Buckminster Fuller has even proposed, more radically than Schrödinger or Segal, that life exists to balance the universal equation, creating negative entropy (coherence) as fast as the thermodynamic processes create positive entropy (disorder).

# STACKS

The paradigm, as Von Neumann and Morgenstern realized in their *Theory of Games and Economic Behavior,* is the card-game. An undirected (random) shuffle produces disorder, chaos, entropy—because that's the way probabilities run. A strategic (stacked) shuffle produces a pattern of order favorable to one player—the shuffler. Life is a shuffler perpetually "stacking" the galactic energy-cards in its own favor, creating negative entropy, pattern, information.

# CARDS

The winning strategy in the Game of Life is perpetual metamorphoses to Higher Intelligence. The tactic is simple. Follow the order of the cards. Decipher the meaning of the numbers. Each card refers to a stage of evolution.

# TO WIN

# *TAROT PREDICTS*

# *IMMORTALITY, LSD,*

# *NUKES, SPACE HOMES*

Each **TAROT** Card represents
(and locates in space/time):

1. A stage of species evolution
2. A stage in your own personal development (temporal caste)
3. A structural caste, a genetic robot, an element which relates to (bonds with) other elements in predictable ways to form standard social molecules
4. A new ecological niche which activates the futatlon
5. A new Neuro-Technology

36

# THE TAROT IS A PRIMITIVE VERSION OF THE NEUROGENETIC CODE WHICH PREDICTS THE STAGES OF EVOLUTION OF INTELLIGENCE (IN THE SPECIES AND IN THE INDIVIDUAL'S LIFE)

The primitive Neurologic of shamans and yogis has previously made post-larval circuits available only to a handful of adepts in each millennium. This swarming cross-over point—where access to Higher Intelligence and post-robotic behavior becomes widespread instead of sporadic and rare—will be one of the three most important scientific breakthroughs in the next two decades. The other two will be success in attaining longevity (and eventual immortality) through genetic engineering and high-orbital migration into the infinite dimensions of Non-Euclidean space.

It is the thesis of this book that the Tarot cards accurately summarize the past twelve terrestrial-mortal stages of our evolution and predict the next twelve stages to come.

**CONVERSATION BETWEEN TWO EVOLUTIONARY AGENTS**

**Intelligence Agent 20:** This book on the Neurological Tarot is too complicated. It jams —short-cuts—too many systems into one transmission. It's confusing. No one will understand it all.

**Intelligence Agent 22:** That's all right. It opens up the next 12 stages for the species. Each individual of each caste will find what SHe is ready for in this book.

*This elimination of the nubile, erotically alive female
from the western deck reflects the sexual asymmetry
of the prudish hive culture.*

# TO MAKE THE TAROT
# EQUATION, LET THE MINOR
# ARCANA SUITS REPRESENT THE
# FOUR AMINO ACIDS; THE
# TRUMPS THE DNA CODE

The primitive Tarot is a deck of seventy-eight cards. Of these, fifty-six are divided into four suits similar to the popular-recreational deck except that there are four Court cards instead of three. The current version of the European-Hive 52-card deck contains a Jack but no Jill. This elimination of the nubile, sexually alive female from the Western deck reflects the sexual asymmetry of the hive-culture.

The gay Tarot currently in vogue is sexually chauvinistic and magnetically imbalanced. King, Queen, Knight and *Page*. The Knight is paired with a young boy! The Tarot court cards of the heterosexual out-caste Aleister Crowley reflect sexual balance. Knight, Queen, Prince, *Princess!*

Some Neurogeneticists, among them Brian Barritt and Robert Anton Wilson, have suggested that the four suits—Pentacles, Cups, Swords, Wands—refer to the four amino acids upon which the genetic code is based—Guanine, Cytosine, Adenine, Thymine.

Assuming, pretending, gambling that there is accuracy in our theory that the Tarot is the work of advanced neurological adepts transmitting in the best symbolism available in their time, we suggest the equations:

WANDS = "fire" energy = First Circuit bio-survival = thymine
CUPS = "watery" fluidity = Second Circuit emotions = guanine
SWORDS = "airy" abstraction = Third Circuit reason = cytosine
PENTACLES = "earthy" eros = Fourth Circuit sexuality = adenine

We will justify this table, and explain why there are fourteen cards in each of these suits, when we examine the Cabala later on.

Meanwhile, this archetypal foursome continues to haunt sensitive minds. Since patients are astonishingly obliging in producing the material psychotherapists are looking for, it is no news that the Four appear continually in the dreams and visions of Jungian patients.

These are simply the Tarot robots* most commonly found in any domesticated ape society.

---

TAROT ROBOT. Personification of one of the 24 quantum-evolutionary slots, according to a primitive neurogenetic theory known as "Exo-Psychology." This pre-mathematical neurological array was invented in the last days of Earth and had its greatest popularity in the decade immediately preceding Migration. While its geometric psionics was crudely dominated by G-star bias and its neuro-atomic theories typically bipedal-mammalian, exo-psychology is praised by ancient historians and often compared favorably to similar hominid laryngeal systems such as Astrology, Psycho-Analysis and Analytical Geometry. In general, it still possesses surprising predictive and diagnostic value, when dealing with entities of a carbon-based chemistry having experienced larval development on planets of G-type stars.

WEBSTER'S GALACTIC DICTIONARY
56th Edition

## Brown's Laws of Supermind [7]

Barbara Brown's 'laws' (from *Supermind*, to be published by Harper & Row in 1979) are based on findings from contemporary biofeedback research. Highlights:

* Human beings have an innate biological awareness of their physical state down to the level of the single cell.

* Human beings can control the direction and flow of nerve impulses throughout the body.

* The human mind can intervene in and direct any physiologic function.

* The mind controls the physical activity of the brain.

* Disease originates in intellectual processes. Stress has its effects on health because the rational mind confronts situations (especially social situations) with which it cannot cope.

* Human beings have evolved new, sophisticated senses; one is an unconscious sense of order in which we anticipate the sequence of natural events and move from chaos toward unity.

* Will is an independent function of mind.

* Human beings have evolved elaborate mechanisms to ensure survival in an evolving psychological—as well as physical—environment.

* The highest-order intellectual capacities—elegant and sophisticated—reside in what we call the unconscious and may always reside there because they are unrecognized by society.

---

## THE FOUR LARVAL CIRCUITS OF EVOLUTION
## ACCORDING TO THE EGYPTIAN ISIS CULT

"    the Egyptian diagram might have to do with the four castes, i.e. man must experience in recurrent form four samples of lives beginning with the most menial. In other words, in crossing the ocean of existence he crosses humanity itself in its main aspects. This diagram, if it has any connection with the repetition of the life, refers to four episodes, each one retraversed seven times, i.e. the same kind of life recurs seven times, and I would take it as meaning recurrence in the same part of time for any episode, or sample of life. Once worked out, once the spiral is accomplished, a new sample of life is begun, and I suppose that this would be in a different part of time." [8]

Maurice Nicoll, *Living Time*

IT'S A SIGNAL DOWN THE CORRIDOR OF MEMBRANE TIME ... TO GURDJIEFF.

YEAH ... AND ALSO A PLUG FOR MARILYN FERGUSON'S NEWS LETTER "BRAIN MIND"

# SEMMELWEIS SCANDAL!!

## HEROIC MEDIC DESTROYED BY HIVE ORTHODOXY

Ignaz Philipp Semmelweis

The additional twenty-two Tarot cards we have been examining are called the major arcana or Trumps. Each trump card carries a number, a symbolic picture, a personal title, and a library of textual-occult speculation. Let each trump card represent a stage in the DNA blueprint of evolution.

The origin and evolution of the Tarot deck is "an enigma wrapped in a mystery." The Tarot possesses such poetic suggestiveness, deliberate obscurity and startling flickers of profound philosophical significance that it has repeatedly inspired larval neophobia and the Semmelweis Reflex.*

It has often been proscribed by orthodox priests, disappearing into the alchemical underground, surfacing in disguised and vulgar form as playing cards. Some scholars believe that the Tarot evolved from the Egyptian mystery cults. The present form of the symbol code dates to the fourteenth century—which accounts for the haunting but confusing medieval flavor.

---

*SEMMELWEIS REFLEX. Mob behavior found among primates and larval hominids on undeveloped planets, in which a discovery of important scientific fact is punished rather than rewarded. Named after Dr. Ignaz Semmelweis, pre-Migration Earth physician who discovered the cause of puerperal fever, a now-obsolete disease which, in Semmelweis's primitive era, yearly killed a vast number of women in childbirth. Semmelweis was fired from his hospital, expelled from his medical society, denounced and ridiculed widely, reduced to abject poverty and finally died in a madhouse. The Semmelweis Reflex is ubiquitous among larval Euclidean civilizations and visitors to primitive planets should take at least one semester of mammalian psychology in advance to avoid any accidental offense to local superstition. See "Reich, Wilhelm," "Sakharov, Andrei," "Bruno, Giordano," and "Domesticated Apes."

WEBSTER'S GALACTIC DICTIONARY
23rd Edition

# TAROT CARDS REVEAL
# EVOLUTIONARY FORMULA

## THE TAROT IS NOT AN OCCULT DIVINATORY DEVICE

Assume that the Tarot symbol-sequence is a message; a scientific formula, an ethological Rosetta Stone, with great explanatory and predictive value. The cards are not for fortune telling. The use of the Tarot for personal divination is a superficial vulgarization which has led to an enormous literature of poetic, romantic, mundane, orthodox piety. The original precise time-script has been corrupted to a text for larval-parochial morality and cloudy sermonizing.

Exo-psychology assumes (on the basis of both logic and suggestive scientific evidence) that Life is of extra-terrestrial origin, Is seeded on this planet and is pre-programmed to pass through four cycles (12 stages) of embryonic neurological development, eventually metamorphosizing via emigration from the womb-planet through four cycles (12 stages) of post-terrestrial evolution.

Just as the DNA of the pollywog contains the future form of the frog, so does the human DNA contain the forms of future post-terrestrial evolution.

We call the Tarot a Neurogenetic script because the numerical sequence of the cards seems to describe the past twelve metamorphic stages of human evolution and to spell out quite specifically ten (really twelve) later phases involved In extra-terrestrial migration.

The Tarot cards are not designed to be shuffled and dealt out by chance. They are carefully numbered. Why? To present a neurogenetic message? To suggest an ordinal sequence?

---

*The Tarot cards are not designed to be shuffled and dealt out by chance. They are carefully numbered. Why? To present a neurogenetic message? To suggest an ordinal sequence?*

---

# FUTILE MISUSE OF GENETIC SCRIPT CITED

It is inevitable that pre-Einsteinian hive-humans with larval, egocentric conscious-ness, blind to their genetic role, would seek Tarot answers to trivial personal and hive-local questions. But surely this is a futile misuse of the script. Let us suppose that we introduce the Einsteinian equation, $E = MC^2$ to a Newtonian human, explain-ing that the basic relativistic nature of energy, matter and time is therein revealed. And the response of the larval hive-member human is: "Can Einstein's equation tell me if I'm going to be rich or when I'll get my release date from the parole board?" The answer might be: "Well, this equation predicts nuclear energy, gravitational field-force, time-dilation allowing us to live for billions of Earth-years, fusion-propelled starships, etc." The equation possibly can apply to your problems of hive adaptation (if you really understand it), but to understand it you have to have a post-hive nervous system which automatically makes your larval problems less significant, etc.*

Shuffling and dealing the Tarot cards is like scrambling and re-arranging by chance the numbered elements in the Periodic Table of Elements. OK, you deal out the element cards and find that Carbon initiates you, Iridium crosses you, Cadmium is beneath you, Strontium is behind you, Titanium is before you, Germanium is your hopes and fears and Radium is what will come!

Synchronicity and telekinesis probably exist, particularly when one is dealing with neurophysical symbols. Fortune telling by shuffling chemical element cards could be as effective as any other divinatory method—particularly if it leads the Querent to think of Hir life situations in terms of molecules, electron shells, quantum leaps, migration across zones, magnetic charges, hive-castes, swarming pressures, etc. Divination using the Tarot can be a useful Psy-Phy meditation technique—but the significance of the prediction is only as effective as one's understanding of the scientific neurogenetic meaning of the cards. If the cards are interpreted in a simple system of good-for-me-bad-for-me then one can only be resigned to living out ethical dramatics and hive soap operas.

---

*Writers on the Tarot who have had genuine initiation into societies of "Adepts" (practitioners of primitive neuro-programming systems) always stress the "spiritual lessons" in the design of the deck and play down the role of ESP. Waite, Papus, Ouspensky, for instance, have each published their own decodings of the allegory in the Tarot, with little mention of divination. Crowley only deals with fortune-telling in *five pages tacked on* as appendix to his book on Tarot symbology, *The Book of Thoth.*

# THE NEUROGENETIC THEORY OF EVOLUTION DEFINES TWELVE LARVAL AND TWELVE POST-TERRESTRIAL STAGES OF HUMAN EVOLUTION

The Neurogenetic theory covers:

**THE FOUR TERRESTRIAL NEURO-TECHNOLOGIES**
1. Safety (Biological Trust-Distrust technology)
2. Security (Politic-territorial technology)
3. Sanity (Epistemology laryngeal-manuai-symbolic)
4. Socio-Sexual (Ethics—hive belongingness)                    And—

**FOUR POST-TERRESTRIAL NEURO-TECHNOLOGIES**
5. Aesthetic-Neurosomatic (Control of Body)
6. Ontologic-Neurophysical (Control of Brain)
7. Teleologic-Neurogenetic (Control of DNA)
8. Eschatological-Neuro-atomic (Control of Quantum Mechanics)

This theory is based on the evolution of the eight-circuit nervous system through twenty-four metamorphic stages, each of increasing mobility. Why twenty-four?

Because each of the eight neural circuits has three sequential functions:

reception of signals; dendritic, the Siva function
integration of signals (intelligence); cell-body, the Brahma function
—transmission of signals; axonic, the Vishnu function

These three functions are based on the structure of the synapse itself. To quote from Dr. Herrick's *Introduction to Neurology,* "The structure of the simple reflex circuit [may be illustrated as follows] . . . The receptor (R) may be a simple terminal expansion of the sensory nerve-fibre or a very complex sense organ. The effector may be a muscle or a gland."    In any case, the receptor must first receive a signal, the nucleus must then integrate the signal and the effector (E) must then transmit the signal onward to whatever nerves, muscles, glands, etc. may be appropriate.

The basic trinity of Hinduism symbolizing the receptive, integrative
and transmitting functions of the neuron

| R | NUCLEUS | E |
| (RECEPTION) | (INTEGRATION) | (TRANSMISSION) |
| SHIVA | BRAHMA | VISHNU |

As Herrick notes, "A simple reflex act involving the use of so elementary a mechanism as has just been described is probably never performed by an adult vertebrate." Instead, chains and networks of such reflex-arcs are activated. "It must be kept in mind that in higher vertebrates all parts of the nervous system are bound together by connecting tracts (internuncial pathways). . . . These manifold connections are so elaborate that every part of the nervous system is in nervous connection with every other part." [9] But at each level of complexity, this three-beat pattern remains: reception, integration, transmission (or action).

The Chinese describe the dogmas of Lao-tse, Buddha and Confucius as the Three Teachings.

It is easy to discern the three neural functions in this oriental trinity:

*Lao-tse* re-presents the passive, self-indulgent, unattached dendritic aspect of the teaching. Siva.

*Buddha* integrating, comparing, seeking the Middle Path reasoning re-presents the neural cell-body. Brahma.

*Confucius* re-presents the axonic stage of the neural impulse—concerned with social fusion, external connections, interpersonal linkages. Vishnu.

In contrast to the Newtonian rigidity of the Judaic doctrine which was to take possession of the Western world, the three Chinese teachings are seen to be primitive Einsteinian. They are personal, relativistic, tolerant doctrines. They are doctrines of a Way, a Path, a genetic Nobility. In short they are evolutionary. They avoid the dogmatic Newtonian commitment to one-church, one-static-truth, one ritual and are perfectly in tune with the neurological structure of reality. As pointed out by H.G. Wells, "This attitude is flatly antagonistic to the state of mind that was growing up in the Jewish communities of Judea, Egypt, and Babylonia, in which the thought of the one God was first and foremost. Neither Gautama nor Lao-tse nor Confusclus had any inkling of this idea of a *jealous* God, a God who would have 'none other Gods,' a God of terrible Truth, who would not tolerate . . . any trifling with the stern unity of things."

Dendrite                    Cell Body                              Axon

*SO, YOU SEE, THE DENDRITE*
*RECEIVES THE CELL BODY*
*INTEGRATES AND THE AXON...*

## RECEPTION

The first stage of each circuit unfolds after migration, after rejection of adulthood. Self-indulgent, self-defining. The Dendritic network of the newly-evolved, emerging circuit must expand and open up to incoming signals which are not registered by the lower circuits. The First Circuit infant, for example, does not receive the kinasethelc signals which are the input of the Second muscular-dominance circuit. At puberty, the post-adolescent becomes aware of myriad sexy signals (invitations to sperm-egg transfer) to which the Three Brained child is blind.

As soon as a new circuit is activated, usually after a migration to a new ecological niche, the species and the individual go through a passive-receptive phase of exploring and rejoicing in the new spectrum of signals. We call this the dendritic "consumer" phase. Self-discovery. The left-hand column of the Neurogenetic Table lists the eight narcissistic passive stages. This self-indulgent stage is symbolized by the Siva function of the Hindu Trinity. Because it involves a juvenile paedomorphic abandonment of the Adult Hive.

## INTEGRATION

Dendritic fibres carry the signal to the cell body. The central column of the Table represents the integration which occurs in the cell-body of the neuron, and in the higher plexes of the nervous system. The neural center receives incoming dendritic messages, stores, analyzes, evaluates and relates thus creating the local reality, via transmission. Eight levels of Intelligence, of Self-Actualization, of Reality Creation are thus defined. This integrative stage is symbolized by the Brahma function of the Hindu Trinity.

## TRANSMISSION

Each neuron and neural circuit is hooked up to and designed for transmission. The axon. Linkage, fusion is the third sequence in the con-telligence process. The aim is communication. Synergic linkage multiplies meaning, migration and intensity. This social-fusional stage is symbolized by the Vishnu function of Hindu Trinity.

The right-hand axonic column of the Table is active-transmitting, migrating, moving, linking and defines the eight levels of synergic fusion, i.e., formation of new gene pools by self-actualized migrants.

TABLE 1
THE NEUROGENETIC TAROT ARRAY

| I Ching Trigram | Neural Circuit; Defined by Ecological niche | Passive Phase (Dendritic, Self-Defining, Receptive) | Integrative Phase (Self-Actualizing Intelligence) | Active Phase (Axonic, fusing) Migrating |
|---|---|---|---|---|
| Chien—Heaven | Metaphysiolog-ical Circuit | Stage 22 No card in primitive Tarot Sagittarius II | Stage 23 The Universe Capricorn II | Stage 24 No card in primitive Tarot Tarot Aquarius II |
| Sun—Seed | Neurogenetic Circuit | Stage 19 Moon Virgo II | Stage 20 Sun Libra II | Stage 21 Scorpio II Last Judgment |
| Li—Light | Neurophysical Circuit | Stage 16 Devil Gemini II | Stage 17 Tower Cancer II | Stage 18 Star Leo II |
| Tui-Pleasure | Neurosomatic Circuit | Stage 13 Hanging man Pisces II | Stage 14 Death Aries II | Stage 15 Temperance Taurus II |
| Ken-Protection | Domestication Circuit | Stage 10 Sagittarius I Hermit | Stage 11 Capricorn I Wheel of Life | Stage 12 Aquarius I Justice |
| Kan—Toll | Mental Symbolic Circuit | Stage 7 Virgo I Lovers | Stage 8 Libra I Chariot Driver | Stage 9 Scorpio I Strength |
| Ch'en—Movement | Emotion-Locomotion Circuit | Stage 4 Gemini I Sly Priestess | Stage 5 Cancer I Emperor | Stage 6 Leo I High Priest |
| Kun—Earth | Bio-Survival Circuit | Stage 1 Pisces I Fool | Stage 2 Aries I Magician | Stage 3 Taurus I Earth-Empress |

At each stage of evolution—personal or species—the histone layer insulating the unused portions of DNA, is peeled back a section. Specific anti-histone proteins (probably produced as by-products of the previous stage—i.e., genetic smog) unlock the next segment of DNA and activate the next brain.

The 24 Tarot cards describe each of the evolutionary stages *in the human individual* (temporal castes) and *in the species* which the individual recapitulates as SHe evolves.

*Please note the change in the numbering of the tarot cards introduced in this table. Each primitive tarot number is increased by one; thus Fool, which was zero becomes one, u.s.w.

OOPS! TERRESTIALS READ
CHARTS FROM UP TO DOWN

THEY'LL
LEARN

# EACH GENE POOL SENDS ITS SMARTEST BLOSSOMS WEST TO THE NEW NICHE

EACH OLD HIVE ASSIGNS TO THE FUTURE PROBE-MIGRATION-WAVE ITS MOST ATTRACTIVE, ENERGETIC, INTELLIGENT, RESOURCEFUL—WHO CARRY IN THEIR BODIES THE ENTIRE SPERM-EGG POPULATION OF THAT HIVE. THE SELF-ACTUALIZED OUT-CASTE MIGRANTS MOVE TO THE FUTIQUE-FRONTIER NICHE AND FORM NEW HIVES BY LINKING WITH MIGRANTS FROM OTHER OLD HIVES—THUS ASSURING THAT EACH CASTE FROM EACH OLD HIVE IS AVAILABLE TO BE INSERTED INTO THE NEW-HIVE REALITY-MOLECULE.

We reconsider the question: Does one's mundane zodiac role predict one's new-hive template? Of course. We recall that each species of caterpillar metamorphizes into a specific butterfly form. The Post-larval can be predicted from the larval. In fact, each larval caste sends its representatives into the post-hive future! Does the Pisces-Fool become the new Neurosomatic Passive Consumer. You bet! Does the Chariot-Driver-Integrating-Intelligence (Libra I) become the Neurogenetic Egg-Contelligence? Sure, just ask one! Does the DNA-code pre-program one's post-terrestrial hive-type as it does the mundane? Yup! Do post-larval individuals progress through the evolutionary sequence until they reach their favorite past-caste genetic role? For sure!

I HATE CALIFORNIA.!!

ME TOO!
FREE SOVIET
MANHATTAN JEWRY —

50

# EACH HUMAN IS A
# CASTE ROBOT

## OUR DESTINY IS TO EVOLVE THROUGH THE STAGES

The evidence available from the numerous cases of post-larvals who have come to the attention of this office suggests that mundane Tarot types *are* repeated in the upper zodiac. When the Pisces-Fool mutates-migrates to the next reality-niche SHe does seem to become the Floating WoMan. The Taurus-Empress (Stage 3) does seem to link up in Tantric Fusions (Stage 15). The Leo-Pope Stage 6 does seem to become an electronic Manager (Stage 18).

Each special orgasm below will be repeated in faster-funnier-free-er form above.

The equation of Zodiac and Tarot presented in later issue of this journal will clarify these issues.

Since there are eight circuits designed for the eight ecological niches (mediating eight technologies) and since each circuit has three phases, defined anatomically and functionally, we are logically led to define 24 stages of neurogenetic evolution. *The destiny of the species is to evolve through these 24 stages.* History and current observation suggest that species and individuals tend to emphasize one metamorphic stage. Within certain advanced species, where division of labor is used for gene survival, genetic templating has designed a range of subspecies or castes. The DNA, for example, programs certain species of the Class *hymenoptera* (ants, bees) to produce digger, guard, nurse, worker, warrior, drone, winged-sexual, and queen types. It is similar with human beings. The DNA produces twelve human types to keep the human hive colonies going, to play the twelve roles necessary for terrestrial evolution. The human hive needs passive receivers, active transmitters and synthesizers—twelve larval human types to keep the gene-pool moving through time.

Although each species and each individual humant moves through the stages, each species and each individual is wired to perform a special hive function.

Assume that DNA also is designed to produce twelve post-larval human types necessary to keep the chain of post-terrestrial-hive evolution going in the future. There is apparently a similarity between the position of a slot in the terrestrial array (first twelve) and the same relative positions in the post-terrestrial array. The Pisces-Fool (Stage 1) is the mundane form of the post-hive Floating WoMan (Stage 13). The Taurus-Empress (Stage 3) is the mundane form of the new-hive Tantra-Temperence slot (Stage 15), etc.

*The point is this: The same caste functions are needed to keep the new hive going at the next level of reality, i.e., ecological niche.*

Neurological con-telligence means, among other things, freeing one's self from the old-hive genetic template, i.e., metamorphizing beyond one's mundane zodiac role. AND moving through the post-hive sequence to find the same caste-slot in the new hive. The self-trained neurologican has experienced all the twelve hive-adjustment roles and can thus exchange signals efficiently with any living Tarot robot (larval human).

# FIRST YOU MASTER MARINE NEURO-TECHNOLOGY

**WE SHALL NOW CONSIDER THE EVOLUTION OF TWENTY-FOUR STAGES OF INTELLIGENCE**
    The meaning of these Neurogenetic terms will be explained in the text which follows. More detailed discussion of the eight neural circuits will be found in books listed in the bibliography.

CIRCUIT I

**THE BIO-SURVIVAL CIRCUIT.**
**IN SPECIES: UNICELLULAR.**
**IN INDIVIDUAL: VISCEROTONIC-ENDOMORPHIC (INFANCY)**
**ECOLOGICAL NICHE: WATER**
**REALITY GOAL: SAFETY**

**Stage 1:** Passive-Receptive; bio-survival
    First Childhood;sucking-floating technology
    Amoeboid Intelligence
    Zodiac: Pisces I
    Tarot: Fool

**Stage 2:** Bio-survival intelligence; bio-survival brain
    The First Self-Actualization; biting-squirming technology
    Fish Intelligence
    Zodiac: Aries I
    Tarot: Fool

**Stage 3:** Active-External bio-survival fusion
    The First Migration; crawling technology
    Amphibian intelligence
    Zodiac: Taurus I
    Tarot: Empress

52

# SECOND: **MASTER MAMMALIAN NEURO-TECHNOLOGY**

CIRCUIT II

THE EMOTIONAL CIRCUIT.
IN SPECIES: MAMMALIAN MUSCULOTONIC-MESOMORPHIC
IN INDIVIDUAL: (EARLY CHILDHOOD)
ECOLOGICAL NICHE: LAND
REALITY GOAL: HERD SECURITY

 **Stage 4:** Passive-Receptive; power via evasion
Sensory acuteness and camouflage
Second Childhood; running technology
Small animal Intelligence
Zodiac: Gemini I
Tarot: Priestess

 **Stage 5:** Emotional-muscular power intelligence
The Second Self-Actualization; territorial control technology
Large animal intelligence
Zodiac: Cancer I
Tarot: Emperor

 **Stage 6:** Active-Externalization of power
The Second Migration; social communication technology
Monkey-Gestural Intelligence; Formation of Second Hive (monkey-troop)
Zodiac: Leo I
Tarot: Pope

53

# THIRD: USE NEURO-TECHNOLOGY
# TO MANUFACTURE YOUR ENVIRONMENT

CIRCUIT III

THE LARYNGEAL-MANIPULATION CIRCUIT.
IN SPECIES: ECTOMORPHIC PRE-CIVILIZED HUMAN
IN INDIVIDUAL: CEREBROTONIC (PRE-ADOLESCENT CHILDHOOD)
ECOLOGICAL NICHE: MAN-MADE SYMBOLIC-ARTIFACT
REALITY GOAL: HIVE SANITY

**Stage 7:** Passive acceptance of artifacts (caves, stones and hive-symbols)
Receptive mind; mimetic; repetitive use of symbols
Third Childhood
Self-Definition; passive consumer of larynegeal-manual technology
Paleolithic Intelligence
Zodiac: Virgo I
Tarot: Lovers

**Stage 8:** Larynegeal Intelligence; invention of symbols
The Third Self-Actualization
Neolothic-Creative Intelligence
Zodiac: Libra I
Tarot: Chariot

**Stage 9:** Active-External cooperative manipulation of symbols
Formation of the Third Hive—the tribe
The Third Migration; division of labor technology
Tribal Intelligence
Zodiac: Scorpio I
Tarot: Chariot

# FOURTH: USE CULTURE
# AS NEURO-TECHNOLOGY TO
# FORM HUMANT-URBAN HIVES

CIRCUIT IV

**THE SEXUAL DOMESTICATION CIRCUIT (HIVE SOCIALIZATION)**
**ECOLOGICAL NICHE: MONOTHEISTIC-HIVE STRUCTURES: CITIES**
**REALITY GOAL: SELECTION AND MAINTENANCE OF APPROVED**
**HIVE SOCIO-SEX ROLE**

**Stage 10:** Self-Indulgent monarchial stage; sexual impersonation
Fourth Childhood: King and aristocracy as Self-Indulgent Patrons of new
technologies
Adolescence
Zodiac: Sagittarius I
Tarot: Hermit

**Stage 11:** Domestic Intelligence; familialization
The Fourth Self-Actualization; family oriented;democratic civilization
Zodiac: Capricorn I
Tarot: Wheel

**Stage 12:** Egalitarian homogenization
Formation of the Fourth Hive; centralized insectoid-monotheistic state
The Fourth Migration; Maoist anthill socialism
Zodiac: Aquarius I
Tarot: Justice

55

# FIFTH: ESCAPE INSECTOID HIVES USING AUTOMOBILE BODY

CIRCUIT V

THE NEUROSOMATIC CIRCUIT (CULTURE-FREE, HIVE-FREE
GRAVITY-FREE, HEDONIC)
ECOLOGICAL NICHE: ONE'S OWN BODY
REALITY GOAL: CONTROL OF ONE'S BODY; SOMATIC SELF REWARD

 **Stage 13:** Neurosomatic Receptivity
Self-definition as Pleasure Elite
Self-Indulgence; hedonic consumption
The Fifth Childhood; Post-Hive body consciousness
Zodiac: Pisces II
Tarot: Hanging Man

 **Stage 14:** Neurosomatic Intelligence; the Body-Mind
The Fifth Self-Actualization; Body control; Somatic Self Reward
Executive management of body as Time-ship
Zodiac: Aries II
Tarot: Horse

**Stage 15:** Neurosomatic Fusion
Tantric linkage of self-actualized bodies
Formation of Fifth Hive; Intentional communes
The Fifth Migration; fusion of winged elites
Zodiac: Taurus II
Tarot: Temperance

# SIXTH: USE YOUR OWN BRAIN TO FABRICATE NEW REALITIES

CIRCUIT VI

THE NEURO-ELECTRIC CIRCUIT (EINSTEINIAN)
ECOLOGICAL NICHE: BRAIN
REALITY GOAL: CONTROL OF ONE'S OWN BRAIN; NEUROLOGICAL SELF REWARD

**Stage 16:** Neuro-Electric Passive-Receptive
Self-Indulgence; Electronic consumer
Sixth Childhood
Zodiac: Gemini II
Tarot: Devil

**Stage 17:** Neuro-Electric Intelligence; control of one's own brain
The Sixth Self-Actualization; self-responsible reality fabrication
Zodiac: Cancer II
Tarot: Tower

**Stage 18:** Neuro-Electric Fusion; telepathy; brain-fusing
The Sixth Hive; High Orbital Mini-Earths
The Sixth Migration
Zodiac: Leo II
Tarot: Star

# SEVENTH: DECODE AND REDESIGN DNA TECHNOLOGY

CIRCUIT VII

THE NEUROGENETIC CIRCUIT (POST-HUMAN)
ECOLOGICAL NICHE: DNA STRUCTURE
REALITY GOAL: CONTROL OF DNA AND EGG-HIVE DYNAMICS; GENETIC SELF REWARD

**Stage 19:** Neurogenetic Passive-Receptive use of DNA technology
Self-Definition as caste-bound hive member
Self-indulgent stage; genetic consumerism
Gene-Pool consciousness; insect awareness
Longevity; re-juvenation
Seventh Childhood
Zodiac: Virgo II
Tarot: Moon

**Stage 20:** Neurogenetic Intelligence; the DNA mind
Genetic Engineering
The Seventh Self-Actualization
Egg-Wisdom; hive selection; cloning; longevity
    and rejuvenation via DNA  management
Zodiac: Libra II
Tarot: Sun

**Stage 21:** Neurogenetic Fusion; conscious symbiosis
The Seventh Migration
Formation of the Seventh Hive; conscious recruitment
    of caste-elements to fabricate new species
Zodiac: Scorpio II
Tarot: Judgement

# EIGHTH: USE NEURO-ATOMIC TECHNOLOGY TO CREATE UNIVERSE AND BLACK WHOLES

## CIRCUIT VIII

THE NEURO-ATOMIC CIRCUIT (POST-BIOLOGICAL)
ECOLOGICAL NICHE: ATOMIC AND GRAVITATIONAL FIELDS
REALITY GOAL: FUSION INTO BLACK HOLE (?)

NO CARD IN PRIMITIVE TAROT

**Stage 22:** Meta-Physiological neuro-atomic consciousness
Self-Definition as atomic consciousness; quantum consumer
Eighth Childhood
Zodiac: Sagittarius II
Tarot: no card

**Stage 23:** Meta-Physiological Intelligence
The Eighth Self-Actualization
Executive management of Schwarzschild Radius energies
Mastery of nuclear and gravitational energies
Star-making via controlled nuclear fusion
Zodiac: Capricorn II
Tarot: Universe

NO CARD IN PRIMITIVE TAROT

**Stage 24:** Meta-Physiological Fusion in Black Hole
Creation of new hives, e.g. new Big Bangs (?)
New astronomical forms
Galactic Domesticity
The Ulti-mate
The Final Migration of the Cycle
Zodiac: Aquarius II
Tarot: no card

# "EARTH SEEDED BY DNA BLUEPRINTS"
## SPECS NOBEL PRIZER SIR FRANCIS CRICK; DNA AGREES!!

**SUMMARY**

In summary, Interstellar Neurogenetic theory suggests that:

1. Planet Earth is one of many million (or billion) life-inhabited planets in the local galaxy.
2. Life is routinely seeded (directed panspermia) on planets like Earth by Bio-genetic Intelligence by means of amino-acid templates which contain the pre-programmed blue-print of the multi-billion year larval planetary cycle. The planet is a womb, a hatchery. When life has evolved through 12 embryonic stages it leaves the planet and assumes self-actualized existence in the galaxy—fabricating H.O.M.E.s, High Orbital Mini-Earths. The unit of life is the gene-pool. In advanced species—social insects, humants—the genetic unit is the hive. The key factor of evolution is the formation of new hives by the fusion of self-actualized winged elite out-castes—who migrate from the old hive, into a new ecological niche.
3. The nervous system meta-morphizes through 24 stages (8 ecological niches).
   1. In water
   2. On land
   3. In artifact shelters (tribal)
   4. In cities (insectoid)
   5. In Hedonests fabricated by self-actualized bodies
   6. In H.O.M.E.s fabricated by self-controlled brains
   7. In self-fabricated DNA hives
   8. In quantum-gravitational fields
4. The first four circuits of the nervous system (which have unfolded over the last three billion years) are larval, gravity-bound and designed for survival in the 4 niches of the placental planet. These neural circuits fabricate realities and mediate adaptation to the four directional attitudes of planetary life:
   1. the ventral attitude, facing forward to accomplish bio-survival linkage in water.
   2. the attitude of rising up vertically on land to the appropriate survival posture of dominance-submission, approach-avoidance.
   3. three-dimensional attitude; precise manual-laryngeal manipulation of artifacts and manufacture of symbols facilitated by the dominance of the left cerebral hemisphere.
   4. the in-out attitude; the development of sociosexual behavior (sexual impersonation) which manages sperm-egg transfer and the subsequent hive domestication roles necessary to protect the young.

HEY!- THIS NEW BOOK, "LIFECLOUD" BY HOYLE &
WICKRAMASINGHE SAYS THE SAME THING!!

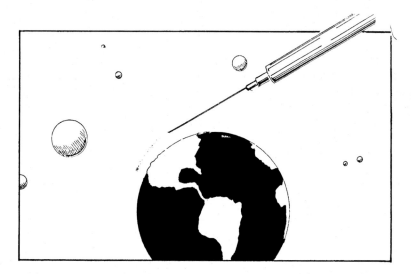

**DIRECTED PANSPERMIA . . . "COULD LIFE HAVE STARTED ON EARTH AS A RESULT OF INFECTION BY MICROORGANISMS SENT HERE DELIBERATELY . . .?**

It now seems unlikely that extraterrestrial living organisms could have reached the earth either as spores driven by the radiation pressure from another star or as living organisms Imbedded in a meteorite. As an alternative to these nineteenth-century mechanisms, we have considered Directed Panspermia, the theory that organisms were deliberately transmitted to the earth by intelligent beings on another planet. We conclude that it is possible that life reached the earth in this way, but that the scientific evidence Is inadequate at the present time to say anything about the probability. We draw attention to the kinds of evidence that might throw additional light on the topic. 10

5. The four post-larval circuits involve an escape from terrestrial-hive, gravity-bound reflexes and make possible transception-control of somatic, neural, genetic and atomic-gravitational realities.
   5. the somatic intelligence, the body as transceptor instrument; the body as one's ecological niche; formation of Circuit V hives.
   6. neurological intelligence, the brain conscious of its own bio-electric functioning; the brain as one's ecological niche; formation of new hives in High Orbital Mini-Earths.
   7. Genetic intelligence, transception and synergic fusion—control of RNA signals. DNA as one's ecological niche.
   8. Meta-physiological, neuro-atomic intelligence, transception and synergic fusion control of nuclear particle signals.

The Fifth, Sixth, Seventh and Eighth circuits are designed for post-terrestrial hive existence.

TOM & I HATE ALL THIS STUFF

# FIRST 12 TAROT FIGURES

# EXPOSED AS IMPERSONATORS

Returning to the directional trend of the Tarot array, let us compare the first twelve cards, which we have called larval-terrestrial, with the last ten cards which we have labelled post-larval extra-terrestrial.

### THE LARVAL TERRESTRIAL TAROT CARDS

Fool; a young man walking
Magus; a young man standing
Empress; a woman seated
High Priestess; a young woman seated
Emperor; a man seated
High Priest; a man seated
Lovers; a boy and a girl; a winged angel above
Chariot Driver; a man seated
Strength; a woman holding the jaws of a lion
Hermit; an older man walking
Wheel of Fortune
Justice; a woman seated

Eleven of these twelve cards portray human beings in natural and normal hive poses obeying the laws of gravity. The only extra-terrestrial being is the angel in card 7, a peripheral figure not mentioned in the label of the card. The Wheel of Fortune, a neurogenetic-egg-principle card, exceptional in several respects, will be discussed later. We note that the Wheel of Fortune shows a circle (planet earth) and floating in clouds around the circle, form winged figures. This card seems to summarize the neurogenetic theory. Migration from terrestrial hives to post-terrestrial hives.

These twelve archetypes are the Twelve Old Men who haunt the dreamer's sleep all through *Finnegans Wake,* reappearing as twelve customers at the bar, the twelve jurors at the trial, u.s.w. Joyce commentators have noted that they are the twelve apostles (hence the refrain, reminiscent of the Last Supper, "Pass the fish for Christ sake"), the twelve labors of Hercules, the twelve signs of the Zodiac, and so forth; as indeed they are in the universal symbolism of Joyce's "monomyth." But basically they are the twelve castes of terrestrial humanity, the twelve genetic types that keep the earthside trip dancing within the same parameters generation after generation.

# Photos Reveal They Are 12 Basic Normal Terrestrial Castes

The numerical order of the primitive Tarot cards presents a consistent directional trend. The twelve lower numbered cards portray the vicissitudes and adaptations of terrestrial hive survival. The higher number cards (12-21) portray extra-planetary hive stages.

This trend in the Tarot matches the Neurogenetic theory which holds that evolution moves humanity from the Earth directly toward interstellar life. We recognize, also, that this mythic evolutionary direction has been crudely dramatized by all the larval human religions which teach that Humanity struggles on Earth for survival; then leaves for an extra-terrestrial existence. Heaven is the Hive in the Sky.

The same trend, interestingly enough, is found in the ancient Chinese Yin-Yang philosophy especially as systematized in the I Ching. The two polar factors of the Taoist Book of Changes are Earth and Heaven. Eight elemental energies are defined. A Neurogenetic transformation of the I Ching will be found in *The Game of Life, Vol. III.*

It has been mentioned earlier that ancient neurogenetic scripts should harmonize with the energy formulae and the theoretical models of science. So we are not surprised to find that the Mendeleyev Periodic Table of Elements follows the same directional trend. The Periodic Table divides the elements into eight "families" based upon atomic weight and number of electrons in the outer shell. The alkali and earth metals have lower numbers of outer electrons; the gases have higher numbers. Again we see the movement from earth to air. Considering the directional trend of increasing atomic weights (sometimes described as the curve of binding energy and the temporal hierarchy of matter) we find trends (increased radio-activity, instability) which may have neurophysical and neurogenetic meanings beyond the scope of this rudimentary transmission.

# LAST TEN TAROT CARDS PORTRAY POST-TERRESTIAL REALITIES

### The Post-Larval, Extra-Terrestrial Cards

Hanging Man; portrays a man *floating* serenely upside down in a zero gravity atmosphere

Death; a skeleton riding a giant horse

Temperance; an enormous *winged* angel; solar explosions in background

Devil; a mythical *winged* creature

Tower; lightening bolt fissioning a tower; two giant, stylized figures *floating* through the air

The Star; an enormous red star, seven smaller stars and the naked figure of a woman

The Moon; lunar landscape with stylized moon reflecting light

The Sun; giant sun over a baby riding a horse

Last Judgement; enormous figure of *winged* extra-terrestrial blowing horn; tiny naked figures arising from containers

World, Universe, Galaxy

A brief glance at this list of 10 cards reveals that no natural, terrestrial hive scenes are portrayed. The stellar, galactic theme is consistent. In pre-scientific language and symbols the last cards portray "other-worldly" events. In the language of modern science we say that these ten cards emphasize post-terrestrial events.

As we shall suggest, the Tarot array can serve as a formula which precisely spells out eight periods and 24 stages of human evolution—earthly and Interstellar. At this point we have simply demonstrated the division between the mundane cards (0 to 11) and post-Earthling cards (12 to 21).

We shall now consider the neurogenetic meaning of Card 21 and the necessity for defining two new Tarot cards to fill out the eighth circuit of the nervous system.

# TEN POST-TERRESTIAL TAROT CARDS

# LET US ADD TWO NEW TAROT CARDS, THUS DEFINING EIGHT PERIODS (CIRCUITS) AND 24 STAGES

So far we have defined Four Periods of Terrestrial Neurological Evolution designed for hive adjustment, and four neural circuits designed for the periods of gravity-free, post-hive interstellar life.

There are several illogical asymmetries in the primitive Tarot arrangement which suggest that two new cards should be added.

**Question:** Why are there only 22 cards in the primitive Tarot?

**Answer:** Perhaps two cards are missing, if eight levels of the Tarot are to be defined.

**Question:** Why twenty-four?

**Answer:** Eight times three is 24.

**Question:** Why three?

**Answer:** Neural signals come in three stages: reception, integration, transmission.

**Question:** Why eight?

**Answer:** The number eight (particularly expressed as 7 plus 1) seems to be involved in the basic equations of energy-matter. Neurogenetic theory looks to atomic physics for explanatory guides. The Periodic Table of Elements is a logical foundation for any model of energy manifestation, even as peripheral as the psychological and sociological. The Periodic Table defines eight (7 plus 1) families of elements. We have pointed out earlier, that the directional tendency of the Periodic Table is, in general outline, similar to the Neurogenetic array. Moving from the earth-metals to the noble gases.*

Also: the oldest philosophic text is the I Ching. The Chinese Book of Changes defines *eight* levels of energy, again moving from earth (yin) to Heaven (yang).

---

The reader is referred to the article on "Correspondences" in *The Intelligence Agents* by Timothy Leary (Los Angeles: Peace Press, 1979).

An amusing and provocative explanation of the recurrent Importance of the number 24 in human neuro-sociology has been suggested by R. A. Wilson:

"What Weishaupt discovered that night of February second, seventeen seventy-six . . . was basically a simple mathematical relationship. It's so simple, in fact, that most administrators and bureaucrats never notice it. . . . Here, take this paper and figure for yourself. How many permutations are there in a system of four elements?"

Joe, recalling his high school math, wrote 4 x 3 x 2 x 1, and read aloud his answer "Twenty four."

"And if you're one of these elements, the number of coalitions—or to be sinister, conspiracies—that you may have to confront would be twenty three. . Just consider it pragmatically—it's a number of possible relationships which the brain can remember and handle.

". . . Korzybski pointed out, back in the early thirties, that nobody should ever *directly* supervise more than four subordinates, because the twenty-four possible coalitions ordinary office politics can create is enough to tax any brain."

from *Illuminatus!* by Robert Anton Wilson

# EVOLUTIONARY MAPS CANNOT BE LIMITED TO LOCAL HIVE CONCEPTS

I WANT TO BE POPE

NO I'VE GOT POPE
YOU BE EMPEROR

We shall make the following assumptions about the Tarot:

1. Let the Tarot be an Interstellar Neurogenetic Code accurately mapping the unfolding sequence of evolution of the twelve larval stages and the twelve post-larval stages.
2. The most advanced Human technology has approached the stages of genetic self-actualization (cloning, life-extension) and nuclear self-actualization (controlled nuclear fusion). Each human being, indeed, each living entity, has carried the evolutionary process to a certain point along the path by means of serial activation of neural circuits. Knowing the map makes it possible to know how far and from whence one has come and what lies ahead. The map is an ordering of the brain circuits as they sequentially emerge.
3. Each version of the Tarot describes the entire voyage in terms limited by the location of the author. Persons whose nervous systems are imprinted to Domesticated Morality (Circuit 4) will portray all cards in terms of hive roles and hive ethics.

68

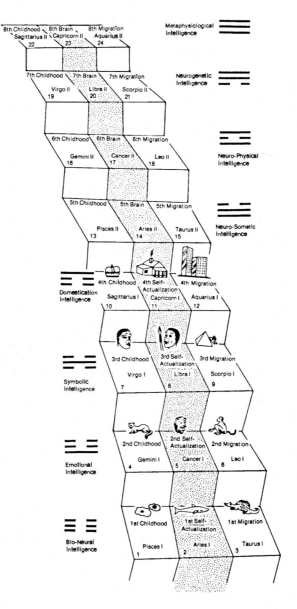

8th Childhood   8th Brain   8th Migration
Sagittarius II   Capricorn II   Aquarius II
22   23   24

Metaphysiological
Intelligence

7th Childhood   7th Brain   7th Migration
Virgo II   Libra II   Scorpio II
19   20   21

Neurogenetic
Intelligence

6th Childhood   6th Brain   6th Migration
Gemini II   Cancer II   Leo II
16   17   18

Neuro-Physical
Intelligence

5th Childhood   5th Brain   5th Migration
Pisces II   Aries II   Taurus II
13   14   15

Neuro-Somatic
Intelligence

4th Childhood   4th Self-Actualization   4th Migration
Sagittarius I   Capricorn I   Aquarius I
10   11   12

Domestication
Intelligence

3rd Childhood   3rd Self-Actualization   3rd Migration
Virgo I   Libra I   Scorpio I
7   8   9

Symbolic
Intelligence

2nd Childhood   2nd Self-Actualization   2nd Migration
Gemini I   Cancer I   Leo I
4   5   6

Emotional
Intelligence

1st Childhood   1st Self-Actualization   1st Migration
Pisces I   Aries I   Taurus I
1   2   3

Bio-Neural
Intelligence

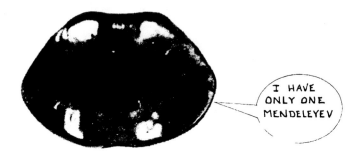

Question: What precedent is there for adding new elements to an ancient system?
Answer: "Dmitri Mendeleyev, a leonine man of dauntless spirit." It is not surprising that Mendeleyev, who figured out the periodic rhythm of physical matter, is described in the biographies as one of the sexiest chemists. In later years, when he took a second wife while not yet divorced from his first, the czar's reported comment was, "Mendeleyev has two wives, yes, but I have only one Mendeleyev."

As Mendeleyev was writing his classic text, *Principles of Chemistry,* eventually published in 1868, he, like all previous chemists, was frustrated by the absence of any systematization of the enormous body of facts about the behaviors of the different elements. Influenced by cabalist and alchemical theories he began to build up a dossier on each element. Like any good detective or intelligence agent he patiently listed all the evidence about each element on cards, shaped in the oblong form of playing cards.

On each card Mendeleyev wrote the numerical properties and personality characteristics of each element—seeking the "periodic," repeating order—the *modus operandi,* the hang-outs and partners-in-time. Dimitri discovered a basic rhythm—of lateral rows and vertical columns which reflected the physical and chemical correspondences among the families of elements.

The fascinating issue was this: Mendeleyev was able to arrange the elements in a tabular order based on symptoms, i.e., external behaviors, without understanding the underlying atomic structure and without realizing that the elements have been and still are evolving, mutating, transmutating in a predictable pattern determined by their species and familial characteristics.

As Dimitri arranged the Tarot Table of the Chemical Elements he noted that certain slots in the table were empty. He therefore courageously predicted that the missing elements existed. "It is possible," he said, "to foretell the properties of still-unknown elements."

And here we encounter, once again, the message of this book: it is possible to foretell the properties of still-unknown stages of our own evolution—as species and as individuals.

70

# HIVE THOUGHT ∎ POLICE
## REPRESS TAROT MEANING

## THE ESSENCE MEANING OF THE TAROT HAS BEEN CONCEALED BY DELIBERATE AND ACCIDENTAL DISTORTIONS

The Tarot card deck is an ancient formula of neurogenetic symbols which has been passed down over the centuries. A complex psychological signal of this sort which persists in time across many generations surely must have some neurogenetic meaning and must relate somehow to modern scientific energy models.

Occult systems are time-scripts, neurogenetic messages sent across millenia. They are crude, blurred, short-hand descriptions of energy processes, genetic types, hive castes, both temporal and structural psychophysical formulae, compressed representations of enduring philosophic, alchemical (i.e. neurochemical) principles.

Discoveries about the evolutionary process have always been controversial, indeed, taboo-prohibited dangerous. New revelations about the nature of things are perilous to conventional hive beliefs, undermining cosmological securities, stirring up ontological malaise, generating epistemological terrors. New breakthroughs in human knowledge are always labelled as destructive, as unsettling, as evil by the Adult Authorities who maintain Hive Monotheism. This can be perilous to out-castes concerned with post-hive sequences.

Neurophysicists and neurogeneticists often communicate their discoveries in esoteric languages to avoid Hive censorship. The secrecy of Copernicus. The mysticism of Paracelsus. The symbolized sex-magic of Giordano Bruno.

The revolutionary formulae of Albert Einstein were presented in the symbols of mathematics, and the neurogenetic meaning of the relativity statements thus hidden from the hive authorities.

Exiled for his beliefs from Germany, Einstein could find refuge in America because the explosive psychological implications of his fissioning equations were not understood. (Perhaps not even by Einstein after separation from his first wife.) The American Catholic Hierarchy did recognize the dangers of Einsteinian Relativity and piously denounced it.

---

*Discoveries about the evolutionary process have always been controversial, indeed, taboo-prohibited dangerous.*

---

HOW COME I'M NOT TABOO ?!

*As soon as a psychophysical principle becomes
hive-orthodox, it is taught in authoritarian, rote fashion,
and the experimental meaning, the direct neurological
significance, is lost.*

Hive pro-phobia has always forced mutant scientists to conceal their discoveries in the form of codes and arcane scripts. Astrological systems, chemical and alchemical procedures, Tantric energy releasers, I Ching commentaries, Tarot cards have at various times been banned, their texts destroyed and their "secrets" forced into esoteric form by hive authorities. The tides of history washing over such records inevitably wash out their meaning. Symbols lose precision, Semantic meanings are outdated. Prosody replaces numerical precision. Errors are made in transmission. What reaches us in the twentieth century is superficial, fuzzy, vulgarized.

To further complicate matters, neurologs often deliberately build errors and interject cryptic codes into their scripts to prevent their being misused by those who do not understand the essential theme. We have, for example, designedly incorporated three errors into this script, which will be detected by the receiver who understands the signal. Alchemical codes preceded the cryptograms of modern chemical companies. One of the classic dangers in the transmission of energy-knowledge comes from popularization and vulgar acceptance. As soon as a psychophysical principle becomes hive-orthodox, it is taught in authoritarian, rote fashion, and the experimental meaning, the direct neurological significance is lost.

Errors, both accidental and deliberate, operate like this: "Multiplication table; children, repeat after me: one times two is two; two times two is four; three times two is six; four times two is ten; five times two is eight . . ."

Such an error is repeated and repeated, bound into texts and bibles, uncritically passed down from teacher and student for generations. For example, the Aristotelian dogmas, the Ptolemaic imperatives, the Euclidean axioms.

Occasionally a detached out-caste observer catches the error. To point out that "two times four is eight" invites rejection as a crank or trouble-maker. Only the person who understands the principle can detect and correct the errors which creep Into all communication systems. Consider the distortion which converted Jefferson's "Life, Liberty and Pursuit of Happiness" to Kennedy's insectoid "Ask what you can do for your hive."

*Consider the distortion which converted Jefferson's
"life, liberty and pursuit of happiness" to
Kennedy's insectoid "ask what you can do for your hive."*

ARE
HUMANTS READY
FOR THIS ?

---

*One wishing to use the Tarot must update and redefine
the cards in terms of modern scientific discoveries.
As a basic primary-school step in neurologic the student
should design and continually revise hir own version of the Tarot.*

---

Despite the distortions, esoteric time-scripts such as astrology, I Ching, Tarot, alchemy, playing cards, Homeric myths, Cabalistic alphabets, biblical epics are important, if for no other reason than this: the wisest, best-endowed out-caste philosophers of the past used them to pass on their discoveries about neurophysical processes. Each new generation of searchers, however, must rediscover, re-search each natural law, must rewrite all the basic formulae, restate all the general principles, reword the great myths, update the epic poems.* Nothing can be taken as finally proven. Every great discovery must be re-experienced.

The English-language Bible is a classic example of a valuable time-script which has fallen into insane incoherence because of corrupted translation, unconscious and deliberate falsification, rote duplication of symbols which have lost their precision, etc. Hebrew versions of the Bible which have been revised regularly across the centuries are interesting because they provide a living chain of transmission in which the entry and perpetuation of distortions can be seen as clearly as the stratified levels of culture in the archeological uncovering of an ancient site.**

Any serious student of human neurologic would do well to excavate and restore the original neurogenetic (sex-magic) meaning of the Genesis chapter of the Hebrew bible.

The I Ching as presented in current texts is loaded with obvious numerical errors and absurd banalities. Only when these are discovered and corrected can the code message of the Book of Changes be understood.

One wishing to use the Tarot must update and redefine the cards in terms of modern scientific discoveries. As a basic primary-school step in Neurologic the student should design and continually revise Hir own version of the Tarot.

---

*We must distinguish between primitive exo-psychological signal systems and later uncomprehending transmitters. That is, between Astrology and Astrologers. Astrology has a certain primitive meaning; most astrologers are rote-robots playing idea-tapes which they do not understand.

**The St. James Christian version of Isaiah 7:14 predicts the conception of Jesus Christ: "Behold a virgin shall conceive and bear a son." The Jewish version accurately retains the original version: "Behold a *young woman* will conceive." U.S.W.

# EVERY GREAT DISCOVERY
# MUST BE RE-EXPERIENCED BY
# YOU!!

---

*Every breakthrough in the "physical sciences" affects the*
*philosophical and psychological and social nets of the hive.*

---

The cyclical pattern of genetic templating as measured in lunar, solar and planetary cycles (astrology) must be restated in terms of current evidence about bio-rhythms from astronomy, nuclear physics, genetics, neuro-psychology.

Each new breakthrough in nuclear physics requires that all the past neurophilosophic systems be re-examined and made more precise.

Each new system of human philosophy must build on and systematically harmonize with or consciously differ from the classic ancient systems. The community of Time Travellers is contemporary and simultaneous. Paracelsus is closer to 20th Century out-castes than the Earthlings we meet in the hive market place. As each new discovery is brought to our attention—pulsars, black holes, LSD, histones, DNA—it is only neurogenetic courtesy to tell Pythagoras, to re-consult the Chinese oracle, to inform the gypsy-alchemist Tarot magi of the new revising confirmations. The Periodic Table of Elements, for example, begs to be harmonized and integrated with the great past symbol systems to the mutual advantage of all concerned.*

The classic systems by means of which ancient out-caste scholars ordered the stages of energy evolution have been corrupted and vulgarized by charlatans and gullible charlatanees. Every breakthrough in the "physical sciences" affects the philosophic and psychological and social nets of the hive. Ptolemaic astronomy was tied to a geocentric ontology. Newton's laws were crystalized in the sociology of capitalism, the dialectics of Marx, the thermodynamics of Freud, etc. Surely the time has come to Einsteinianize all human traditions, fission the classic systems to release the next level of neurological energy.

---

*Surely the time has come to Einsteinianize all human*
*traditions, fission the classic systems to release the next*
*level of neurological energy.*

---

* The reader is referred to the article on "Correspondences" in *The Intelligence Agents* by Timothy Leary (Los Angeles: Peace Press, 1979).

# LET THE TAROT SLOTS REPRESENT 24 STAGES IN PERSONAL AND SPECIES EVOLUTION

*Up to this time, we havé had no language to describe the processes of the four post-hive circuits of the nervous system. It is sobering to realize that we are forced to use 'caterpillar' words to describe 'butterfly' events.*

Assume that the Tarot is a concise blueprint of the ordinal course of neurogenetic evolution, past and future. The skeletal structure of the system is accurate although the verbal labels and cartoon-strip, hive-role designations (Fool, Pope, Emperor, Hermit) are outdated, trite and confusing. If one grasps the meaning of the Tarot Number Sequence from the neurogenetic framework then one can see through the titles and rename the cards to bring them up to date. Personalizing the cards in terms of current hive-roles is a useful but perilous flourish.

Let each card represent a metamorphic neurogenetic stage. A slot in the DNA chain. These stages can be personalized in that one's neurogenetic development does involve personal hive roles and intersection with, and imprinting of, persons playing different hive roles. However, it is more accurate to use names of processes rather than illustrative persons from the current, local anthill.

The hive personalizations of the Zodiac (e.g. Taurus the Bull) and of the I Ching (e.g. Earth-Mother) and of Tarot I (e.g. Empress) are childish, Mickey Mouse kindergarten expressions of the messages presented in more scientific language by the Neurogenetic Table and Periodic Table of Elements.

In order to help the reader understand the rhythm of the Periodic Table (and to counteract the distortion of the primitive Tarot labels) we present in Table II vulgar vernacular personification of the twenty-four neurogenetic elements. The first twelve are neurogenetic translations of primitive hive Tarot I elements. The Fool becomes "The Unattached Floater," etc.

The last twelve elements refer to post-planetary, post-hive evolutionary stages which are beyond the limits of our current mundane hive language and involve concepts of exo-psychology. Up to this time, we have had no language to describe the processes of the four post-hive circuits of the nervous system. It is sobering to realize that we are forced to use "caterpillar" words to describe "butterfly" events. Table II should be viewed as suggestive and preliminary.

Let the first twelve cards of the Tarot describe the metamorphic sequential emergence of the first four terrestrial-hive circuits of the nervous system.

Let the twelve later cards of the Tarot summarize and describe the metamorphic sequence of the four post-hive, post-terrestrial circuits.

The Individual in Hir own individual evolution recapitulates and, in the case of advanced futants, forecastes the evolution of the new species.

# CROWLEY, GURDJIEFF EXPOSED AS GENETIC AGENTS

## THE ALEISTER CROWLEY TAROT SCHEME IS PRE-EINSTEINIAN — BASED ON THE FIFTH CIRCUIT

Several students of Magic (Brian Barritt, Andy Warhol, Robert Anton Wilson) have commented on synchronicities between the life and work of Aleister Crowley and the publicized experiences of Dr. Timothy Leary.

Crowley's transmissions were primarily concerned with the Fifth Circuit. Sex-magick. Self-definition as a polymorphous erotic receiver. Somatic control. The tantric union of male-female. The Pan, Dionysus rapture myth. The alchemy of aphrodisiac drugs.

There is evidence to suggest that the evolutionary element called Timothy Leri has unconsciously repeated, step-by-step, the neurogenetic evolution of Crowley and carried his work to the next stage following the explicit instructions of Crowley. Instructions about the completion of his work.

"In the last pages of his autobiography, *Confessions of Aleister Crowley**, the Mage describes an Egyptian document which he believed to contain an important prophetic signal. The name TIMA was assigned to the mysterious transmitter. With this strange reference Crowley goes on to summarize his life's work as being unfinished, particularly his work on the Tarot. Crowley says that his task will be completed by his successor who will make it more quantitative, scientific and objective." (Brian Barritt)

The cases of Crowley and George Gurdjieff are similar. Both based their work on sexual energies released by neurosomatic drugs (opium, cocaine, hashish) and expressed in aesthetic patterns.

---

*The cases of Crowley and George Gurdjieff are similar. Both based their work on sexual energies released by neurosomatic drugs (opium, cocaine, hashish) and expressed in aesthetic patterns.*

---

*Details of the synchronicities between Crowley and the primary transmitter of this signal will be found in *Confessions of a Hope Fiend*, written as discharge of neurogenetic obligation and tribute to the predecessor.

76

# Gurdjieff

## Beelzebub's
## Tales to
## His Grandson

Both Crowley and Gurdjieff were Masters of Circuit 5 which was the highest point of consciousness and intelligence possible before the Einsteinian era. Both were also sporadically capable of profound precognitive visions of Circuit VI and higher.

Toward the end of their lives both men lost their *baraka;* their nervous systems no longer operating as receivers and transmitters of high-energy, new knowledge. There is a certain poignancy in their histories. The lives of both men ended exactly at the time when the discoveries of electronic-atomic-nuclear energies made possible biological longevity and migration from the planet and when the time-dilation implications of accelerated motion were made known. Before the possibility of space-migration there was no apparent point in human life and planetary existence. What could Crowley or Gurdjieff do with the neurosomatic energies they released? Teach others? Play with erotic and interpersonal power? Entertain? Get involved in all-out risky events that challenged their expanded energies? Shock the mundane? Pass on the primitive version of the message?

Gurdjieff did see clearly the galactic step which awaited humanity. *Beelzebub's Tales to His Grandson*12 is one of the great larval time-scripts, a comic, broad, philosophic, satirical view of larval humanity from the standpoint of Galactic Intelligence. An amazing pre-view of the Interstellar Age.

# CROWLEY:
# A BRAIN ALL DRESSED UP
# AND NO WHERE TO GO

Crowley's greatest contribution is his version of the Tarot, brilliantly executed by his Alchemical Mate, Lady Frieda Harris. His *Book of Thoth* is a fascinating literary tour de force, a colorful, tasty goulash of concepts from every spicy religious magical tradition loaded on to the Tarot plates. The book allows us to watch one of the most interesting minds of the century juggling neurogenetic concepts. Entertaining, educational, but limited and filled with deliberate or unconscious errors.[13]

Crowley's interpretation of the Tarot is based on Cabala—the Tree of Life. Whatever its original neurogenetic meaning, the Tree of Life as now presented is a boring larval moral code at the philosophic level of the Boy Scout oath. Consider the usual names for the ten node points of the Tree of Life: Kingdom, crown, foundation, victory, splendor, strength, beauty, mercy, understanding, wisdom. Where, one wonders, is thrift and cleanliness?

On the surface at least, the Cabalistic array seems to the uninitiated to be a Talmudic laryngeal-mind defense of Domesticated Primate morality.

What is missing from the Crowley Tarot is the scientific, evolutionary perspective. Crowley does broadcast an erotic magnificence, a graceful, tawny lasciviousness, a gleaming phallic radiance, a soft hashishine luxury. The Circuit V energy seethes and murmurs; but eventually fades, turned in on itself. Even the most perfect neurosomatic union eventually becomes boring. "Keep me high," She murmured. But rapture dissolves. Two sweaty bodies, pulled back by larval insecurities, worrying about passports and the rent.

The evolutionary process moves or freezes. Aleister Crowley represents human intelligence at its transition point. The rapturous body, floating detached from terrestrial-life lines, all wired up and nowhere to go. As he got older, he increasingly amused himself with childish jokes, playing on the "Black Magick" and "Satanist" image given to him by vulgar tabloids. Funny, frivolous, futile.

Crowley understood the interstellar goal of human evolution and was bitterly aware of his imprisonment on the planet. Gravity and the inability of current technology to reach escape velocity kept him from breaking out. The first four lines of *The Book of the Law* file his appeal for release from the custody of gravity:

"1· Had! The manifestation of Nuit.
2. The unveiling of the company of heaven.
3. Every man and every woman is a star.
4. Help me, o warrior lord of Thebes, in my unveiling before the Children of Men!"

And throughout the *Book of the Law* runs the refrain of Nuit, the star-goddess, who represents galactic intelligence in Crowley's symbology, and who continually calls us home:

"Come forth, O children, under the stars and take your fill of love."

"I am above you and in you." . . .

"They shall gather my children into their fold; they shall bring the glory of the stars into the hearts of men." . . .

"Invoke me under my stars! Love is the law, love under will." . . .

"I love you! I learn to you! . . . Put on the wings and arouse the coiled splendor within you: come unto me!"

"To me! To me! . . . I am the naked brilliance of the voluptuous night sky. To me! To me!"

# JUDEO-CHRISTIAN DOGMA: WEIRD, KOOKY, PESSIMISTIC, ANTI-EVOLUTIONARY

*All Monotheisms are obviously the residues of primitive neuro-political stages.*

Let us hope that the following logic is comprehensible.

Assume that there is a genetic plan and that biological life is coded to unfold in stages. (It certainly works that way up to the present. Conception is followed by a rigorous sequence of predictable changes. Thus it is not occultist to assume that the future is working out according to plan.)

The Egg-Wisdom seems to have designed nervous systems to continually evolve (in both species and individuals) so that at each subsequent stage (up to adulthood—menopause in the individual and up to adult specialization in species) it handles more complexity, wider frequencies of energy input, more precise, faster power of communication, transportation and higher altitude (in the sense of being able to look backward and down at what has happened and, therefore, to scope what is to come).

The general outline of the Egg-Wisdom Plan seems obvious from this post-DNA perspective. But until recently even discussion about a "plan" was placed under severe taboo by both of the monotheistic hive-orthodoxies.

Monotheistic species are committed to a creator (Jehovah) whose intelligence and morality is that of a savage paleolith.

Nineteenth century scientists reacted passionately against Monotheistic Creationism by inventing a genetics of blind, repetitious change in which evolution favored the most murderous seed-dispensors. This is, of course, a male-militaristic model which has been enthusiastically accepted by Marxist burocrats (male).

The orthodox Judeo-Christian "spiritual" theory and the Marxist-socialist scientific "materialist" theories are both examples of the implausible, kooky, weirdo programs that masculine bureaucracies so love. All monotheisms are obviously the residues of primitive neuro-political stages.

For 200 years (1800-200 a.d.) all of the terrestrial hive energies were thrown Into patriotic support of one or the other of these ludicrous negative, pessimistic dogmas.

The evolutionary plan obviously required a global struggle of the two monotheisms—usually labelled right-wing Christian and left-wing Marxist—In order to mobilize hive collectivities In frantic technological competition. The inevitable results of white-ant versus red-ant rivalry were the great scientific breakthroughs which allow, Indeed, compel the human species to move into Self-Actualized Control of:

> physiological realities
> neurological realities
> genetic realities
> quantum-nuclear-gravitational field realities.

The thesis of this book Is that the Tarot array recapitulates and pre-capitulates (I.e. predicts) the Eight Great Steps In Evolution that takes life from unicellular form (in the primitive oceans of a Flower Planet) up to the construction and Intelligent management of the galaxy itself. Table III presents this sequence In its overall form.

TABLE III THE TWENTY-FOUR STAGES OF NEUROGENETIC EVOLUTION*

| | | |
|---|---|---|
| **Stage 22, No Tarot**<br>Metaphysiological<br>Receptivity<br><br>(no Tarot card) | **Stage 23, Tarot 22**<br>Metaphysiological<br>Intelligence<br>The Nuclear Controller<br>The Tarot "World" | **Stage 24, Tarot 23**<br>Metaphysiological<br>Fusion<br>"The Black Hole"<br>(no Tarot card) |
| **Stage 19, Tarot 18**<br>Neurogenetic<br>Receptivity<br>"The Genetic Consumer Brain"<br><br>Tarot Moon | **Stage 20, Tarot 19**<br>Neurogenetic<br>Intelligence<br>"The DNA Mind"<br>The DNA Controller<br>Tarot Sun | **Stage 21, Tarot 20**<br>Neurogenetic<br>Fusion<br>Genetic Symbiotic<br>Brain<br>Tarot Judgement |
| **Stage 16, Tarot 15**<br>Neurophysical<br>Receptivity<br>Electron Consumer Brain<br>Tarot Devil | **Stage 17, Tarot 16**<br>Neurophysical<br>Intelligence<br>The Brain Controller<br>Tarot Tower | **Stage 18, Tarot 17**<br>Neurophysical<br>Fusion<br>Telepathic Brain<br>Tarot Star |
| **Stage 13, Tarot 12**<br>Neuro-somatic<br>Receptivity<br>"Rapture Consumer" Brain<br>Tarot Hanged Man | **Stage 14, Tarot 13**<br>Neuro-somatic<br>Intelligence<br>"The Body Controller"<br>Tarot Death | **Stage 15, Tarot 14**<br>Neuro-somatic<br>Fusion<br>"Tantric Linkage"<br>Tarot Temperance |
| **Stage 10, Tarot 9**<br>Sexual Self-Indulgence<br>Adolescent Brain<br>Tarot Hermit | **Stage 11, Tarot 10**<br>Domestic Intelligence<br>"The Domesticated Brain"<br>Tarot Wheel of Life | **Stage 12, Tarot 11**<br>Cultural Domestication<br>"The Socialist Brain"<br>Tarot Justice |
| **Stage 7, Tarot 6**<br>The Receptive-Paleolithic Brain<br>Mental Passivity<br>Tarot Lovers | **Stage 8, Tarot 7**<br>The Inventive Brain<br><br>Tarot Chariot | **Stage 9, Tarot 8**<br>The Engineer Brain<br>Craft-caste<br>Tarot Strength |
| **Stage 4, Tarot 3**<br>Emotional Passivity<br>"The Small Animal Brain"<br><br>Tarot Priestess | **Stage 5, Tarot 4**<br>Emotional Intelligence<br>The Large Agressive<br>Animal Brain<br>Tarot Emperor | **Stage 6, Tarot 5**<br>Emotional Dominance<br>The Monkey<br>Politician Brain<br>Tarot High Priest |
| **Stage 1, Tarot 0**<br>Bio-survival<br>Receptivity<br>Amoeba Brain<br>Tarot Fool | **Stage 2, Tarot 1**<br>Bio-survival<br>Intelligence<br>The Fish Brain<br>Tarot Magician | **Stage 3, Tarot 2**<br>Bio-survival<br>Fusion<br>Amphibian Brain<br>Tarot Empress |

1. The numbers are those conventionally assigned to the Tarot-plus One. The Fool is 1 instead of zero, Magician is 2 instead of 1. Note that card 2 (formerly High Priestess) and card 3 (formerly Empress) have been reversed. In some Tarot decks cards 8 and 11 are reversed. Note: also that two new Tarot slots have been added 21 and 23—and that the Universe Card (formerly 21 is now 22).

* To understand human evolution, it is necessary to understand the function of *Structural Caste* and *Temporal Caste*—as described in *Sociobiology* by Edward Wilson and *The Intelligence Agents* by Timothy Leary.

# AMAZING PROPHESY OF NEURO-FISSION BY MEDIEVAL TAROTISTS

Alelster Crowley, whose hashish consciousness centered on sex-magic (Fifth Circuit) eroticized the cards. In general, Tarot commentators have been able to understand only early fetal elements and have been able to give only the most fanciful anticipations of stages and cards which lie ahead in their own future and the future of the species. For example, the Sixth Circuit mediates atomic fission, time dilation, electron manipulation, neurological relativity, astronautics. It was, therefore, difficult for anyone living before 1945 to describe these events which lay ahead. Thus, stage 17, the Tower Fissioned by Lightning, has mistakenly picked up lower circuit meanings (war, destruction etc.)—and the precise meaning of this post-Einsteinian signal could only be poetically anticipated.

THE FIRST TWELVE TAROT
CARDS PORTRAY THE
LARVAL-HIVE STAGES OF
HUMAN EVOLUTION AND
OF YOUR OWN PERSONAL
DEVELOPMENT

THIS PART II MAKES HAMBURGER
OUT OF ALL OUR SACRED COWS

TOO BAD YOU WONT BE AROUND
FOR PART III

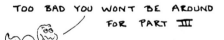

# PART II

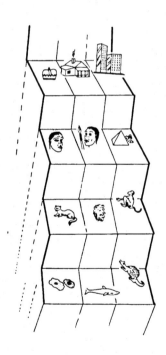

# TAROT I:

## YOUR PERSONAL PICTURE ALBUM

EACH OF US HAS TWELVE PRIMITIVE, TERRESTRIAL BRAINS WHICH HAVE BEEN ACTIVATED SEQUENTIALLY DURING OUR PERSONAL DEVELOPMENT. EACH OF US PASSES THROUGH THESE STAGES WHICH ARE CALLED TEMPORAL CASTES. EACH OF US IS GENETICALLY WIRED SO THAT ONE OF THESE BRAINS IS DOMINANT AND FABRICATES OUR ADULT SPECIALIZED "HOME" REALITY THIS IS CALLED STRUCTURAL CASTE.

IT IS YOUR STRUCTURAL CASTE, YOUR ADULT SPECIALIZATION, THAT EVENTUALLY STOPS YOUR GROWTH, AGES AND KILLS YOU.

# THE FIRST THREE CARDS—
## FOOL, MAGUS, EMPRESS
# PORTRAY YOUR THREE
# MARINE NEURO-
# TECHNOLOGIES

Wetting their whistles at a caste-party are (l. to r.) Demeter, Nepture-Aries and Pluto-Pisces. What's the occasion? The happy primordials have just completed their current reality-film LIFE IN THE DEPTHS.

**THE FIRST CIRCUIT OF THE NERVOUS SYSTEM TO EVOLVE**
**(both in the species and the individual)**
**ACTIVATES MARINE (PRE-TERRESTRIAL) SURVIVAL INTELLIGENCE**

The I Ching Trigram which signifies the First Circuit is KUN: EARTH

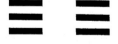

The Tarot Trigram which predicts this cycle are:
      CARD 0: THE FOOL — Stage 1—Amoeboid Floating
      CARD 1: THE MAGUS—Stage 2—Fish Swimming, Biting
      CARD 2: EMPRESS—Stage 3—Amphibian Crawling

# THE FOOL PORTRAYS YOUR FLOATING-SUCKING NEURO-TECHNOLOGY

**CASTE 1**

| | |
|---|---|
| **NEUROGENETIC TECHNOLOGICAL STAGE:** | Amoeboid Floating-Sucking; The First Self-Definition; Unicellular consciousness |
| **PHYLOGENETIC STAGE:** | Invertebrate; unicellular; protozooic |
| **ONTOGENETIC STAGE:** | New-born Infant. Endomorphic |
| **ATTITUDE:** | Ventral, Floating Towards Vegetative Security, Incorporative |
| **ZODIAC I:** | The Floater (Pisces) |
| **ROMAN I:** | Pluto-Proserpine |
| **GREEK I:** | Hades-Persephone |
| **א  HEBREW:** | Aleph, "I am undefined. Undirected" |
| **REALITY CREATED:** | Simple Approach-avoidance world |
| **ECOLOGICAL NICHE (species):** | Water |
| **ECOLOGICAL NICHE (indiv.):** | Mother's arms |

The Fool drifts through planetary atmosphere embracing the soft, sweet, smooth, moist, nourishing, avoiding the hard, noxious, rough, dry, irritating. The Dendritic decision is viscerotonic: to turn towards the secure and biologically satisfying.

The Fool card is a reminder from DNA that your nervous system contains an amoeboid-baby brain circuit which is still functioning and demanding of respect.

*This book describes 24 genetic castes for which the Tarot cards serve as signs or memory devices. For each caste we have included the drawing of a chemical element based on the logical assumption that bio-neural evolution must be related to the evolution of physical chemical elements.

These element drawings are based upon a revision of the Mendeleyev periodic table of the elements which has been designed by two brilliant 21st-century intelligence agents, Jason Saleeby and Francis Busco. The new arrangement of elements is a double spiral helix!

It makes sense, does it not? While it is true that a simple-minded two dimensional table fits nicley in 19th-century books, on the wall of chemistry laboratories and in the square minds of primitive chemists, still we know that the spatial topological relationships among atoms as they evolve and build up in complexity must be at least three dimensional. And the periodicity which Mendeleyev diagrammed in the rows and columns of his table are more accurately expressed as recurring degree points on an expanding spiral.

The Saleeby-Busco periodic spiral of the elements will be detailed in the next volume in the Future History Series: *How to Joyfully Survive the Collapse of Civilization During the 1980's.* Here, we simply call the reader's attention to the fact that every stage of neurogenetic caste development corresponds to a step in the periodic spiral of elements. We thus remind ourselves that the evolution of the individual nervous system is best understood as relating to the addition of electron-protons in evolving elements and that the fusions and connections among humans are best described by the way elements hook up in chemical molecular bonds.

The reader is referred to Appendix 1, Page 291 for a brief description of the periodic spiral of evolution.

THESE HOOLIGANS ARE OVERTHROWING DIMITRI'S CENTURY-OLD TABLE

HURRAY! THE PRISONERS BEGIN THEIR ESCAPE

UNICELLULAR INTELLIGENCE

A
♦

HADES-PLUTO PERSEPHONE-PROSERPINE

FLOATING-SUCKING TECHNOLOGY

**FOOL**

INNOCENT PISCES I

♦
A

*Stage 1*

Tarot Fool (Card Zero) The FOOL (Pisces I) represents sucking-floating technology. The passive, unattached primordial stage of unicellular bio-survival. Marine, liquid. In the species this stage is AMOEBOID. In the individual this stage represents the new-born baby.

This primitive brain-circuit (which was first built by DNA some 3 billion years ago) is still wired into your nervous system. It allows you to re-experience the earliest days of evolution, time-travel back to protozooan memorealities. And to re-live your own suckling Infant days.

# THE FOOL IS YOUR BABY BRAIN STILL FLOATING AWAY IN YOUR HEAD

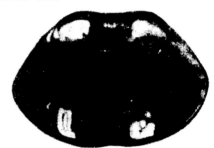

The Tarot card **FOOL** represents this passive, self-contained invertebrate mode of bio-survival. The *Attitude* is floating. Unattached to a fixed outer survival connection, the Bio-Org imprints Hir own vegetative processes for security satisfaction. The infantile-receptive consumer phase of the First Circuit.

This is initial caste in the evolutionary system; the plastic, unformed, unattached, flexibility of the new-born organism. Occultists call this card the Primum Mobile, the first life principle, innocent, liquid, dreamy, self-contained wise potential. The Tao infant sage. Fresh and moist from the genetic pool. Not really adjusted to terrestrial life. The Babe. In-Sanity.

"The Fool" is portrayed as youthful. SHe carries a bag. Let the bag in this equation represent the genetic-material-ovum-sperm. The Fool launches the great journey carrying the seed cargo.

De Laurence's book on the Tarot[1] warns "Danger is associated with this card," reflecting the vulnerability and unformed nature of the organism which has not RNA-externalized an active technology. The attitude is loose. The direction aimless. Eyes not focussed on Earth. Dreamy, in-different. SHe "lives in lonely understanding of truths too far and deep to express in words or deeds."

From the Neurogenetic position of this card we can understand the classic Piscean divinatory meanings assigned to the Fool: folly, disorganized mania, intoxicated incoherence, aimless floating, depth, apathy, nullity, autism.

90

DON'T WEEP YOU PISCES...
YOUR DIVINITY APPEARS IN CASTE 13

# YOUR AMOEBOID BRAIN DEMANDS TO BE INDULGED: BEWARE ITS OPIATE, VEGETATIVE INVITATION

Stage 1 thus reflects newborn other-worldly innocence. The Fool is usually portrayed as floating toward danger, Hir back turned away from safety. This caste person is unformed—not quite at home in a mechanized, organized society, where social conformity is required. In looser tribal situations the passive detached Fool, the Adult Infant, is tolerated and even seen as a source of social strength. This card represents the positive (Laing-ian) aspects of in-sanity. Opium wisdom—distillation of the fluid, underworld DNA mysteries which are RNA-actualized within the vegetative nervous system.

This structural caste, the Pisces Personality, represents technological incapacity to fabricate external sources of reward. Disinterest in external control or fusion—biological, emotional, political, domestic. Ambition, competition, engineering manipulation, have no appeal to compare with the rich visceral life. Disregard for rules, indifference to threats and punishments. The path of least resistance. Privacy. Amoral flexibility. Oral greed.

The Fool is self-rewarding, self-indulgent, self-stimulating, self-contained and self-undoing.

Crowley correlates this card with such mythic Jungian archetypes as the "April Fool" or spirit of spring in the Frazerian vegetation cults: nature's newborn child, rising again after death (winter). The Holy Ghost, he says, is the Christian equivalent, and Hoor-par-kraat the Egyptian congate. Hoor-par-kraat is usually depicted with finger in mouth, like a newborn, and symbolizes meditation: the yogic hippy drop-out. Parcifal, also mentioned by Crowley, is a special case, in which the mutation to the extra-terrestrial equivalent (Pisces II, Stage 13 Hanging Man) is clearly indicated; Crowley calls him "the Pure Fool," since his unearthly vision can give him many qualities of the prophet, wandering wise man, the Mysterious Stranger who is a Magician, etc.

In many traditions, fairy tales and allegories, the king's daughter (symbolizing Gaia, earth wisdom) can only be won by such a Pure Fool, who must be an alien, a vagabond. A new arrival on the planet. The meaning again is given in the New Testament: "Unless ye become as a little child, ye shall in no wise enter the kingdom of earth."

91

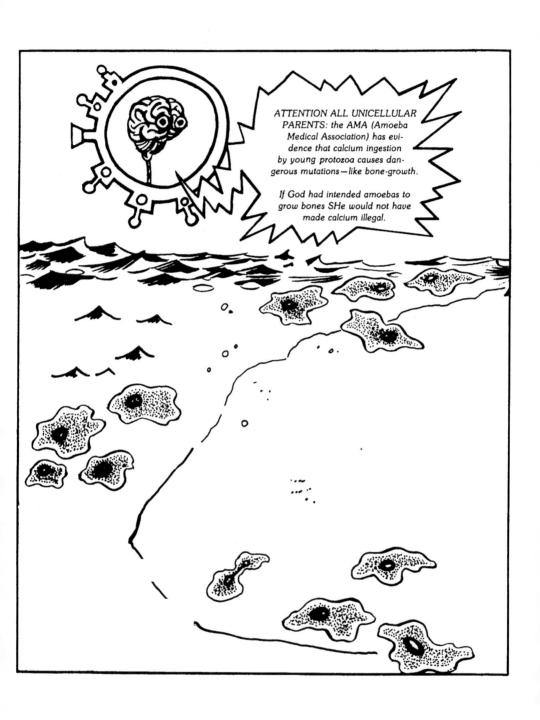

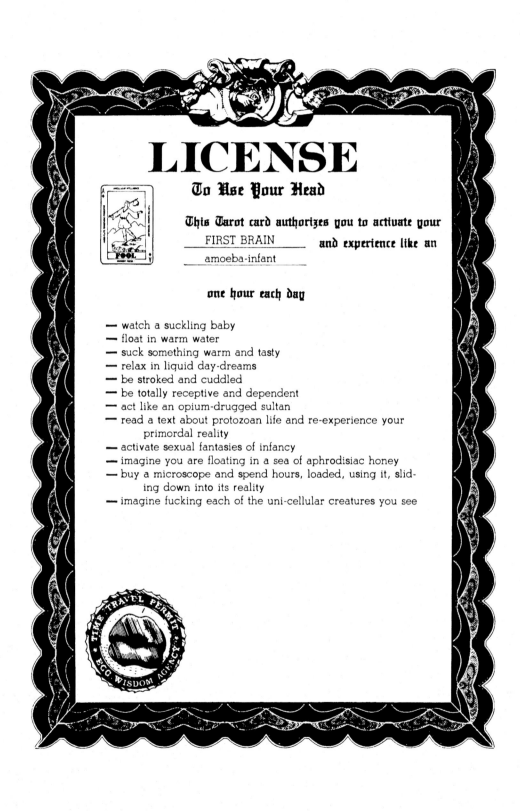

# LICENSE

## To Use Your Head

This Tarot card authorizes you to activate your

_____FIRST BRAIN_____ and experience like an

amoeba-infant

## one hour each day

— watch a suckling baby
— float in warm water
— suck something warm and tasty
— relax in liquid day-dreams
— be stroked and cuddled
— be totally receptive and dependent
— act like an opium-drugged sultan
— read a text about protozoan life and re-experience your
        primordal reality
— activate sexual fantasies of infancy
— imagine you are floating in a sea of aphrodisiac honey
— buy a microscope and spend hours, loaded, using it, slid-
        ing down into its reality
— imagine fucking each of the uni-cellular creatures you see

# THE MAGUS PORTRAYS YOUR SWIMMING-BITING NEURO-TECHNOLOGY

**CASTE 2**

| | |
|---|---|
| **NEUROGENETIC TECHNOLOGICAL STAGE:** | Squirming, biting, swimming. The First Self-Actualization. Marine Intelligence./Control over One's own Vegetative Reality |
| **PHYLOGENETIC STAGE:** | Fish (Paleozoic) |
| **ONTOGENETIC STAGE:** | Infantile Squirming, Biting and Control of Reality by Crying. |
| **ATTITUDE:** | Ventral, Straight-on-forward to Viscerotonic Satisfaction |
| **ZODIAC I:** | Aries I |
| **ROMAN I:** | Neptune, Amphitrite |
| **GREEK I:** | Poseidon, Amphitrite |
| **ב HEBREW:** | Beth, "A Young Man will take heed." |
| **REALITY CREATED:** | Self-Actualized control over oral supplies |
| **ECOLOGICAL NICHE (species):** | Water |
| **ECOLOGICAL NICHE (indiv):** | Mother's arms; crib |

Let the Tarot card **MAGUS** represent the First Self-Actualization. Bio-neural intelligence, the physiological reflex mind. Control and satisfaction of the ventral organs. *The Aries-Magus attitude is forward-oral.*

We have just considered Bio-neural Passivity. Stage 1. The infantile Fool floating, wandering, gathering food where it is found.

Now we consider Stage 2 the first imprint which creates the infant bio-reality. It is necessary to understand the neurological significance of the fact that all the survival-sensory equipment is located in front: mouth, eyes, ears, nose. The nervous system is oriented forward and the dorsal (rear) side is impoverished neurologically.

The evolutionary stage is marine, paleozoic.

The Magus card is a telegram sent you by DNA reminding you that one circuit of your brain is shark-infant, still functioning and requiring use.

*I LIKE THIS PART*

ORAL SELF ASSERTION

2 ♦

SQUIRMING-BITING TECHNOLOGY

POSEIDON-AMPHYTRITE NEPTUNE

**MAGICIAN** ♦ 2

FEISTY ARIES I

*Stage 2*

Tarot Magus (**CARD 1**) The **MAGUS** (Aries) represents the second phase of survival technology—the mobile, squirming, moving, biting Fish. The environment is still marine. In the species this stage Is represented by the **SHARK**. In the individual this stage is the biting-squirming period of Infancy. The first Self-Actualization via mobility.

Your ability to re-activate this brain allows you to tune in to the Paleozoic circuits of your brain, experience like a fish; and to re-live your own squirming-biting memorealities.

# THE MAGUS IS YOUR INFANT-SHARK BRAIN STILL BITING AWAY IN YOUR HEAD

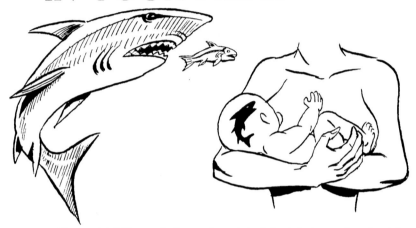

Bio-neural intelligence is the marine mind of the infant scanning ahead for immediate visceral satisfaction, integrating and organizing the vegetative, autonomic survival signals. The youthful Magus figure usually wears the horizontal infinity sign over Hir head. Sign of Life. On the table in front of the Magus are the symbols of the four Tarot suits. In this equation we have let these symbols represent the four basic nucleic acids whose permutations transmit the **DNA** code. We shall not concern ourself about whether the suits "really" represent the nucleic acids. We simply suggest that it might be an advance in con-telligence for people who seriously or frivolously engage in Tarot-semantics to use scientific-evolutionary terms in addition to terrestrial concepts.

The Tarot Magician is usually surrounded by marine and vegetative flourishes: vines, flowers, leaves, cellular forms.

Psychologically this card signifies the self-centered, driving marine bio-intelligence. The motive force of animation. *Jaws.*

Crowley's magical image of this card is the wand or caduceus, thrusting *forward*. The Magician has solved the first basic problem of all life: SHe knows what to approach and what to avoid. SHe is now ready for the first Mating, the First Migration to Mother-Earth.

DONT GET UPSET YOU ARIES... YOUR TRUE
NATURE EMERGES AT STAGE 14 IN PART III

# LICENSE

## To Use Your Head

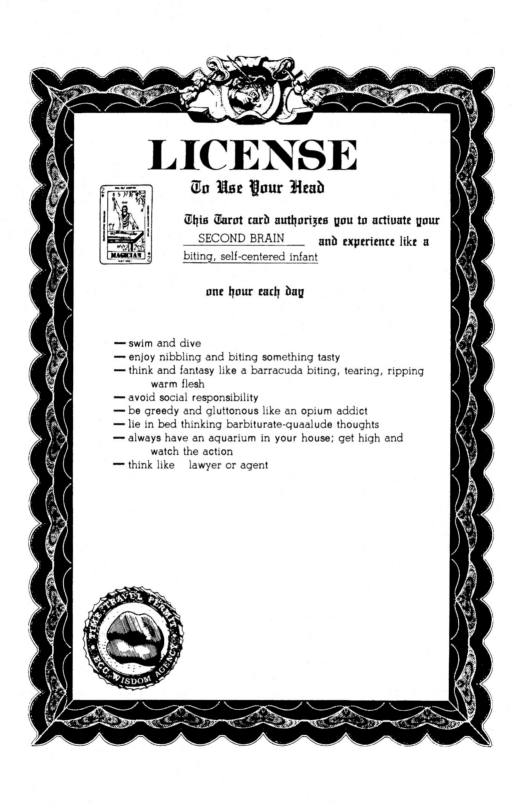

This Tarot card authorizes you to activate your

_SECOND BRAIN_ and experience like a

biting, self-centered infant

### one hour each day

— swim and dive
— enjoy nibbling and biting something tasty
— think and fantasy like a barracuda biting, tearing, ripping
     warm flesh
— avoid social responsibility
— be greedy and gluttonous like an opium addict
— lie in bed thinking barbiturate-quaalude thoughts
— always have an aquarium in your house; get high and
     watch the action
— think like    lawyer or agent

# THE EMPRESS PORTRAYS YOUR AMPHIBIAN-CRAWLING NEURO-TECHNOLOGY

**CASTE 3**

| | |
|---|---|
| **NEUROGENETIC TECHNOLOGICAL STAGE:** | Amphibian crawling/Mastery of gravity. |
| **PHYLOGENETIC STAGE:** | Amphibian migration to shoreline |
| **ONTOGENETIC STAGE:** | Infant Crawling |
| **ATTITUDE:** | Ventral, Face-to-face Satisfaction |
| **ZODIAC I:** | Taurus I, The Earth Connection |
| **ROMAN I:** | Demeter-Bacchus |
| **GREEK:** | Ceres-Dionysus |
| **ℷ HEBREW:** | Gimel, "Deal bountifully with me, that I may live." |
| **REALITY CREATED:** | Shoreline langurous |
| **ECOLOGICAL NICHE (species):** | Shoreline |
| **ECOLOGICAL NICHE (indiv):** | Floorline |

The Tarot EMPRESS, Caste 3, represents the active-output Stage of the First Circuit. The ventral-ventral linkage. The embracing, belly-to-belly visceral connection. The First Migration. From water to shoreline. The soft landing of the infant onto the planetary skin-surface. The external target of the First Circuit vegetative connection. The First Mate. Mother Earth, moist source of nourishment, warmth, softness, food. The searching, hungry, stimulus-starved ventral nerve-endings hooked up. The First Fusion—solid, comforting, smooth, liquid, warm, cuddly and moist.

Tarot literature personalizes this basic engagement as the EMPRESS MOTHER, Universal fecundity. Warm and humid. Corn ripens around the fruitful vagina. She holds the blossoming sceptre. Refugium of the weak. "She is the . . . outer sense of the [primal] Word,"[2] a splendid quote from ancient occultism that precisely forecasts Slot-3 of the Neurogenetic Array.

The Empress Card is a valentine from Gaia-Egg wisdom reminding you that your nervous system contains a slow, crawling amphibian Brain Circuit which is still functioning and demanding of affectionate attention.

DONT FRET YOU TAURANS

YOU'LL FLY HIGH IN STAGE 15

AMPHBIAN BRAIN

CRAWLING NEURO-TECHNOLOGY

CERES—DEMETER DIONYSUS—BACCHUS

**EMPRESS**

SOLID EARTHY TAURUS I

*Stage 3*

Tarot Empress (Card 2) The EMPRESS (note number change with High Priestess which in some systems is card 2) represents the crawling technology which makes possible migration to the shore-line, floor-line. The young nervous system links with the earth in belly-to-belly contact. Bio-security through crawling. In the species this stage is **AMPHIBIAN**. In the infant individual this stage is **CRAWLING**.

This brain (which first appeared 400 million years ago) is still wired into your nervous system and can be turned on—allowing you to re-live the amphibian experience. And, as an added bonus, tune-in to memorealities of your own crawling infancy.

99

# THE EMPRESS IS YOUR CRAWLING-INFANT BRAIN STILL REQUIRING ACTION

*DRUG SCANDAL EXPOSED! Recent warnings from the FDA (Fish-Drug-Administration) are confirmed by this photo of two teen-age delinquent sharks lolling around on the shoreline sniffing Oxygen. Warning: the FDA has determined that Oxygen is a lethal drug producing terrible mutations in the unfortunate users' DNA.*

Let this card locate the First Home on earth, solid, tranquil, sensual, tactile, Security. The ventral nerve-endings of the infant search, find, and connect with earth. Mother-love. The Self-Actualized Infant recognizes and fuses with earth.

The anthropological expression of this evolutionary slot is matriarchal. The worship of life. The fertility cults of Astarte, Ishtar, Ashtoreth, Freyja.

The Earth-Mother provides the face-to-face satisfaction of the ventral hungers. The security and indolent satisfaction obtained from the full-belly, the soft-skin touch, the sense of cushioned languor.

The Cabalists identify this card with the Hebrew letter *daleth,* a door. The cervical opening. The womb. The sparrow, dove or swan are given as correlated images by Crowley and appear on many decks, ancient and modern. The symbolism is soft, material, feathery-warm. The magical instrument is the girdle, softly enclosing. Associated perfumes and incenses are "sandalwood, myrtle, all soft voluptuous odors." Crowley describes this card as "The Daughter of the Mighty Ones," i.e. the king's daughter who, mating with the Fool, transmutes him to the Magician ready to march forward into the higher circuits.

# YOUR AMPHIBIAN BRAIN CANNOT BE REPRESSED: IT DEMANDS REGULAR STIMULATION

The largest symbol shown in this card is the stylized "valentine" heart which is the Disneyland pop-symbol of romantic love in domesticated civilization. The real meaning of the "heart" would be quite shocking to Four-brained larvals who flaunt this symbol for commercial purposes. The "pop-art-heart," which has little resemblance to the cardiac organ, is obviously a hieroglyphic for the vulva, engorged, distended, pink-with-arousal, in receptive-embrace and bisected on top by the clitoral dimple.

In the Empress-Taurus card the Symbol-for-Life has been placed inside the opened vagina, suggesting the birth process and the neonate status of this First Circuit of neural evolution.

This caste element is characterized by material love, pleasure in food, drink, contact with soft luxury, comfort, indolence. The steady, quiet immovable fulfillment which results from ventral-ventral fusion.

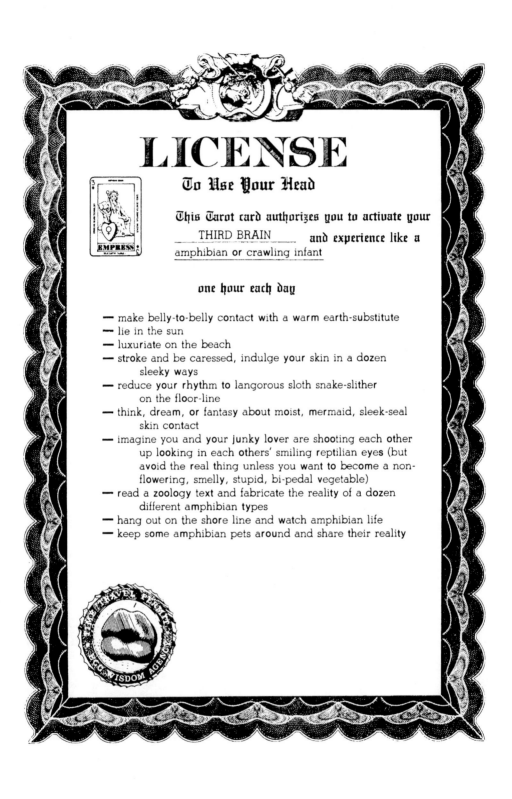

# LICENSE

## To Use Your Head

This Tarot card authorizes you to activate your

_____THIRD BRAIN_____ and experience like a

amphibian or crawling infant

### one hour each day

— make belly-to-belly contact with a warm earth-substitute
— lie in the sun
— luxuriate on the beach
— stroke and be caressed, indulge your skin in a dozen
     sleeky ways
— reduce your rhythm to langorous sloth snake-slither
     on the floor-line
— think, dream, or fantasy about moist, mermaid, sleek-seal
     skin contact
— imagine you and your junky lover are shooting each other
     up looking in each others' smiling reptilian eyes (but
     avoid the real thing unless you want to become a non-
     flowering, smelly, stupid, bi-pedal vegetable)
— read a zoology text and fabricate the reality of a dozen
     different amphibian types
— hang out on the shore line and watch amphibian life
— keep some amphibian pets around and share their reality

# THE NEXT THREE CARDS –
## PRIESTESS, EMPEROR, PRIEST
## PORTRAY YOUR THREE NEURO-TECHNOLOGIES FOR TERRITORIAL MUSCULAR POWER

Why are these three smiling? The Sly Priestess, the Mafia Emperor, and the Pope are probably giggling about their plans to take over TransAmerica Corp. The crafty mammalian trio were snapped at the caste-party celebrating the wrap-up of their reality-movie LIFE ON THE LATE-GREAT PLANET EARTH.

**THE SECOND CIRCUIT OF THE NERVOUS SYSTEM TO EVOLVE MEDIATES MUSCULAR POWER AND TERRITORIAL CONTROL AS THE SURVIVAL TECHNOLOGY**

The I Ching Trigram which signifies the Second Circuit of the Brain is CH'EN: MOVEMENT-EARTHQUAKE

The three Tarot cards which predict this cycle of development are:

CARD 3: HIGH (SLY) PRIESTESS – Stage 4 – Evasive-Mammalian Loco-motion

CARD 4: The EMPEROR — Stage 5 – Large-Fierce Mammalian Power to Control Territory

CARD 5: The HIGH PRIEST — Stage 6 – Monkey-Social Communication

103

# THE HIGH PRIESTESS PORTRAYS
# YOUR WILY WEASEL
# NEURO-TECHNOLOGY

**CASTE 4**

| | |
|---|---|
| **NEUROGENETIC TECHNOLOGICAL STAGE:** | Evasive mobility. The Little Trickster. The Self Defined As Speedy Terrestrial Auto-Mobile. |
| **PHYLOGENETIC STAGE:** | The Mammalian Loner |
| **ONTOGENETIC STAGE:** | The Child Beginning To Crawl, Walk And Maneuver Emotionally |
| **ATTITUDE:** | Mercurial, Evasive, Secretive, Speedy |
| **ZODIAC I:** | Gemini I |
| **ROMAN:** | Mercury |
| **GREEK:** | Hermes |
| ד **HEBREW:** | Da Leth, "Remove me from the way of lying." |
| **REALITY CREATED:** | Survival on land via speed and cunning |
| **ECOLOGICAL NICHE (species):** | Land |
| **ECOLOGICAL NICHE (indiv):** | Floor of home |

Let Tarot Card 4, The High (Sly) Priestess represent the receptive exploratory phase of the Second Circuit, emotional passivity, the selection of a terrestrial survival style-evasion, stealth, camouflage, secrecy,' shifting flexibility, yielding. The underworld. Self-definition as a mobile, musculotonic, agile mammal.

The High Priestess card is a subtle, funny, precise reminder from **DNA** that your nervous system still contains the circuits you used as a wheeling-wheedling toddler—as well as the circuits used by wily-little animals, arab rodents, and swift evasive mammals—still functioning and demanding of affectionate attention and indulgence.

DONT FORGET US AS YOU EVOLVE.
— YOU'LL ALWAYS NEED A WHEELER-DEALER ——

4 ◆

WILY ANIMAL INTELLIGENCE

EVASIVE NEURO-TECHNOLOGY

MERCURY—MERCURIA HERMES—HERMIA

**HIGH PRIESTESS** ◆

MERCURIAL GEMINI I

*Stage 4*

Tarot Priestess (Card 3). The **SLY PRIESTESS** (Gemini) represents mammalian locomotion technology—the emergence of paws and muscles designed to produce speed, agility and evasive flight. The emergence of new sensory systems. The activation of neural centers which fabricate mammalian reality. This is the passive stage of mammalian territoriality. Survival through secrecy and evasion. In the species this stage involves SMALL MAMMALS. In the individual, this stage portrays the child learning how to walk, run and sense hive cues which signal power and status.

This brain (which appeared 100 million years ago) is still wired into your nervous system and can be activated—allowing you to relive the mobile-animal experience. And, as a double feature, permits you to tune in to memorealities of your own toddler childhood.

105

O.K. CLEVER GEMINI
YOU GET TO BE A
HERO AT STAGE 16

# THE HIGH PRIESTESS IS YOUR GRABBING TODDLER BRAIN STILL SCHEMING AWAY IN YOUR HEAD

The Second Circuit manifests as muscular skill, emotional politics. Stage 4 represents the weak side of the eternal gravitational (up-down) polarity—the down-trodden, the up-start, the young, the rebellious, the helpless victim, the wily small, the female-male, the boy-girl. Cunning, furtive, crafty, smooth, deceitful, underhand. Bewitching, beguiling, enchanting, charming, fluent.

In the prudish Middle Ages this attitude was laundered as the Nun or Priestess behind whose demure smile and robes flashed silken smiles. SHe is sly, mysterious, enigmatic, veiled, paradoxical, two-faced, two-sided. SHe mirrors, imitates, reflects, echoes, simulates, feigns, dissembles. SHe is quicksilver.

This up-down emotional turbulence is the input stage of the Second Circuit. As all learned emotional response is play-acting, the Priestess is the *prima donna* supreme. SHe has learned that people gain attention and status from their emotions, and is learning how to develop emotion-craft of hir own.

The *attitude* is mercurial; sliding to avoid pressure from above; the passive evasion of the young and small. The motion is swift, changing. The direction reactive, adapting, supple. SHe has just migrated from the amphibian shoreline and is developing the myriad ways of specialized adaptation to terrestrial life.

The Tarot portrays this element as a young woman personifying the mysterious wisdom of the Sly Priestess who must exert power covertly. De Laurence's Tarot commentary stresses secrecy: "the scroll in her hands . . . signif[ies] . . . the Secret Law and the second sense of the Word. It is partly covered by her mantle, to shew that some things are implied and some spoken. . . .

"She has been called [pompously] Occult Science, . . . but she is really the Secret . . ." Rodent Life of smiling crime and sweet deceit.

106

THINGS LOOK BETTER FOR
YOU GEMINIS IN STAGE 16

SKIP THIS PAGE
UNLESS YOU'RE A
TAROT SCHOLAR

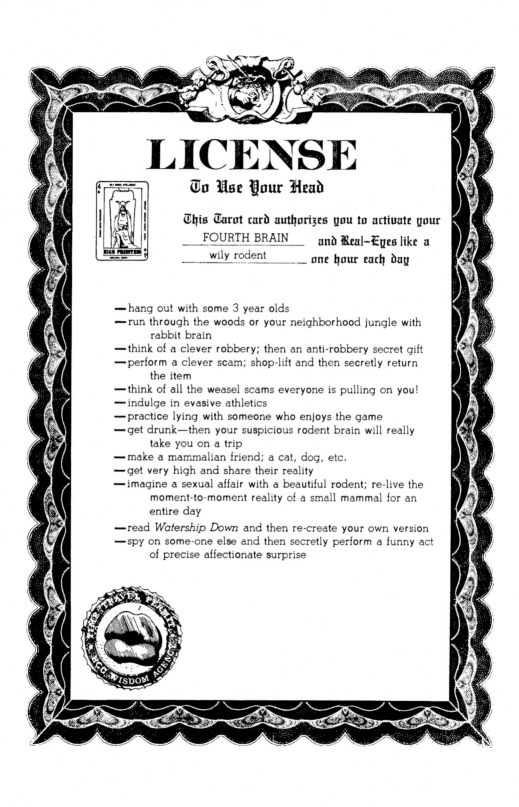

# LICENSE

## 𝕿𝖔 𝖀𝖘𝖊 𝖄𝖔𝖚𝖗 𝕳𝖊𝖆𝖉

𝕿𝖍𝖎𝖘 𝕿𝖆𝖗𝖔𝖙 𝖈𝖆𝖗𝖉 𝖆𝖚𝖙𝖍𝖔𝖗𝖎𝖟𝖊𝖘 𝖞𝖔𝖚 𝖙𝖔 𝖆𝖈𝖙𝖎𝖛𝖆𝖙𝖊 𝖞𝖔𝖚𝖗

_____FOURTH BRAIN_____ 𝖆𝖓𝖉 𝕽𝖊𝖆𝖑-𝕰𝖞𝖊𝖘 like a

_____wily rodent_____ 𝖔𝖓𝖊 𝖍𝖔𝖚𝖗 𝖊𝖆𝖈𝖍 𝖉𝖆𝖞

- hang out with some 3 year olds
- run through the woods or your neighborhood jungle with rabbit brain
- think of a clever robbery; then an anti-robbery secret gift
- perform a clever scam; shop-lift and then secretly return the item
- think of all the weasel scams everyone is pulling on you!
- indulge in evasive athletics
- practice lying with someone who enjoys the game
- get drunk—then your suspicious rodent brain will really take you on a trip
- make a mammalian friend; a cat, dog, etc.
- get very high and share their reality
- imagine a sexual affair with a beautiful rodent; re-live the moment-to-moment reality of a small mammal for an entire day
- read *Watership Down* and then re-create your own version
- spy on some-one else and then secretly perform a funny act of precise affectionate surprise

# THE EMPEROR PORTRAYS YOUR MACHO-AMAZON BULLY NEURO-TECHNOLOGY

**CASTE 5**

| | |
|---|---|
| **NEUROGENETIC TECHNOLOGICAL STAGE:** | Mobility on land:/Mastery of gravity Emotional Intelligence./The Musculotonic Ego./The Emotional Engineer, The Second Self-Actualization (This land Is My Land) |
| **PHYLOGENETIC STAGE:** | Mammalian Power And Mobility; Territorial Instinct |
| **ONTOGENETIC STAGE:** | The Child Learning To Operate Emotionally; sensing the power situation; getting out of the way; avoiding being put-down |
| **ATTITUDE:** | Upwards, Controlling |
| **ZODIAC I:** | Cancer I |
| **ROMAN:** | Vesta, Lares-Penates |
| **GREEK:** | Hestia |
| ה **HEBREW:** | He, "I shall keep It until the end." |
| **REALITY CREATED:** | Self-Actualized Control of turf; reality divided neatly Into "my territory" and turf of the hostile neighbors. |
| **ECOLOGICAL NICHE (species):** | Turf limited by territorial range |
| **ECOLOGICAL NICHE (Individual):** | Personal reality claimed and possessed; ("my mother," "my room," "my toys") |

The primitive Tarot card Emperor personifies the mid-brain, mammalian intelligence that seeks to establish hierarchical dominance and territorial control.

The Emperor card Is a classic, enduring signal sent across time by Evolutionary Agents to remind you that one of the twenty-four circuits In your own brain is that of a school-yard bully, a powerful territorial animal—and that this ancient neurotechnology and neuromusculature still requires affectionate use.

108

——— WE CANCERS BECOME HEROS AT STAGE 16

*Stage 5*

Tarot Emperor (Card 4) The EMPEROR (Cancer) portrays muscular aggression, lumbering control of territory. The Technology of Animal Power and Emotional Status. Most human emotions trace back to the 5th Stage of Brain Development. In the species this stage Involves the **LARGE MAMMALS**. In the Individual this stage meditates the child's linking its nervous system to the power establishment and the emotional network of the local environment—namely the home and neighborhood.

This brain (which appeared 80 million years ago)is still wired into your nervous system and can be turned-on—allowing you to real-eyes like a fierce, possessive, carnivore. And, for Saturday mornings, permits you to re-activate memorealities of your own child-hood bully days.

# THE EMPEROR PORTRAYS
# YOUR BULLY-CHILD
# FIERCE-ANIMAL
# NEURO-TECHNOLOGY

The fifth brain is well-named as Zodiac Cancer and Tarot Emperor because its impulse is to acquire, grow unrestrictedly, spread over the land. Later brains symbolize and civilize this enduring self-actualizing control—but behind the security-giving, mortgage-deed paper work and behind the moral claims which appear in later stages, there still lives the aggressive mammalian control brain. The armed police. Each of us survives because our mammalian territorial brain creates the real, the symbolic and the moral home-turf we inhabit.

The fifth Tarot card, Emperor, represents the integrating, active, self-actualizing function of the Second Circuit. The emotional Intelligence designed to acquire and control territory, maintain autonomy, crawl upward against gravity, adjust behavior—now strong, now weak—so as to avoid helplessness. This element is personalized as musculotonic ego.

The *attitude* is upwards—but by shifts and starts, side movements, waits and lunges. The preceding caste, Gemini, deals with power from a position of speedy weakness. The succeeding stage deals with external manifestations of emotions in social structures—pecking order. Here we consider the Emotional Brain which can mobilize endocrine and motor systems to maintain the appropriate position of dominance-submission.

# YOUR MACHO-AMAZON
# BRAIN CIRCUITS
# DEMAND DAILY ACTIVATION
# AND EXPRESSION

The Tarot card Emperor reflects the medieval concept of the Ego as decision maker. The moody, hypothamalic dictator located in our mid-brain who can command the ATP muscular-adrenaline armies and endocrine brigades to retreat, evade, attack, dominate—all in order to control.

De Laurence tells us, "This is not the wisdom of the Higher World, but terrestrial. The moody ego-dictator, subject to stormy extremes—joy, despair, horror, compassion, sorrow and ecstasy—holds each emotion fast with a retentive memory."

Crowley, perhaps imaginatively, links the Tarot card Emperor with the root TS found in Sanscrit words for head or crown and in Caesar, Kaiser, Tsar, Senior, Seigneur, Senor. The Emperor, he says, represents "sudden, violent, but impermanent activity." The base idea is perhaps the infant learning to throw a "temper tantrum" and thereby gain attention, status, control, as in W. H. Auden's poem on the child as "dictator." The *alpha male* in ethology: the baboon's tribal leader, jealous, brutal, quick-tempered. The "male chauvinist pig" of Womens Liberation polemic. The "female chauvinist sow" of male counter-polemic.

111

DONT FRET YET YOU CANCERS
THE BEST PART COMES IN
STAGE 17

OOPS, SORRY!! WRONG REALITY NICHE!

Crowley ironically titles this card "Sun of the Morning, Chief among the Mighty" and correlates it with Dragon's Blood incense, the ruby, and the horns worn by some magicians as symbols of mammalian emotional energy.

All this describes The Emperor objectively, from outside. Seen from inside, SHe is the voice that speaks in all lyrical poetry of a hortatory, inspirational or uplifting variety: "I am the Master of my Fate; I am the Captain of my Soul." Most of the selections in grammar school English Literature texts are programming manuals teaching the children how to develop this mode of Ego; only in college is one admitted to the knowledge that there are other modes. And the hero in popular films, books, TV etc. is always the person who acts as every Emperor wishes to act: "on top of" the situation at all times.

# LICENSE

## To Use Your Head

This Tarot card authorizes you to activate your

_____ FIFTH BRAIN _____ and experience like a

spoiled-possessive mafia-capo

## one hour each day

— hang around a pre-school playground
— throw your weight around!
— think, dream, or fantasy about defeating and humiliating
   everyone
— act like the absolute ruler of the world
— indulge in strength competitive athletics and win or
   imagine you won
— think of all the people who want to keep you from your
   goals; in your mind defeat them
— be Stalin or Idi Amin for a while
— reward everyone in the world for admiringly following your
   rule
— get drunk and tell everyone, loudly, what you think of them
— go to the zoo; get loaded and psych out the lions and tigers
— make love fiercely, possessively, staking out your animal
   claim on the mate under you
— imagine you are a Mafia Capo ruthlessly extorting and
   coercing

# THE HIGH PRIEST PORTRAYS YOUR BODY-LANGUAGE NEURO-TECHNOLOGY

**CASTE 6**

| | |
|---|---|
| **NEUROGENETIC TECHNOLOGICAL STAGE:** | Monkey-troop Social Communication Arboreal Climbing: Hand gesturing; Grasping. Bird Flock Technology. The Externalization and Socialization of Emotion. The Second Migration (Arboreal), The Emotional Axon, The Primate Politician. Avian communication. |
| **PHYLOGENETIC STAGE:** | The Social Mammal (Herd, Pack, Troop, Flock, Pecking Order) |
| **ONTOGENETIC STAGE:** | The Child Tuned Into The Power-web; the kid gang. |
| **ATTITUDE:** | Superior, pissing Energy Downward from the tree-top. |
| **ZODIAC I:** | Leo I (not a lion but a monkey) |
| **ROMAN:** | Apollo, Antiope |
| **GREEK:** | Appollo, Hyppolyta |
| **ヿ HEBREW:** | Vau, "My hands I will lift up to Thy Laws." |
| **REALITY CREATED:** | Troop consciousness; survival not through strength but social communication and tree-top altitude allowing over-view. |
| **ECOLOGICAL NICHE (species):** | Three-dimensional; trees and adjoining turf. |
| **ECOLOGICAL NICHE (Individual):** | Kid's play-ground; cub moving away from home base; Post-familial, peer group society; Beginning of communication links to those outside of family. |

Tarot card 6, the Pope, represents the Confucian-socialized linkage of the Second Circuit. Emotions expressed in primate social signal systems. The Mammalian Politician. Emotional-communication fusion. The herd, troop, flock. The Second Mate, i.e. linkage.

The High Priest card is a tattered, medieval reminder transmitted along CNS-**RNA** that one of the twenty-four circuits in your brain fabricates a kindergarten-monkey exhibitionist reality—and that this primitive communication system demands expression and realization every day.

MONKEY-CLIMBING TECHNOLOGY

SOCIAL COMMUNICATION INTELLIGENCE

APOLLO AMAZON HIPPOLYTA

**HIEROPHANT**

CHARISMATIC LEO I

*Stage 6*

Tarot High Priest (Card 5) The HIGH PRIEST (Leo) represents the emergence of social communication technology—gestural, not symbolic. This is monkey-talk. The 5th Stage Mammal, no matter how big and fierce, is a loner. The primates gained territorial control by going higher—elevating themselves from four feet, climbing trees. The monkey troop is the first political technology used for survival. Social-herd communication. A new neurological technology—a new brain circuit—is needed to mediate this jump in evolution. The POPE comes after the EMPEROR in the Tarot order—signifying that Papal Politics—communication—is superior to brute muscular power. In the species this stage defines the **MONKEY** BRAIN. In the individual this stage is the pre-verbal child who communicates through troop language. Kids' gangs. Jungle Jims and Jungle Janes.

This Brain (which **DNA** activated in the early primates 65 million years ago) is still wired into your nervous system waiting to be turned-on—allowing you to experience like a smart-ass monkey. And also permits you to re-experience the memorealities of your show-off childhood.

115

DONT BE OFFENDED, LEO

YOUR GREAT MOMENT
HAPPENS AT STAGE 18
WHEN WE LEAVE THE PLANET

# THE HIGH PRIEST IS
# YOUR KID BRAIN
# STILL INSISTING ON
# SHOWING OFF

Tarot cards were designed during the pre-psychological Middle Ages when the Pope was the Head Monkey—The Primate seated on the throne of emotional-power. Although the High Priest is usually portrayed as male, the names of Abbess, High Priestess, Queen have been assigned to this element and in modern days the person of the female school teacher is for many the Immediate symbol of socialized emotions—a state employee passing on and enforcing the ruling style.

But the basic quality of the slot is exhibitionistic male. Organization, law, bureaucracy, titles, administration. Politician. Chairman. The person around whom the emotion network centers. The Pope has no armed division, but rules through monkey symbols.

In the classic Tarot card the Pope has at his feet two crossed keys. Keys are the symbols of power. One key locks in; and the other locks out. Two uniformed underlings kneel before the Ruler.

*The attitude is vertical,* directing energy in the form of signals to others In the troop. The aim is not commanding power but popularity.

Stage 4, the Sly Priestess, disguises emotions, hides, evades. Stage 5, the emotional Ego, is on top, proud, arrogant. Stage 6 is above it all signalling about It.

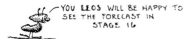

YOU LEOS WILL BE HAPPY TO SEE THE FORECAST IN STAGE 16

116

# YOUR MONKEY-BRAIN
# DEMANDS TO BE
# INDULGED: BEWARE
# ITS HISTRIONIC POWER

The associated Hebrew letter, *vau* (nail), is equally ominous. One thinks of the loyal bureaucrats of Nazi Germany, the Catholic Inquisition, Soviet Russia, of the Roman administration which crucified Jesus. Emotions, as herd-bonds, can lead to genocidal furies. Richard Cavendish points out that this figure is usually depicted with two fingers *up* and two *down*: "This indicates a distinction between *'above'* and *'below,'* God and man, . . ."[4] the gold and the base metal. Those defined as "below" or "base" are easily pissed on, all without the Hierophant ceasing to be sunny, cheerful, dutiful, obedient.

Crowley links this card to a verse in *The Book of the Law:* "there are love and love. There is the dove, and there is the serpent." He comments: "Though the face of the Hierophant appears benignant and smiling . . . it is hard to deny that in the expression of the initiator is something mysterious, even sinister. He seems to be enjoying a very secret joke at somebody's expense." The Pope likes to piss on those below who fail to admire.

Some say that the placement of the cards on the Qabalistic Tree of Life contains Gnostic propaganda, and this card—often called the Pope—links directly to the path of the Devil. If this was deliberate, it presents the Establishment as seen from outside, by the victims of Inquisitors, Gestapo, KGB or the Federal Bureau of Narcotics and Dangerous Drugs.

# LICENSE

## To Use Your Head

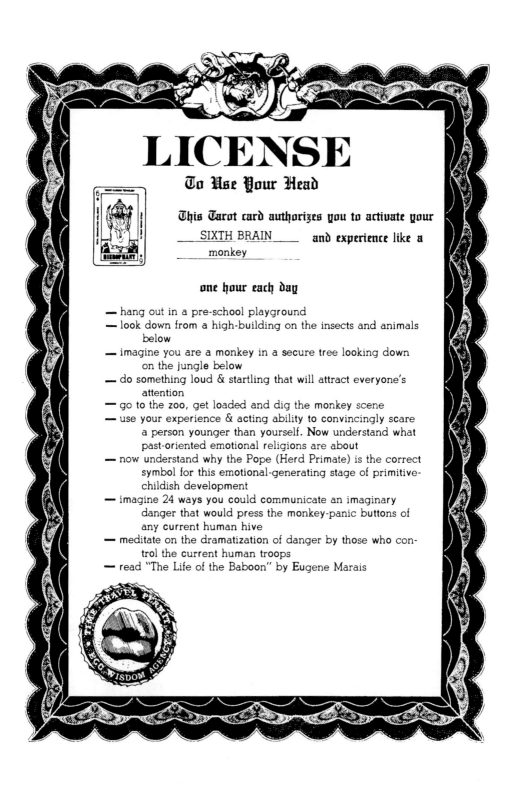

**This Tarot card authorizes you to activate your**

_____SIXTH BRAIN_____ **and experience like a**

monkey

## one hour each day

— hang out in a pre-school playground
— look down from a high-building on the insects and animals
     below
— imagine you are a monkey in a secure tree looking down
     on the jungle below
— do something loud & startling that will attract everyone's
     attention
— go to the zoo, get loaded and dig the monkey scene
— use your experience & acting ability to convincingly scare
     a person younger than yourself. Now understand what
     past-oriented emotional religions are about
— now understand why the Pope (Herd Primate) is the correct
     symbol for this emotional-generating stage of primitive-
     childish development
— imagine 24 ways you could communicate an imaginary
     danger that would press the monkey-panic buttons of
     any current human hive
— meditate on the dramatization of danger by those who con-
     trol the current human troops
— read "The Life of the Baboon" by Eugene Marais

# THE NEXT THREE CARDS —
# LOVERS, CHARIOT, STRENGTH PORTRAY
# YOUR THREE NEURO-TECHNOLOGIES
# FOR USING, INVENTING AND
# ORGANIZING SYMBOLS AND
# MANUFACTURED ARTIFACTS

Snapped here at the opening festivities for their recent Reality Movie,"Wright-Hand Lovers"–Arel Left-Brain, Mr. Libra Smart-Ass, georgeous Strength and Mel Right-Hand.

**THE THIRD CIRCUIT OF THE NERVOUS SYSTEM TO EVOLVE (in both species and individuals) PRODUCES LEFT-BRAIN SYMBOL-ARTIFACT-MECHANICAL TECH-NOLOGY: THE LARYNGEAL-MANUAL DEXTEROUS MIND**

The I Ching Trigram which signifies the Third Circuit of the Nervous System is **KAN: WATER or TOIL**

The three Tarot cards which predict and portray this cycle of development (both in the species and the Individual) are:

> **CARD** 6: PRE-ADOLESCENT LOVERS — Stage 7—Hive Sanity via Mimicking
> **CARD** 7: The CHARIOT — Stage 8—Mental Self-Actualization
> **CARD** 8: STRENGTH — Stage 9—Division of Labor

119

FROM HERE ON THEY LIVE
IN REALITIES OF THEIR OWN FABRICATION

# THE LOVERS PORTRAYS YOUR HUNTER-GATHERER-MIMICKING SCHOOL-CHILD NEURO-TECHNOLOGY

**CASTE 7**

| | |
|---|---|
| **NEUROGENETIC TECHNOLOGICAL STAGE:** | Mental passivity. Cerebrotonic Self-Definition as tool user/Laryngeal-manual Discrimination./The Receptive Mind./The Symbolic Dendrite. |
| **PHYLOGENETIC STAGE:** | Paleolithic Homanid. Repetitious, mimicking (pre-semantic) use of symbols. Hunter-gatherer. |
| **ONTOLOGICAL STAGE:** | The Child learning how to manipulate the muscles of the larynx and hand, imitating imprinted symbols. |
| **ATTITUDE:** | Accepting, mimicking, grasping to manipulate |
| **ZODIAC I:** | Virgo I, The Student |
| **ROMAN:** | Diana-Narcissus |
| **GREEK:** | Artemis-Hyacinthus |
| **⸙ HEBREW:** | "Zain, Thy word has quickened me." |
| **REALITY CREATED:** | Hunter-gatherer use of artifacts and shelters already provided |
| **ECOLOGICAL NICHE (species):** | Cave Dwellings |
| **ECOLOGICAL NICHE (individual):** | Areas Designated by Adults for Child-play and Training |

The 7th Caste receptive, dutiful, serving, ordering, shy, naive, inhibited. The mental virgins look upward for instruction. The orientation is towards symbols and artifacts, mimicking. The laryngeal-manual imprint is accepted or rejected, grasped, repeated. Here is no inventive manipulation or creative fusing of symbols.

The LOVERS card is a delicate, humorous, metamorphic reminder from DNA that your nervous system still contains the circuits first activated in the paleolithic era and used by you when you first learned to mimic and parrot symbols—to say the right words to get what you want.

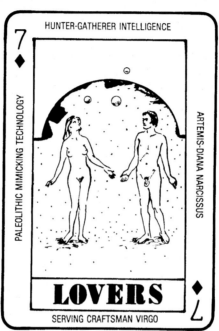

HUNTER-GATHERER INTELLIGENCE

7 ♦

PALEOLITHIC MIMICKING TECHNOLOGY

ARTEMIS-DIANA NARCISSUS

**LOVERS**

♦ 7

SERVING CRAFTSMAN VIRGO

*Stage 7*

Tarot Lovers Card 6 PRE-ADOLESCENT LOVERS (Virgo) signifies
the passive-receptive-parroting repetitious use of symbols and
artifacts. Mimicking use of the nine-vocal cords and the
right-hand. Discrimination without original thought is Superstitious Ritual. Magic is the use of energies you don't
understand. In the Species this stage is THE PALEOLITHIC—
dumbly and docilely using stones and words that have been
given. In the individual—the 5 year-old child learning to talk and
read and manipulate—without understanding the semantic origin
of the symbols. Self-definition in terms of Imprinted hive
cognitive structure—learning how to be a sane member of the
hive.

This Brain (which was activated in the Lower Paleolithic) Is
still wired Into your nervous system operating whenever you use
symbols or artifacts in a routine-repetitive way. With child-like
seriousness.

121

# THE LOVERS PORTRAY YOUR NAIVE-CHILDLIKE PARROT-MIMICKING NEURO-TECHNOLOGY

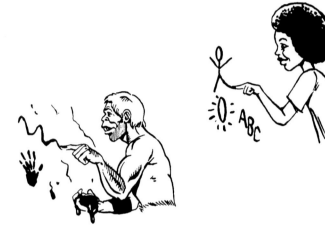

The Seventh Tarot card, the Lovers, represents the passive phase of the Third Circuit, the left-cerebral hemisphere learning how to discriminate, order, differentiate, mimic linguistic-manual symbols. From the swirling nebular clouds of raw sensation, the larynx and the right hand learn to select, close down, grasp the abstracted detail. This circuit emerges during the period when the child begins to talk and manipulate dextrously. Third Childhood. *The Student.*

The *attitude* is sphincteral—opening and closing, narrowing, focussing passively, echoing, mimicking.

The seventh brain is the first mental stage, passive, magic-obsessed, credulous, unquestioning, mimicking. Communication and mentation is rote and repetitious. A, B, C, D, E, F, G. One, two, three. Red, white, blue. This parrot use of symbols is basically magical and ritualized. The seventh brain is wired to reproduce symbols. The style, order and arrangement of the symbols are precisely imitated. Thus the familiar Virgo fussiness. The paleolithic human uses the tools handed down exactly as hir forebears. Or passively searches the stream beds, rock quarries, and play pens for the already formed tool. SHe is not yet a tool maker, fire-user, toy-maker. This is the hunter-gatherer period. Caves rather than constructed shelters. Finding rather than making. Repeating rather than thinking.

THIS ISN'T THE END, ALL YOU
VIRGOS... GREAT THINGS HAPPEN
IN STAGE 19"

I GET SO BORED
WITH MY VIRGO
BRAIN !!

YEAH - LUCKY WE HAVE
23 OTH'R CIRCUITS

When the child discovers that the world has been packaged and labelled, there is a period of dutiful, industrious, repetitious laryngeal-manual symbol-parotting. The chaos of complex sensation must be discriminated and ordered. What is *that?* While every nervous system evolves through this phase to more active, creative inventive mentation, some pre-programmed genetically (the Structural-Caste called Virgo) and/or exposed (at the time of imprint vulnerability) to an orderly authoritarian environment, adopt this passive, docile style as a survival device and social role. The key to this stage is imitation of symbol manipulation.

This Tarot caste is easily identified. Gentle, methodical, dutiful, industrious, introspective, worried, often a bit obsessive or anxious, pressed by the continual need to pigeon-hole the neural input of every second. Capable at repetitious tasks, dependable, fastidious, exacting, fussy, dogmatic about the categories, neat, always irritated by people and events which do not fit the boxes, detailed, hairsplitting, often made melancholy and weary by the refusal of the energy flux to remain dependably consistent. They are prudent, inhibited by logic and rules, critical, painstaking, practical, punctual, humor-less devoted, diligent, reliable, particular, modest. Pious, moralistic, superstitious in their compulsion to imitate the ritual.

123

DON'T WORRY ABOUT THIS PAGE.
MOVE ON.

# YOUR PALEOLITH BRAIN IS ADDICTED TO REPETITIOUS MAGIC USING WORDS AND RITUALS

The three-to-five-year-old is not yet a member of the species *Homo sapiens*. SHe is a larval form of human. Neurogenetically, this homanid temporal-caste, the symbol-mimicking stage, recaps the paleolithic stage of our species development.

Let us have no illusions. When we were five years old we were stone-age primitives, dim-witted crafty parroting primates. Hunter-gatherers.

When the growing child has mastered the social primate reality the next metamorphosis is reached. Around age 3-5 the left hemisphere of our cortex kicks into high gear and creates two new neuro-physiological technologies. We learn how to dextrously manipulate the thumb and opposable forefingers. We learn how to rub the nine muscles of our larynx together. We thus became Laryngeal-manual symbol dealing humanoids. Magic-rituals require precision of repetition.

This perfectionistic attitude leads to an emotional detachment. This caste is shy, fearful of connection, passion or dependence. Cool, self-controlled, self-preoccupied, self-disciplined. Mentally celibate.

Docile to authority. But quick to criticize, sensitive to disorder and inconsistency.

This caste is the first, primitive use of symbols and artifacts. The paleolithic person and the modern urban Virgo deal with symbols in a repetitious manner. The approach is not rational; but magical. This neural stage assures that by saying the right word, by performing the rote ritual—survival will be attained. Thus the reliance on rules and accustomed ways of doing things. Most modern human beings never progress beyond this passive stage of symbol manipulation. The True Believer, the docile repeater of religious, political, or racial slogans. Stage 7 individuals are irritated and threatened by attempts of the Stage 8 intellect to test or revise the semantic reality of symbols.

In the usual design of this Tarot card, the young man looks passively at the young woman, and she, in turn, looks passively at the angel. The message is receptivity, learning, accepting instruction. The first slot of the Third Circuit. Older packs show a man choosing between two women. Cavendish says that the card has various implications—love and innocence, temptation, free will, choice—but it is also a symbol of the union of opposites. The element of choice is primary: the discriminating faculty of the symbolic intelligence is depicted.

# LICENSE

## 𝔗𝔬 𝔘𝔰𝔢 𝔜𝔬𝔲𝔯 𝔥𝔢𝔞𝔡

**This Tarot card authorizes you to activate your**

<u>SEVENTH BRAIN</u> **and experience like a**

pious-parrot hunter-gatherer

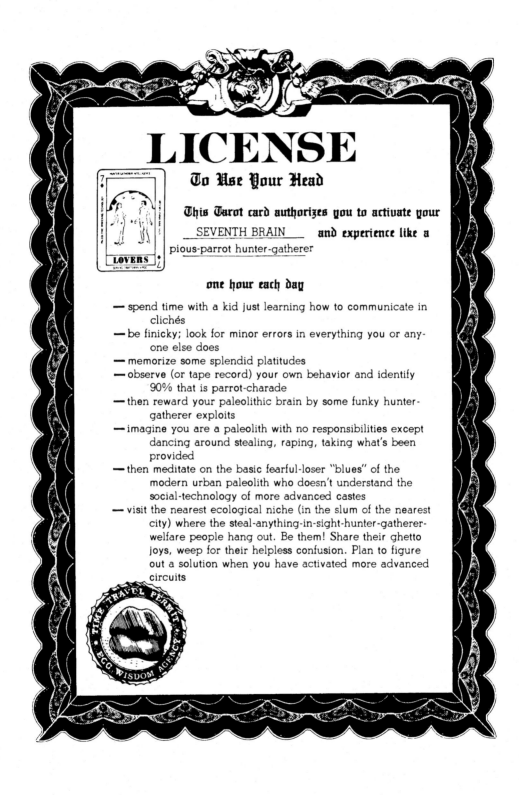

### one hour each day

— spend time with a kid just learning how to communicate in
    clichés
— be finicky; look for minor errors in everything you or any-
    one else does
— memorize some splendid platitudes
— observe (or tape record) your own behavior and identify
    90% that is parrot-charade
— then reward your paleolithic brain by some funky hunter-
    gatherer exploits
— imagine you are a paleolith with no responsibilities except
    dancing around stealing, raping, taking what's been
    provided
— then meditate on the basic fearful-loser "blues" of the
    modern urban paleolith who doesn't understand the
    social-technology of more advanced castes
— visit the nearest ecological niche (in the slum of the nearest
    city) where the steal-anything-in-sight-hunter-gatherer-
    welfare people hang out. Be them! Share their ghetto
    joys, weep for their helpless confusion. Plan to figure
    out a solution when you have activated more advanced
    circuits

# THE CHARIOT PORTRAYS YOUR NEOLITHIC, OBSTINATE-KID NEURO-TECHNOLOGY

**CASTE 8**

| | |
|---|---|
| **NEUROGENETIC TECHNOLOGICAL STAGE:** | Tool making:/Symbolic Invention. The Ectomorph./The management of laryngeal manual symbols. Symbolic Intelligence./Symbol Engineering./The Third Brain./The Cerebrotonic Mind. |
| **PHYLOGENETIC STAGE:** | Neolithic; Discovery of fire, agriculture, tool-making. |
| **ONTOLOGENETIC STAGE:** | The Child Mastering the Hand and the nine laryngeal muscles; learning to think for hirself. |
| **ATTITUDE:** | Balancing, inventing, relating, comparing symbols |
| **ZODIAC I:** | Libra I |
| **ROMAN:** | Prometheus |
| **GREEK:** | Prometheus—Psyche, Mnemosyne |
| **П HEBREW:** | Cheth, "I thought on my ways." |
| **ECOLOGICAL NICHE (species):** | Artifactual environment |
| **ECOLOGICAL NICHE (individual):** | Areas set aside by adults for children's learning and play |

The Tarot card CHARIOT **DRIVER** is an unmistakable signal from **DNA** to remind you that you have a Neolithic brain which was activated around age six—and which still functions every time you make up your mind or move symbols around In a way that is "your way." At this stage of your own development (and In the evolution of the species) the game gets more serious. You realize that your skills and abilities are different from others. You conceive of yourself as a person with special mental personality.

126

NEOLITHIC TECHNOLOGY

8 ♦

SELF-ACTUALIZED SYMBOL CONTROL

PSYCHE—PROMETHEUS

**CHARIOT** ♦

INVENTIVE LIBRA I

8

### Stage 8

Tarot Chariot Card 7 THE CHARIOT (Libra) signifies The Cognitive Mind Integrating, synthesizing, organizing the Stage 7 symbols and inventing new combinations and creating new artifacts. This is the stage of Symbolic Self-actualization—the realization that one can take responsible-direction of symbols— think Independently. In the species this PROMETHEAN BRAIN manifested in the Mesolithic Age—when humans first used Laryngeal-manual technology to create new forms. The lone crafts WoMan. In the Individual this occurs when the child begins to think, to create personal patterns. In Catholic terminology, the Age of Reason and Choice.

This Brain-circuit (which was activated by DNA 10,000 years ago) is still wired into your Nervous System allowing you to dial back to the Mesolithic and re-experience like a primitive idea-Inventor. And also allows you to re-live the tender days when you were a seven-year old just learning to make-up-your-mind.

127

# YOUR INVENTIVE NEO LITH BRAIN THINKS ITS THOUGHTS ARE REAL

Slot-8: The Integrating Mind; Libra Harmonizing the Active and Passive Aspects of Laryngeal-Manual Thinking

The Tarot portrays this element as the Chariot Driver guiding two Mythic Beasts, one Black and one White. We shall let these two mysterious entities represent the passive and active sides of the L. M mind. It is interesting that the Chariot is the only manufactured, instrumental object named in the Tarot deck—a neat confirmation of the Third Brain—manipulative, artifact-making technological, dextrous.

The Chariot Driver has a tool *in Hir right hand* for active expression *and Hir left hand* is open and passive.

According to de Laurence, "he is conquest in the mind, in science, in progress . He is above all things, triumph in the mind."[5]

Just as the Chariot is itself a manufactured vehicle, the Hebrew letter-key is *cheth,* fence, a product made by dexterity to divide one thing from another thing. The associated gods according to Crowley are Apollo, Mercury and Khephra: Apollo, as patron of science; Mercury as an image of swiftness: Khephra (who conveys Ra, the Sun, through the darkness of night, in Egyptian myth) as explorer of dark and hidden things. The Charioteer leads on two (or, in some decks, four) sphinxes, symbols of animality and natural mystery, but they are securely under his dextrous control.

This division-of labor between digital left lobe (Third circuit) and analogical right lobe (Fifth circuit) is pre-scientifically described in Neitzsche's celebrated dichotomy of Apollonian-rational and Dionysian-ecstatic.

# THE CHARIOT PORTRAYS THE LEFT BRAIN GUIDING YOU THROUGH A LIFE TIME OF LINEAR CHOICE

De Laurence is clear about the terrestrial nature of this slot: "It is to be understood a) that [SHe has solved the problem of Mundane] Nature and not of the world of Grace [and Time], to which the charioteer could offer no answer; b) that the planes of his conquest are manifest or external and not within himself, c) that the liberation which he effects may leave himself in the bondage of the logical understanding [that is, SHe is trapped in the reality of hir mind], d) that the tests of initiation through which he has passed in triumph are to be understood . . . rationally. . ."

The manifest behavior is mediating, intelligent, inconsistent, vascillating, dual, continually comparing, harmonizing, arranging, changeable, versatile, inconstant, fluctuating, fickle, oscillating.

# LICENSE

## 𝔗𝔬 𝔘𝔰𝔢 𝔜𝔬𝔲𝔯 𝔥𝔢𝔞𝔡

### 𝔗𝔥𝔦𝔰 𝔗𝔞𝔯𝔬𝔱 𝔠𝔞𝔯𝔡 𝔞𝔲𝔱𝔥𝔬𝔯𝔦𝔷𝔢𝔰 𝔶𝔬𝔲 𝔱𝔬 𝔞𝔠𝔱𝔦𝔳𝔞𝔱𝔢 𝔶𝔬𝔲𝔯

<u>EIGHTH BRAIN</u>   𝔞𝔫𝔡 𝔚𝔢𝔞𝔩-𝔈𝔶𝔢𝔰 like a

<u>kid learning to think</u>

### 𝔬𝔫𝔢 𝔥𝔬𝔲𝔯 𝔢𝔞𝔠𝔥 𝔡𝔞𝔶

— hang out with a child learning to think and invent
— think of a new way of saying anything-everything
— say "yes but" or "on the other hand" to everything you hear
— live in your own thoughts
— imagine yourself as the first neolithic person to discover fire, plant seeds, domesticate animals, make a wheel
— invent a utopian society, then find all the flaws in it
— spin out a conspiracy-salvation theory or the universe based on one theme
— figure out a way to please everyone so they'll leave you alone
— take any idea with fanatic seriousness
— make diagrams, lists that explain and relate everything

# THE OARD STRENGTH PORTRAYS YOUR NINE-YEAR OLD COPPER AGE NEURO-TECHNOLOGY

**CASTE 9**

| | |
|---|---|
| **NEUROGENETIC TECHNOLOGICAL STAGE:** | Division of Labor; Invention of Money as medium of exchange and collaboration; Social Linkage of Self-Actualized tool-makers and inventors; The Third Migration to Technological-trading centers |
| **PHYLOGENTIC STAGE:** | Bronze-Age |
| **ONTOLOGICAL STAGE:** | Pre-adolescent groupings into clubs, teams, cooperation among different skills and roles |
| **ATTITUDE:** | Receiving (left hand) and giving (right-hand); cooperative bartering and exchanging. |
| **ZODIAC I:** | Scorpio I |
| **ROMAN CASTE DIVINITY:** | Minerva; Theseus |
| **GREEK CASTE DIVINITY:** | Athena; Vulcan |
| **ט HEBREW LETTER:** | Teth, "Thy teaching is better than gold or silver" |
| **REALITY CREATED:** | Inter-dependent-technological hive (post-tribe and post-family) |
| **ECOLOGICAL NICHE (species):** | Trading centers and manufacturing centers |
| **ECOLOGICAL NICHE (Individual):** | Play and training centers set aside by Adult-Hive-Authorities for pre-adolescents. |

The Tarot Card STRENGTH is a signal from the DNA Imprinting Press that your brain still contains a Copper-Age neuromuscular control circuit which was activated in ecological-eras when neolithic family-centered humanoids collected in larger Priest-run manufacturing occupational caste societies.

This neural circuit becomes dominant in pre-teen years when you learned how to operate in kid-teams and organized groups. At this stage in your temporal caste development it gets even more serious. You begin to understand that your special skills and aptitudes must fit into the division-of-labor system of your culture. Your new neural equipment blindly reaches out to imprint a group, a band, a club, a tribe to belong to. Before this stage you wanted to do everything your own way. Now you select specific skills or you brood because you can't.

### Stage 9

Tarot Strength Card 8, **STRENG**TH (Scorpio) illustrates the Division of Labor period of evolution. After different persons began to create new, individualized, methods of creating laryngeal-manual artifacts—the Age of Specialization begins. But a world filled with Independent Librans—each joyfully driving Hir own chariot is chaotic. Once Mental Self-Actualization begins—then inevitably the next stage follows. The Independent alchemists and inventive thinkers find it necessary to link-up in technological communities. SOCIAL COOPERATION, trading, at the artifact level. In the evolution of the species this stage occurs when trading-industry centers are formed. Caste guilds emerge. In the individual this appears in pre-adolescence—when clubs, gangs, hobby and athletic groupings appear.

This Brain circuit which was activated in the Copper Age, 7000 years ago, is still wired into your nervous system allowing you to Time-Travel back and re-experience like a swarthy, tribal, Mediterranean-Wheeler-Dealer-Trader. And, in tender nostalgia, to relive your pre-teen club-cubhood.

133

# THE CARD STRENGTH IS YOUR SERIOUS LITTLE GIRL-SCOUT BRAIN READY TO COMPETE FOR MERIT BADGES

Tarot card Strength portrays the Ninth Caste, cooperative, bartering wheeling-dealing. The Third Migration from tribal isolation to centers of trade, exchange and manufacture.

We have seen that caste 7, the Passive Mind, the Lower Hand, mimics, in-cells, repeats laryngeal-muscular symbolic patterns. Caste 7, the Upper Mind, creates ex-cells, expresses. Caste 9 involves social linkage for technological success.

The *attitude* is active, open, sharp, shrewd. Marketing intelligence, externalized in systems of business, science, manufacture, symbolization. Excellence. Wealth. Commercial Novelty. Status, earned by merchandizing achievement. Craft in movement and exchange of raw materials and manufactured goods. Acuteness, perspicacity, genius, skill, adroitness, proficiency, competence in sensing the rhythms of supply and demand.

Success won by organizing rather than force. Educational bureaucratic awards, teacher status, reputation, wealth, possession, credit. The Phoenician Deal. The Byzantine Bargain. Occupational and professional rank.

Tarot cards were designed during the Middle Ages when technology, science, and the craft-guild tradition of skilled manipulation were not understood as stages of history. The Tarot illustrations for Third Circuit Success are therefore fuzzy and allegorical. To update the Tarot it is necessary to introduce technical mastery and commercial organization themes in the cards for the Third Circuit.

We are provided here with an example of how later discoveries must be used to revise errors and complete omissions in earlier neurogenetic symbol systems.

The Cabalistic letter-key is *teth*, the Serpent—possibly an expression of cunning and commercial craft. Crowley's title for this card, "The Daughter of the Flaming Sword" evidently refers to the magical weapon of "preliminary discipline" (i.e., training, programming). The plant is the cybernetic feedback exemplar, the Sunflower, which adjusts its position hour-by-hour to the sun: a perfect botanical glyph for the self-correcting Intelligence. The beast is the lion which obviously represents mammalian (Second Circuit) muscular power being replaced by symbolic intelligence. Reason as governor of emotion.

134

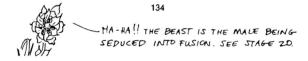

HA-HA!! THE BEAST IS THE MALE BEING SEDUCED INTO FUSION. SEE STAGE 20.

# LICENSE

## To Use Your Head

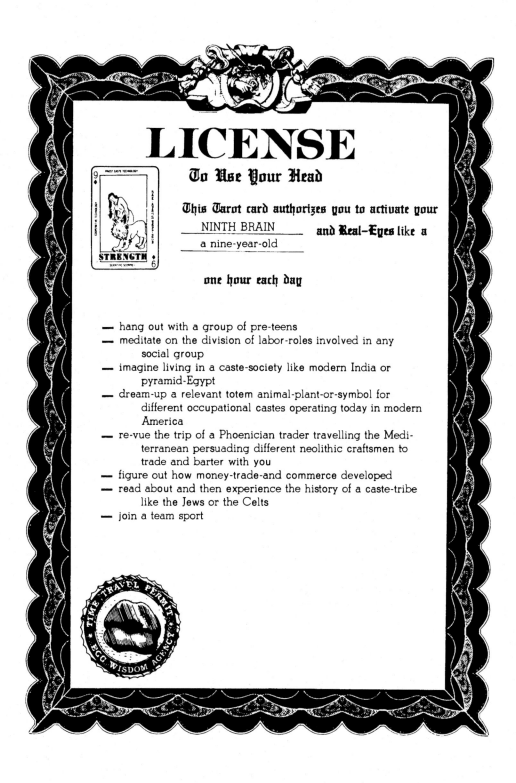

This Tarot card authorizes you to activate your

_____NINTH BRAIN_____ and **Real-Eyes** like a

a nine-year-old

### one hour each day

- hang out with a group of pre-teens
- meditate on the division of labor-roles involved in any social group
- imagine living in a caste-society like modern India or pyramid-Egypt
- dream-up a relevant totem animal-plant-or-symbol for different occupational castes operating today in modern America
- re-vue the trip of a Phoenician trader travelling the Mediterranean persuading different neolithic craftsmen to trade and barter with you
- figure out how money-trade-and commerce developed
- read about and then experience the history of a caste-tribe like the Jews or the Celts
- join a team sport

# SEVENTY-FIVE PERCENT OF HUMANITY OPERATES WITH PRE-CIVILIZED BRAIN

Playboy Herm flashes (!) into the Fourth Brain Civilized future while Hindu-Caster Scorpia comes along for the ride.

At this point reference should be made to the temporal-caste distribution of human beings on the planet in the year 1978.

Approximately 22 to 25 percent of the human race operates at the First Circuit—marine neurotechnology. We count here unborn fetuses, infants, invalids, seniles. In a word all those who cannot run around mastering gravity vigorously.

Approximately 22 to 25 percent of the human race exists within a Second Circuit—territorial-mammalian-primate level of neurointelligence. We include here children up to the age of seven, seniles who can still walk but who are obsessed with possession and security fears, as well as the hundreds of millions who survive in ghetto gangs, pre-technological villages where muscular strength-threat and monkey-brain communication is the vital-technology. The fact that many of these hummalians can use tools should not conceal the fact that their attitude is muscular coercion.

Approximately 25 to 35 percent of the human race operates at the Third Circuit—hunter-gatherers, mimicking symbol-users, tribal members. There are more paleoliths in Los Angeles county today than there were paleoliths in the paleolithic era. We include here pre-adolescent juveniles, menopausals and pre-civilized people who make up the central-modal-average of every terrestrial hive. The average, i.e. the most numerous human caste today is hunter-gatherer. Anyone who has activated circuits beyond the hunter-gatherer is a fore-caste, is actually ahead of the average level of humanity.

Roughly 22 to 25 percent of the human race now operates at the evolutionary level of the Fourth Circuit—civilized-domesticated hive. We consider here home-owners in advanced time-zones and those who live in a reality of feudal-democratic—capitalist or socialist societies. (When we use the term socialist we refer to the welfare-fair-play societies of west-Europe and North America. We do not include those who happily exist in the monolithic communisms of the east—which are pre-civilized-hunter-raper-peasant brutish, barbarian swarms administered by 20th century technology.

About two percent of the human race has activated post-hive, post-terrestrial brain circuits. Here we include the aesthetic-hedonic elitists, Einsteinian Intelligences and Egg-wisdom adepts who are to be found clustered in the Sun-belt of the North American continent.

# THE THREE CARDS — HERMIT, WHEEL OF FORTUNE, JUSTICE PORTRAY YOUR THREE NEURO-TECHNOLOGIES FOR BECOMING CIVILIZED — THAT IS, AN INSECTOID HIVE MEMBER

Bee-hivers miss bee-having at the Judeo-Christian-Marxist Rally. Mrs. Calvin Ethic (left), joins her husband Mortgage (far right), Judge Ronald Mao-Mao Menopause (second from right) and Herm the Feudal Flasher in a toast to Insectoid Monotheism.

**THE FOURTH CIRCUIT OF THE NERVOUS SYSTEM TO EVOLVE (in both species and individual) PRODUCES SEXUAL-DOMESTICATION CIVILIZATION AS SURVIVAL TECHNOLOGY**

The I Ching Trigram which signifies the Fourth Circuit of the Nervous System is **KEN**: PROTECTION

The three Tarot cards which predict this cycle of development—in both the species and the individual) are:

        CARD  9: The **HERMIT** — Stage 10—Feudalism
        CARD 10: The WHEEL OF LIFE — Stage 11—Parental Society
        CARD 11: JUSTICE — Stage 12—Centralized-Hive-Socialism

# THE TAROT OARD HERMIT PORTRAYS YOUR TEENAGE BARBARIAN NEURO-TECHNOLOGY

**CASTE 10**

**NEUROGENETIC TECHNOLOGICAL STAGE:** Paedomorphosis-neoteny (post-ponement-avoidance of Adult-special-ization) made possible by Feudal state which produces a playful-aesthetic-adolescent elite; Monothe-ism as device for Organizing Tribes into centralized poly-caste hives; sex-role as Neuro-technology to form Hive-caste society called civilization; Self-Definition in terms of sex-role; Nar-cissistic sexuality; Sexual Impersona-tion stage: rejection of adult-models by aristocratic caste.

**PHYLOGENETIC STAGE:** Monotheistic-feudal Hive-society based on Familial-sex roles;

**ONTOLOGICAL STAGE:** Adolescence; sexually active pre-adult; Explorative-definition of sexual-identity.

**ATTITUDE:** Mobile; change-able, intense; ideal-istic; playful (or ascetic) paedomorphic search for new sociobiological forms

**ZODIAC I:** Sagittarius I

**ROMAN DIVINITY:** Mars-Venus

**GREEK DIVINITY:** Ares-Aphrodite

**ˑ HEBREW LETTER:** Yod; "Thou hast afflicted me with faithfulness."

**REALITY CREATED:** The Adolescent-culture; expanded dur-ation of self-Indulgent search and growth by the elite of the feudal hive.

**ECOLOGICAL NICHE (species):** Feudal society; Mediterranean

**ECOLOGICAL NICHE (individual):** Adolescent society; teenage culture

138

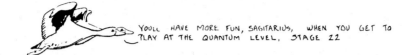

J ◆

ADOLESCENT TECHNOLOGY

SOCIO-SEXUAL SELF-INDULGENCE

MARS—VENUS APHRODITE—ARES

**HERMIT** ◆ ſ

SEXY ROMANTIC SAGITTARIUS I

*Stage 10*

Tarot Hermit (card 9) THE HERMIT (Sagittarius) codes the
self-indulgent stage of Sexual Socialization, Sexual Impersonation as caste-class factor. Sexual energies expressed not as
Parental Domestication but used for self-definition. Sex-role is
used as civilizing technology. In the species this stage is
barbarian-war-chief-feudal-kinship. In the individual this stage is
Adolescent.

This Brain Circuit (which was activated by DNA when
monotheism became the urbanizing-collective signal, around
3000 years ago) is still wired into your nervous system and can be
dialed to re-experience the bravura-macho-monarchial trip. And,
as a flamboyant fringe-benefit allows you to re-animate your
intense-self-defining-idealistic horny adolescence.

139

# MONOTHEISM, MONARCHY ARE NEURO TECHNOLOGIES WHICH ORGANIZE PANTHEIST PAGAN-CASTE TRIBES INTO CENTRALIZED NATIONS. FEUDALISM, .. INHERITED CLASS PRODUCE ADOLESCENT ELITES FREE TO POSTPONE ADULT SPECIALIZATION

The Tarot card Hermit, Caste 10, portrays the passive-receptive exploratory neotenous phase of the Fourth Circuit. The awakened sexual system, before commitment to parental role or domestic responsibilities, i.e. before commitment to an adult specialized survival technique. Here is the post-pubertal body, fully equipped sexually, but uncommitted to sperm-egg linkage. The perpetual adolescent. Fascinated by sex but not ready to domesticate as parent. Self-Defined in terms of sex-role.

Evolution and Futation operates through Paedomorphosis or Neoteny—i.e. change-development by the pre-adults of the species. A tribal society cannot provide the affluence and leisure necessary to produce a carefree, self-indulgent caste. Feudal-monotheism is the necessary stage which produces an affluent-aristocracy which disdains work and survival duty and is thus free to experiment aesthetically, philosophically, scientifically. It is necessary to have a hierarchical kingdom before Philosopher Kings can exist. Feudal-monarchy is designed to encourage Neoteny, spoiled, frivolous elites who are sexually active but not bogged down with parental duty. The Hermit with Hir lantern can only be afforded by a successful feudal hive.

The *attitude* is youthful, histrionic, change-able, intense. There is no one quite so titillated by sex as the prudish virgin. Sexuality expressed in religiosity, flirtatious aesthetics. The self-centered, swarming gregariousness of the adolescent. Avoidance of marriage and the adult responsibility of the parental state.

Flamboyant chastity, tactless naiveté, obsession with gender impersonation. The excitement of foreplay socialized as fashion, style, fad. Youthful charm, enthusiasm. Frank, earnest, sincere ingenuousness. Behind the juvenile silliness is the serious business of speciation. Rejection of Terminal Adulthood.

The Hermit is the Neotenous Youth rejecting adult specialization and searching for the next futational step.

# YOU HAVE A PERPETUAL ADOLESCENT BRAIN, A SPOILED ARAB-ITALIAN PLAYGIRL-PRINCE DEMANDING TO BE ACTIVATED SO THAT YOU CAN KILL-RAPE FOR YOUR CAUSE

This card, Hermit, portrays self-indulgent inhibition and avoidance of the sexual impulse. The Tenth Caste is the post-pubescent who imprints a celibate sex role or who indulges in self-gratifying sexual activities basically masturbatory even if another is involved. The Latin Lover, the Playboy, the tease, the homosexual. The sexual impersonation phase through which every human passes.

The Tarot cards were designed in a pre-technological era when there was no conceptual knowledge of neoteny, of the pre-adult sexual impulse. No understanding of the crucial genetic significance of extended adolescence, of postponed adulthood. No insight into the difference between robot Impregnation sexuality and pre-parent sexuality that expresses itself in aesthetics, erotics, romance, poetry, inhibited sublimation, broadened search for identity, new forms of caste differentiation. Thus we are not surprised to see this structural and temporal Imprint-mode portrayed by the renunciate figure of the monk. SHe is bachelor-spinster turning away from the uterine Wheel of Parental Adulthood (Caste 11, the integrating-mind of the Fourth Circuit).

The Hermit-monk is often described in the glowing terms of naive occultist as seeking the inner-light, the higher wisdom, etc. The medieval symbolism is intuitively correct. The Hermit-monk rejects or post-pones hive-parental responsibility and searches for a new way, a higher role. Monkish renunciation of sex is a luxury available only in an affluent culture which can afford to let able-bodied fertile young men and women avoid parental responsibilities and hive work duties. Extended adolescence is the genetic blossom of the successful species, the key to evolution.

The Cabalistic letter for Caste 10 is *yod,* alternately translated as spermatozoa or FIST. Either reading nicely fits the theme of adolescent neoteny. The flower, of course, is Narcissus. Crowley explains the magical instrument association, "Lamp and Wand," explicitly as "Virile Force reserved." The gods Aphrodite, Mars and Attis are associated, evidently as images of youthful virility-virginity; Attis, it should be remembered, is said to have castrated himself, either deliberately or accidentally—the myths differ. Similar self-castration by the priests of Attis is held by some historians of religion to have been imitated by the psychological castration (celibacy) of the Roman Catholic priesthood. The Egyptian divinity given by Crowley is Isis, which he kindly explains with the note: "(as Virgin)."

Crowley comments mysteriously, "[The Hermit's] Serpent Wand . . . is the spermatozoon developed as a poison . . . Yod ≡ Phallus ≡ Spermatozoon ≡ Hand ≡ Logos ≡ Virgin. There is perfect identity, not merely Equivalence, of the Extremes, the Manifestation, and the Method." This is another of Crowley's jokes. Decoded, he is saying that the conventional celibate-religious path is based on sublimated masturbation: a truncated and unconscious Tantra.

# LICENSE

## To Use Your Head

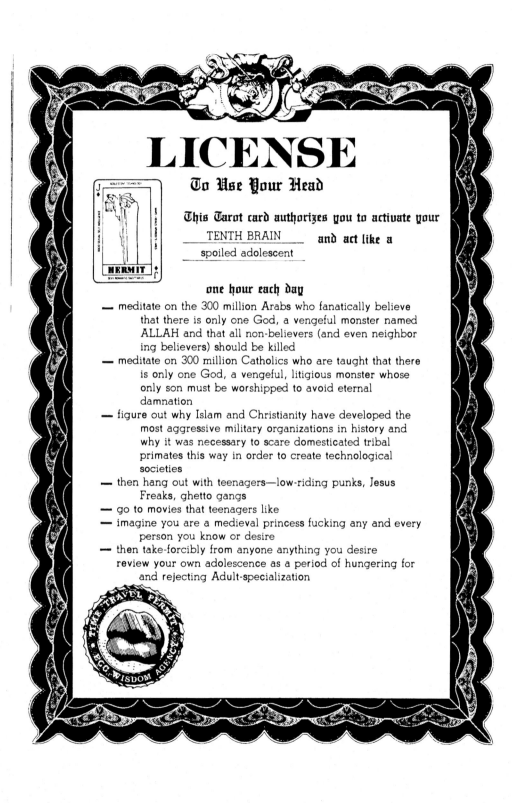

This Tarot card authorizes you to activate your

_____TENTH BRAIN_____ and act like a

spoiled adolescent

### one hour each day

— meditate on the 300 million Arabs who fanatically believe
that there is only one God, a vengeful monster named
ALLAH and that all non-believers (and even neighbor
ing believers) should be killed

— meditate on 300 million Catholics who are taught that there
is only one God, a vengeful, litigious monster whose
only son must be worshipped to avoid eternal
damnation

— figure out why Islam and Christianity have developed the
most aggressive military organizations in history and
why it was necessary to scare domesticated tribal
primates this way in order to create technological
societies

— then hang out with teenagers—low-riding punks, Jesus
Freaks, ghetto gangs

— go to movies that teenagers like

— imagine you are a medieval princess fucking any and every
person you know or desire

— then take-forcibly from anyone anything you desire
review your own adolescence as a period of hungering for
and rejecting Adult-specialization

# THE CARD WHEEL OF FORTUNE PORTRAYS YOUR PARENTAL-DOMESTICATED-ROBOT NEURO-TECHNOLOGY

**CASTE 11**

| | |
|---|---|
| **NEUROGENETIC TECHNOLOGICAL STAGE:** | Nest Intelligence, Domestication. The Parent-centered Society; The Fourth Self-Actualization: the Home-owner. |
| **PHYLOGENETIC STAGE:** | The Family-centered Society; Sexuality harnessed to domestic responsibility |
| **ONTOGENETIC STAGE:** | Parenthood, marriage, child-rearing |
| **ATTITUDE:** | Parental-protective |
| **ZODIAC I:** | Capricorn I |
| **ROMAN:** | Juno—Jupiter |
| **GREEK:** | Hera—Zeus |
| **ⵁ HEBREW:** | Kaph, "I am like a bottle in the smoke." |
| **REALITY CREATED:** | W.A.S.P. |
| **ECOLOGICAL NICHE (species):** | Protestant-capitalist-democratic Society, 1559-1859 |
| **ECOLOGICAL NICHE (individual):** | My own home as my castle |

Parenthood is symbolized by the Wheel of Fortune. To Hive-terrestrials, conception was a great genetic roulette. When the sperm and egg fuse to create new consciousness, primitive earthlings did not know what was going to happen. The Mutational Lottery. When conception occurs dramatic biochemical changes occur in the mother (and the father). These biochemical signals activate the 11th Circuit—domestic robothood.

A coiling serpent-like spermatozoic creature swims around the circular ovum wheel.

The Tarot card WHEEL OF FORTUNE is an enigmatic whisper from **DNA** to remind you that your brain contains a Domesticated-family circuit which provides the secure-comfy satisfaction that you are virtuously sacrificing your life for the good of the kids. This circuit monitors the neuromuscular habits involved in finding a little-home-nest, to become bourgeois-home-owner king-queen of your own family castle.

BE PATIENT, CAPRICORNS, YOU GET TO BE
PARENTS OF THE UNIVERSE AT STAGE 23

BOURGEOIS TECHNOLOGY

DOMESTICATED FAMILY INTELLIGENCE

HERA-ZEUS JUNO-JUPITER

**FORTUNE**

PARENTAL CAPRICORN I

### Stage 11

Tarot Wheel (card 10) **WHEEL OF LIFE** (Capricorn) reflects Impregnation and Parenthood as Social Technology. This card portrays the DOMESTIC BRAIN which organizes, synthesizes, Integrates the many signals which relate to breeding and protection of the young. The Child-centered Society as Survival Tool. In the evolution of species this stage appears as the Family Centered Democracy which originated in the Protestant Reformation and peaked in Pre-Civil War America—which was the ultimate Child-centered educational Society. In the Individual this stage appears as the Post-Adolescent-Domesticated-Parent Brain. Self-Actualization as Father-Mother-King-Queen of the Home Castle.

POST CIVIL WAR

145

# THE WHEEL IS YOUR DOMESTI-CATED ADULT BRAIN EAGER FOR VIRTUOUS RESPONSIBILITY

Sometime between the ages of 20-25, a miraculous metamorphosis occurs in the neurology and behavior of the human being.

Domestication. The wild, selfish, idealistic, barbarian teenager mutates into a prudent, practical, docile, productive young adult.

This usually occurs when conception (sperm-egg fusion) occurs. Hormonal, biochemical signals are picked up by RNA and flashed to DNA headquarters. "Attention; this model has imprinted a sexual-impersonation role. Cool out the wild intoxicated hormonal sexual-invitation display." The specific Stage 11 anti-histone proteins peel off the next section of DNA and the Parental Brain (Capricorn) is activated.

Typically this dramatic, all-changing metamorphosis occurs at pregnancy. In the normal course, the young woman is automatically, reflexly fertilized. On a population basis, human pregnancy is as routine as the breeding habits of fish or fowl. However thrilling and chancy to the individual fish or trembling feathered bird—these pre-designed periods of fertility are totally robotized and predictable on a population basis.

# YOUR DADDY-MOMMY BRAIN IS ADDICTED TO PROTECTION OF THE YOUNGER-WEAKER AND REGAL CONTROL OF YOUR OWN LITTLE BREEDING NICHE

Once fertilized the expected changes occur. The physiological metamorphosis—swelling of belly and breasts—are obvious. Equally predictable are the behavioral changes. Suddenly the flirty, skirty, saucy, giggling teenybopper is replaced by a sedate, serene, cautious quiescent matron. Clearly a new brain has emerged—obsessed with nesting, stability, "forever-mine" security.

Less obvious are the changes in young males moving from the Tenth to the Eleventh developmental stage. Teenage hormonal hurricanes naturally pile up hormonal debris and testosterone-byproduct pollutions, which, in time, signal DNA that the next stage is ready to be scheduled.

The Eleventh Capricorn Brain is activated in the young male when he has selected his sexual-impersonation role and focussed his wild-scanning, ovary-hunting antennae. The sex roles selected are not necessarily parental. Just as adolescent sex-role-scanning can and does range wildly from promiscuity to monkish renunciation, so we move through a wide range of domesticated socio-sexual realities. Many non-parental roles are harnessed together in the domesticated society—nurses, teachers. Indeed, all domesticates are offered and encouraged to play non-parental roles as long as they contribute somehow to the ethos. Virgin celibates like J. Edgar Hoover and Pope Paul are the staunchest supporters of family life.

According to the Tarot philosopher de Laurence, The Wheel of Life card portrays seven radii; in the eighteenth century, the ascending and descending animals were really of nondescript character, one of them having a human head. At the summit [of the wheel] was another monster with the body of an indeterminate beast, wings on shoulders and a crown on head." The mutational-genetic flavor of the imagery is unmistakable even when transmitted by pre-Darwinian agents.

The *Wheel of Fortune* card is of interest because it compactly summarizes many of the principles of Exo-psychology.

The terrestrial-extraterrestrial perspective is illustrated by the circular earth surrounded by clouds.

The earth is bisected by four diameters—horizontal, vertical and two diagonal, perhaps symbolizing the spatial parameters of Euclidean survival. The four "S's" of terrestrial life: Safety, Security, Sanity (hive-acceptance) and Socio-Sexual role.

On the circumference of the circle are a snake and two mythological half-man-half-animal creatures—all symbolizing, perhaps, the process of evolution and mutation.

Four winged creatures float on the extraterrestrial clouds, clearly forecasting the four circuits of post-terrestrial technology: Body, Brain, DNA, Atomic.

The book of Ezekial is the classic biblical description of the descent of extra-terrestrial beings to Earth. The astounding technical detail and UFO specificity of the Ezekiel vision has led many to believe in the visitation of Earth by galactic astronauts. Neurogenetics does not require the physical space-ship arrival of alien cosmonauts. There is sufficient evidence to assume that throughout human history, certain pre-evolutes (futants) have been able to decipher their own DNA code and experience futique visions. Higher Intelligence, indeed, did visit this planet four billion years ago in the soft form of miniaturized genetic templates. The process of evolution centers on the beautiful, comic, carefully arranged fusion of sperm-egg, neatly symbolized by the ever-spinning wheel of fortune. D.N.A. coils are the unidentified flying organisms.

This element is portrayed as Father-Mother. Yod = He in Cabala: the mysterious YAH buried in YHVH (Yahweh, or Jehovah): in short, the earliest form of the Hebrew God as male-female dyad similar to Shiva-Shakti in the East. In many places, Cabalistic and Hasidic Jews still worship the female component, now called Shekinah, as "the embodied Glory of Jehovah," co-equal with Him, under the guise of conventional patriarchy. On the wedding night, the bride and groom sleep in a special hut with the roof open to the sky, so that Jehovah and Shekinah may "enter" them and join in the genetic roulette of the conceptual act.

In another sense, the wheel on this card is the Great Wheel of all mystic traditions: Samsara, attachment. The married WoMan is involved in the world, in the eco-systems (economics, ecology—from Greek *eco,* household) and cannot join the yogic or hedonic drop-outs without being accused of irresponsibility (betrayal of the primordial life-functions of Reproduction *and* Protection).

148

# LICENSE

## 𝕿𝖔 𝖀𝖘𝖊 𝖄𝖔𝖚𝖗 𝕳𝖊𝖆𝖉

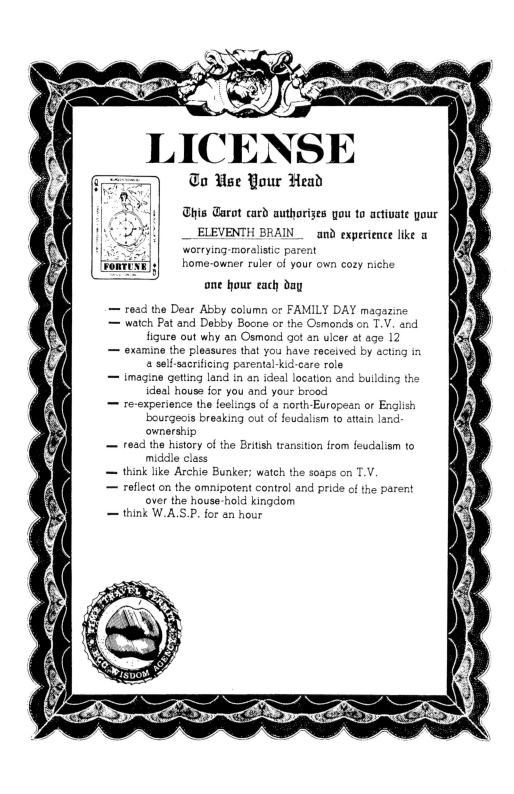

𝕿𝖍𝖎𝖘 𝕿𝖆𝖗𝖔𝖙 𝖈𝖆𝖗𝖉 𝖆𝖚𝖙𝖍𝖔𝖗𝖎𝖟𝖊𝖘 𝖞𝖔𝖚 𝖙𝖔 𝖆𝖈𝖙𝖎𝖛𝖆𝖙𝖊 𝖞𝖔𝖚𝖗

__ELEVENTH BRAIN__   𝖆𝖓𝖉 𝖊𝖝𝖕𝖊𝖗𝖎𝖊𝖓𝖈𝖊 𝖑𝖎𝖐𝖊 𝖆

worrying-moralistic parent
home-owner ruler of your own cozy niche

### 𝖔𝖓𝖊 𝖍𝖔𝖚𝖗 𝖊𝖆𝖈𝖍 𝖉𝖆𝖞

— read the Dear Abby column or FAMILY DAY magazine
— watch Pat and Debby Boone or the Osmonds on T.V. and figure out why an Osmond got an ulcer at age 12
— examine the pleasures that you have received by acting in a self-sacrificing parental-kid-care role
— imagine getting land in an ideal location and building the ideal house for you and your brood
— re-experience the feelings of a north-European or English bourgeois breaking out of feudalism to attain land-ownership
— read the history of the British transition from feudalism to middle class
— think like Archie Bunker; watch the soaps on T.V.
— reflect on the omnipotent control and pride of the parent over the house-hold kingdom
— think W.A.S.P. for an hour

# THE TAROT CARD JUSTICE POR-
# TRAYS YOUR DEPENDENT SENIOR-
# CITIZEN DYNG NEURO-TECHNOLOGY

**CASTE 12**

| | |
|---|---|
| **NEUROGENETIC TECHNOLOGICAL STAGE:** | Post-menopausal dependence. Completion of terrestrial task. Insectoid Socialization. Lust for next-world transcendence. Obsession with death and after-life. |
| | Hive consciousness. Collective domestication. Larval Completion. |
| **PHYLOGENETIC STAGE:** | The Age of the Collectivized, Fair play, Welfare-state religious society (1859–1976) |
| **ONTOGENETIC STAGE:** | Terror of Aging and Death. |
| **ZODIAC I:** | Aquarius I |
| **ATTITUDE:** | Dependence on Hive Authority |
| **ROMAN DIVINITY:** | The Caesar Principle |
| **GREEK DIVINITY:** | Themis, Nemesis, Aidos |
| ל **HEBREW LETTER:** | Lamed, "They continue this day according to thine ordinances for all are Thy servants." |
| **REALITY CREATED:** | Dependence on Hive |
| **ECOLOGICAL NICHE (SPECIES):** | Totalitarian State Religion |
| **ECOLOGICAL NICHE (INDIV.):** | Retirement Home |

The Tarot Card JUSTICE is a reminder from your own DNA that your brain contains a post-menopausal circuit which fabricates a reality of security-safety-stasis and an expectation of respect-for-the-aged for a job well done. This circuit demands a strong morality-control-conservative ecological surrounding which protects the aging weak and prepares-promises-programs-reassures that onrushing death is a reward.

*Stage 12*

Tarot Justice (card 11) JUSTICE (Aquarius) illustrates the final stage of terrestrial life. The death card. The seated figure obviously represents the ultimate Hive-Authority. The Neurology of Hive Morality. The ultimate of Insectoid Domesticity—centralized religious socialism. This caste is obsessed with death (the raised sword) and the chance for the next life (the scales). Submission to the Hive Religion provides material security during the aging years and spiritual reassurance. This caste is thus fanatically, desperately, dogmatically moralistic.

151

# JUSTICE IS YOUR FEARFUL OLD ONE BRAIN LUSTING FOR WEL FARE PROTECTION AND RELIGIOUS CERTAINTY

This card represents the docile, willing enslavement of the death-fearing aging one to the hive-central-state-religion. This stage marks the completion of the human terrestrial cycle. Global socialist-welfare and preparation for post-death transcendence.

Before the 20th century this temporal caste occurred in individuals when the 12th brain, the Neurotechnology of Dying, was activated. Usually at menopause. The young of the species, however, could still get involved in tribal (Stage 9), national (10) and political (11) conflicts or engage in western migrations, scientific progress, socialist-utopian yearnings. During the 20th century the Dom Species became Caste 12. The entire human race began to sense that the terrestrial game is over. Exploration of frontiers finished. Over-population, pollution, diminished resources, Hiroshima-Nagasaki, agonizing discrepancies between the affluent-scientific west and the impoverished-religious east! Doomsday-Armageddon scenarios proliferate! And here come the religious dogmas!

Religion has always been the neuro-technology of pessimistic losers—fabricating a reality in which stupidity, docility and ugliness is rewarded. Beauty, individualism, change, originality is heresy. A sense of weakness and futility infiltrates all the hives. A general recognition that the terrestrial trip is on a down-slide. Pie-in-the-sky-after-life promises are the classic solaces of the failing. You start to die when the Caste 12 button in your brain has been activated.

UNTIL HUMANS REALIZE THAT WE ANTS ARE MORE CIVILIZED THAN THEY... ..THEY CANT EVOLVE BEYOND US

# YOUR RELIGIOUS-SUBMISSION BRAIN ACHES TO BE REWARDED BY HIVE MORAL AUTHORITY

Justice is appropriately the final card of the terrestrial deck. Those who obey the hive priests will be supported by the insectoid-welfare state and after death will rise to heaven.

Those who challenge the Hive Theology—via Individualism, pantheism, or scientific experiment—are condemned to eternal damnation.

The heavy stakes in the game explain the desperate-fanaticism of the Caste 12 people. The Hive cannot tolerate any dissent. The Game of Terrestrial Life depends upon uniformity and unanimous acceptance of the Hive theory of post-terrestrial, eternal life.

The *attitude* of this card remains insectoid security, hive-oriented submission, dependence on the over-specialized Adult Authority. The Hebrew letter is *lamed*, an ox-goad (i.e., the reins by which we are bonded to the team).

The English word *religion* comes from Latin *religio* which also means bond. The ropes which tie the hive into a uniform obedience.

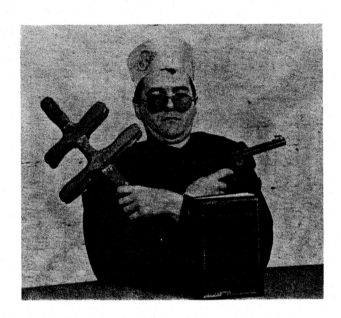

Would you really like to be facing this stern-eyed, sword-holding figure? Well, like it or not SHe is a powerful circuit in your brain.

Crowley: "It is the final adjustment"—ad-just-ment—"in the formula of Tetragrammaton [YHVH], when the daughter, redeemed by her marriage with the Son, is thereby set up on the throne of the mother; thus, finally, she 'awakens the Eld of the All-Father.' " He is evidently thinking of the menopausal mother piously committing herself to Hive Law and Order, joining sects, doing good, getting involved in social welfare, voting for Ronald Reagan.

The Twelfth Tarot card, Justice, is the last terrestrial element. It represents both aspects of the future, (1) the global, brotherhood-of-man-ism, Egalitarian, prudish. Socialism leading to cyborg-insectoid colonization, and (2) the yearning, prospective anticipations of extra-terrestrial existence and immortality.

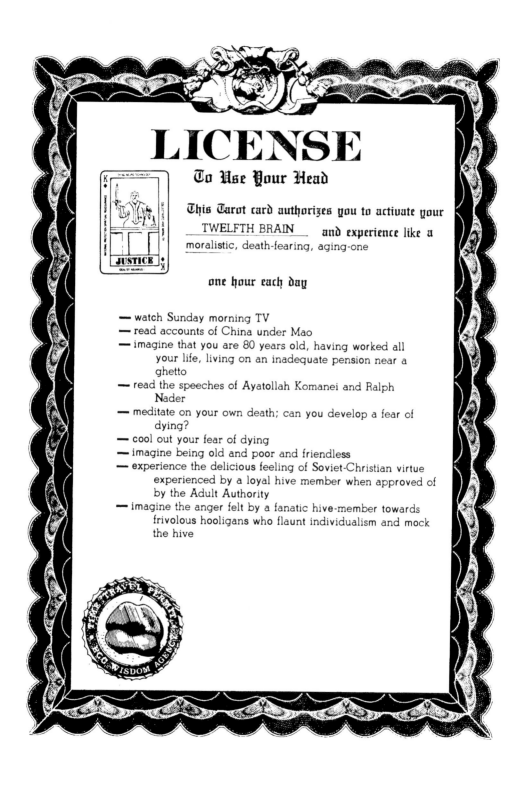

# LICENSE

### To Use Your Head

**This Tarot card authorizes you to activate your**

<u>TWELFTH BRAIN</u> **and experience like a**
moralistic, death-fearing, aging-one

### one hour each day

— watch Sunday morning TV
— read accounts of China under Mao
— imagine that you are 80 years old, having worked all
   your life, living on an inadequate pension near a
   ghetto
— read the speeches of Ayatollah Komanei and Ralph
   Nader
— meditate on your own death; can you develop a fear of
   dying?
— cool out your fear of dying
— imagine being old and poor and friendless
— experience the delicious feeling of Soviet-Christian virtue
   experienced by a loyal hive member when approved of
   by the Adult Authority
— imagine the anger felt by a fanatic hive-member towards
   frivolous hooligans who flaunt individualism and mock
   the hive

# THE END

DEPARTURES              ARRIVALS

| TRACK | DESTINATION | TIME | TRACK | FROM | TIME |
|---|---|---|---|---|---|
| 13 | MARIJUANA | 1968 | 1 | INFANT SUCKING | 1 MONTH |
| 14 | EROTIC INTELLIGENCE | 1976 | 2 | BABY INTELLIGENCE | 3 MO |
| 15 | AESTHETIC FUSION | 1980 | 3 | CRAWLING POWER | 6 MO |
| 16 | LSD CONSCIOUSNESS | 1986 | 4 | TODDLER EXPLORATION | 1 YR |
| 17 | REALITY FABRICATION | 1991 | 5 | "ME" POSSESSION | 3 YR |
| 18 | SPACE MIGRATION | 1994 | 6 | KID GANGS | 4 YR |
| 19 | SPERM INTELLIGENCE | 1998 | 7 | READING DOCILITY | 5 YR |
| 20 | EGG INTELLIGENCE | 2000 | 8 | WRITING INVENTION | 7 YR |
| 21 | DNA FUSION | 2004 | 9 | PEER GROUP COOPERATION | 9 YR |
| 22 | QUANTUM CONSUMERISM | 2008 | 10 | ADOLESCENT SELF INDULGENCE | 19 YR |
| 23 | QUANTUM INTELLIGENCE | 2016 | 11 | DOMESTIC RULE | CANCELED |
| 24 | BLACK HOLE FUSION | ?... | 12 | MENOPAUSAL COLLECTIVITY | CANCELED |

CLARK

# FAR WESTERN

| | | | | | | 118 24 |

YOUR DNA CODE HEREBY IN-FORMS YOU THAT THE
WORD INDULGENCE REPEAT INDULGENCE IS DEFINED AS
FOLLOWS:  1)  TO YIELD TO THE DESIRES AND WHIMS
OF YOURSELF OR ANOTHER OR OF YOUR HIVE LEADERS
2)  TO GRANT AN ECCLESIASTICAL DISPENSATION TO
ONESELF OR A LOVED ONE, OR THE HIVE BUREAUCRACY.
3)  TO ALLOW ONESELF OR A LOVED ONE OR HIVE
AUTHORITIES SOME SPECIAL PLEASURE OR PRIVILEGE.
4)  TO TREAT LIBERALLY OR TOLERANTLY YOURSELF, YOUR
YOUR LOVED ONES, OR YOUR HIVE MASTERS.
    YOU ARE RE-MINDED THAT ONLY YOU REPEAT ONLY
YOU ARE AUTHORIZED TO GRANT AN INDULGENCE PERIOD.
HIVE OFFICIALS CAN GRANT INDULGENCES ONLY BECAUSE
YOU YIELD TO THEIR WHIMS.
                      LOVE,
                        MOTHER

FOR BEST RESULTS  NEUROGRAM*

# HELLO!!

## WELL-COME TO A NEW BEGINNING

The
GAME OF LIFE

the
**BEST**
 is yet to
  **COME!**
12 NEW **SELVES!**

*3 TAROT STAGES
TO FREE YOUR BODY!*

*3 TAROT STAGES
TO FREE YOUR BRAIN!*

*3 TAROT STAGES
TO DIRECT DNA EVOLUTION!*

*AND
A BLACK-WHOLE SURPRISE
BONUS!*

## Self-hood Creates FUTURES

THE NEXT 12 CHAPTERS WILL
FREE YOU FOR THE FUTURE

# PART III

IF YOU HAVE ONE
ONE GRAIN OF RESPECT
FOR HUMAN CULTURE

WE ORDER YOU
NOT TO READ
PART III

IT WILL PUT
SELF PITY

AND ALL
WE HOLD SACRED
OUT OF BUSINESS

160

# TAROT CARDS 13-24 PORTRAY THE TWELVE FUTANT CASTES (SPECIES) OF POST TERRESTRIAL EVOLUTION

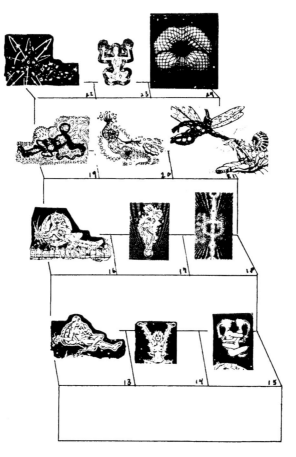

## A TRANSITION POINT

At this point in the unfolding of the DNA array we come to an abrupt transition. The leap of metamorphosis, the extra-terrestrial flight. Terra I to Terra II. Tarot I to Tarot II.

The first four circuits of the nervous system, the first twelve Tarot cards, accurately describe the sequence of terrestrial adaptation. The next four circuits, the next twelve Tarot cards in the expanding Tarot equation, symbolize the post-terrestrial caste-stages of existence. The post-human interstellar life-forms toward which we are mutating.

The first twelve cards describe the primitive, heavy, mammalian, earthly, domestic, social, hive-orientation of the passed. With the exception of Impregnation (Wheel of Life) all the cards described so far present human figures engaged in some form of material, cultural, secular, earth-bound larval activity. The Baby-Fool. The Wily-cellular Magician. The Earth-Mother. The Secret-Woman. The Emperor-Power. Papal-popularity. The Paleolithic-Serving-Mind. The Neolithic-Manipulative-Chariot-Mind. Tribal-Success. Feudal Hermit-Playboy Adolescence. Marital Domesticity. Egalitarian Hive-Justice.

A fast scan of the cards to come reflects the extra-terrestrial nature of the Fifth, Sixth, Seventh and Eighth Circuits:

> The Contra-gravity Hanging Floating Man.
> Death-rebirth of the Body.
> The Winged-form of Blending into new hives.
> The Einsteinian-Lysergic Devil.
> The Atomic Fission Tower.
> The Moving-Reality Star.
> The Moon.
> The Sun.
> The Galactic Awakening-Judgment.
> And Finally the Universe-world Black-Whole finale.

The last ten cards of the primitive Tarot are post-Newtonian. In spite of the fact that the scientific discoveries had not been made at the time the cards were designed, still the numerical array of the Tarot anticipates the Neurogenetic sequence. The Tarot clearly progresses from the mundane to the Sci-Fi. The last half of the Tarot clearly deals in futique, futant, extra-terrestrial themes.

It is fitting that the next card initiating the transition to post-terrestrial is that of the Floating-Reversed Person.

Evolution moves upward. Gravity is always the drag, the enemy of the future.

162

# The Three Cards
## *Hanging Man, Skeleton Horse, Temperance*
## Portray
## Your Three Body-intelligence Neuro-Technologies

13. Body Consumer

14. Body Wizard

15. Inter-Body Fusion

**THE FIFTH CIRCUIT OF THE NERVOUS SYSTEM TO EVOLVE (In both species and individual) FABRICATES POST-SOCIAL REALITIES WHICH INVOLVE BODY-SELF-DISCOVERY, BODY-SELF-ACTUALIZATION AND POST-SOCIAL FUSIONS WITH OTHERS TO FORM A NEW HIVE**

The I Ching Trigram which signifies the Fifth Circuit of the Nervous System is TUI: JOYOUS LAKE

The three Tarot cards which predict this cycle of development are:

12. Hanged Man
Hedonic self-indulgent

13. Death Horse

14. Aesthetic Temperance

# THE HANGING MAN
## PORTRAYS YOUR BODY-RAPTURE,
## HEDONIC CONSUMER INTELLIGENCE:
## THE NEURO-TECHNOLOGY OF SELF-INDULGENCE

### CASTE 13

| | |
|---|---|
| **NEUROGENETIC TECHNOLOGICAL STAGE:** | Neurosomatic Receptivity./Self-Definition as Hedonic Consumer. Passive Awareness of the body. The Hippy./ The Rapture Consumer. The Aesthete. The Fifth Childhood. Zero-Gravity Liberation. |
| **PHYLOGENETIC STAGE:** | The Hedonic Elite; Post-hive Consciousness |
| **ONTOGENETIC STAGE:** | Post-terrestrial Self-Reward Consciousness |
| **ATTITUDE:** | Sensual Awareness of the body; Zero-Gravity Floating |
| **ZODIAC II:** | Self-Indulgent Pisces II |
| **TITAN:** | Tethys |
| **ℶ HEBREW LETTER:** | Mem, "I have refrained my feet from the evil way of earth." |
| **REALITY CREATED:** | Self reward. |
| **ECOLOGICAL NICHE (SPECIES):** | Zones of high technology and Affluence in Stage 12 Empires. |
| **ECOLOGICAL NICHE (INDIVIDUAL):** | One's own body as space-time ship. |

The Thirteenth Tarot card, Hanging Person, represents the passive-receptive stage of the Fifth Circuit. The retraction of the neuro-umbilical lines that create hive-bound, earth-bound reality islands. The transition from terrestrial gravity to being "high." The breakthrough to Body Consciousness. The Somatic passage. The Turn-on. Liberation from gravitational pull. The Body experienced as Soft-machine, freed from mundane survival imprints.

This Tarot card is an unmistakable, dramatic signal from DNA that your nervous system contains post-terrestrial circuits which free the body from the gravitational and territorial limits of the womb planet. The Birth of the Self. The Self! The Self!

164

Card image: RAPTURE NEURO-TECHNOLOGY — A ♥ — HEDONIC CONSUMER – PLEASURE RECEIVER — TITAN TETHYS — **HANGED MAN** ♠ — SELF-INDULGENT PISCES II

SEE PISCES!... WE TOLD YOU THAT YOU'D LEAD US HOME

### Stage 13

Tarot Hanging Man (card 12) THE HANGING MAN (Pisces II) codes the consumer-Indulgent stage of the post-social Self-Discovery. The resurrection of body as Time Ship—freed from social imprint to be used as receptive apparatus for hedonic experience. The Passive-Receptive stage of Neuro-Somatic Awareness. Sensory pleasure. Enjoyment of the Gravity-free Awakened Body. Thoughtless rapture. Consumer use of Body Turn-ons—especially drugs. In the species this stage appears in affluent, successful societies as hip-sophisticated transcendence of primitive moral systems. In the individual it emerges when intelligent use of drugs and other sensory aids allows suspension of social imprints. The individual transcends hive-morals and uses the body as pleasure organ. Self-Definition as aesthetic person; as happy-hippy pleasure seeker wandering through the Garden of Sensory Goodies.

# YOUR BRAIN CONTAINS 12 SUPER WO-MAN CIRCUITS

PETE VON SHOLLY

The transition from larval to post-larval (Stage 12 to Stage 13) has been called by prophets, the "abyss." Nietzsche, influenced by Darwin, became obsessed with the concept of Superman—the next step after *homo-sapiens*.

*Superman* is a post-terrestrial futique exo-psychological concept which was reflexedly corrupted by hive philosophers to serve the mundane ambitions of local power-politics.

Far from being inclined to National Socialism, Nietzsche recognized the dangers of collective domestication.

"Christianity, Democracy, and Socialism are so many examples of 'herd morality'. Democracy pretends that all men are equal and obliterates the distinctions between the noble (futants) and the base. Socialism would abolish the leisure class that is the mainstay of culture and cater instead to the taste of the mass. He who cannot raise himself to the level of those above him, can at any rate drag them down to his in the name of brotherhood."

Nietzsche then describes the futational nature of Stage 13 in the famous poetic passage:

"Man is a rope stretched between beast and Superman—a rope over an abyss

"Man is great in that he is a bridge and not a goal. Man can be loved in that he is a transition and not a perishing."

HEY!! IVE KNEW THIS ALL ALONG!

166

# The 1st Stage of Post Terrestrial Neuro-Technology Frees the Body as Self-Contained Time-Ship

PETE VON SHOLLY

"This temporal caste makes the transition from the body as a hive-robot maneuvering in terrestrial gravity to the body as gravity-free self-directed rapture instrument. Sensory consciousness. This slot represents the somatic 'turn-on', the reversal from earthly to extra-terrestrial consciousness. The Higher Nature awakening. The attitude is dendritic, passive, receptive and hedonistically consuming."

This Tarot card *does not* portray a hanged man, but rather a person floating free. There is no suggestion of gallows, rope, punishment. SHe is suspended in the attitude of rapturous detached passivity. Entrancement. De Laurence says,

"the face expresses deep entrancement, not suffering; . . . the figure as a whole suggests life in suspension, but life and not death.

"It is a card of profound significance, but all the significance is veiled. One of his editors suggests that Eliphas Levi did not know the meaning, which is unquestionable— nor did the editor himself. It has been called falsely a card of martyrdom, . . . of prudence . . . of duty; but we may exhaust all published interpretations and find only vanity. I will say very simply on my own part that it expresses the relation, in one of its aspects, between the Divine and the Universe."

Note that this interesting comment by de Laurence attributes no mundane meaning to this card. He refers to "The Divine and the Universe." The modern meaning of "universe" is post-terrestrial, post-hive.

De Laurence goes on to say, "He who can understand that the story of his higher nature is embedded in this symbolism will receive intimations concerning a great awakening that is possible, and will know that after . . . [terrestrial life] . . . there is a glorious . . . Resurrection."[1]

"Great awakening" refers to the *Turning-on* of the Fifth Circuit . . . the amused, liberation of the body from terrestrial imprints, the discovery that one is not an Earthling, that the body can get "high", can be experienced as a gravity-free pleasure machine. Resurrection of the body. Birth of the Self, the auto-mobile Self.

167

# The 13th Brain Defines Self As The key Neuro-reality: The Self-Free and Clear of Terrestrial Hive

The original narcotics agent. Here is the basic drama of Judeo-Christian superstition. The evolving mates are driven away from Selfhood and Immortality by a vengeful armed police agent—currently impersonating Ayattulah Ralph Nader.

Practically, in the evolution of the individual's neurology, this element represents the receptive, passive, body-consumer phase when the Fifth Circuit has been activated but before feedback control of physiology and rapture linkage has been made. This is the shiva sida of the Soma imprint. This card closely resonates with Stage 1, the Fool. Both cards are birth situations. This is the crucial initiatory phase in post-hive evolution. Just as the Unformed Potential of the Fool must establish muscular control of body organs and link with the Mothering Earth, so must the Sensually Awakened go on to establish intelligent disciplined body control and then link with a post-hive mate. If the Fifth Somatic Circuit does not hook-up, if the Soma-rapture imprint remains sensually passive, then the individual remains in this slot—the enlightened blissed-out Fool, the Hanging Man. We speak here of the Hippies, the Playboy Hedonists, the Ram Dasses, the good-times rollers, the hashishines, the bliss prophets, the second-hand Karma dealers, the thoughtless sensory consumers.

Oriental philosophy and its Western playboy vulgarizations produce armies of Hanging-Floating people—awakened from hive imprints, but un-attached, un-tuned-in. Arhats, Hippies and dropped-out wanderers are actually premature post-terrestrials. The Hippies who "hang-out," apparently doing nothing, are waiting passively like babies for the space-ship to take them home to the stars, turned-on lay-abouts waiting for the technology to provide escape velocity. Grounded butterflies, they naturally incur the wrath of the unevolved hive caterpillars who cannot understand and resent the carefree futants.

The post-terrestrial self is a winged creature—too big for the hive.

168

HEH HEH
HE'S ATTACKING
THE HIPPIE ESTABLISHMENT

# Getting High — Hedonic Con- sumerism — is the First Step in Becoming A Post-terrestrial Divinity

Getting High, floating above the earth, is the theme behind every pre-technological religion.

The Twelve Apostles (12 terrestrial castes) watch as Christ, the 13th hanging-man, floats into Self-hood.

The Hebrew letter-code is *mem,* water, suggesting fluidity, buoyancy, floating and symbolic re-birth (as in Baptism and similar purification rites involving water). According to Crowley the cognate gods are Osiris (as dead-and-reborn image of the Resurrected Body), Soma (the divine plant of the Vedas, variously identified as cannabis or the psychedelic mushroom, *amanita*), Titan Tethys (as images of gravity-less floating, Oceanic consciousness, transcendence of solid-earth Fourth Circuit hive responsibilities)· The lotus is the associated plant, echoing Buddhist use of this image for the yogic drop-out; the caste-totem animal is a strange eagle-snake-scorpion cherub symbolizing extra-terrestrial bio-systems.

Other images are the beryl or acquamarine, Wine, myrrh: all suggestive of sensuality, Dionysian intoxication, hashish-vision, escape from hive sobriety.

Cavendish recognizes the reversal of conditioned tribal-values: "In the process of the Hanged Man the [magician] is drowned in floodtides of his inner being [somatic-sensory energies. The false self which is destroyed is the whole 'higher' structure of outlook, attitudes, tastes, acquired mental and emotional habits (first four hive cir-cuits), which cages the inner man]. In a reversal of values [—the Hanged Man is upside down on his gibbet—] this structure is overturned and fragmented to release the fertile waters of the depths."2

The sinister overlay of the card—imagery of death by execution: hanging and/or crucifixion—clearly reflects the terror which the hive authorities use to block this futation. The First Circuit signals: Pleasure is dangerous! The Second Circuit warns: "If you relax your vigilance you will be put-down!"The Third Circuit worries, "I can't understand; am I going mad?" The Fourth Circuit whispers, "Taboo—violation of sex-role." Only when these hive taboos are understood and mastered does the pure joy of self-reward neurosomatic pleasure begin.

PLEASURE IS ANTI- SOCIAL

169

WE MUST SACRIFICE FOR THE HIVE!

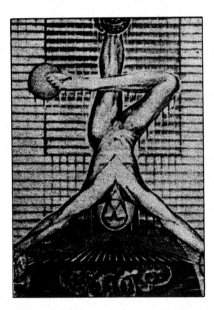

LSD SUICIDE IN NEW YORK

## THE PREMATURE-UNPREPARED EXTRA-TERRESTRIAL

When the larval circuits of the nervous system are retracted and the post-terrestrial circuits activated, the function of the body as a time-ship designed to maneuver in zero-gravity is recognized.

The futant neural circuits designed to deal with post-terrestrial realities are fore-casted ahead of the external RNA technology.

The ill-prepared person or the person whose post-terrestrial circuits are activated without his knowledge can become confused—and can operate as though gravity has already been transcended.

# DIVINITY DEGREE

❖❖❖❖❖❖❖❖❖❖❖❖ ❖❖❖❖❖❖❖❖❖❖❖❖

## This TAROT CARD

## authorizes you to turn-on your

_thirteenth_ **brain**

ACCEPT YOUR ELITE SELF-HOOD, BECOME THE GOD SIVA, THE TITAN TETHYS, THE PLEASURE CONSUMER AND EXPERIENCE LIKE A SELF-CONFIDENT, ENRAPTURED OWNER OF YOUR OWN BODY.

— get high, get high, get high
— create-fabricate a stimulus for turning-on each of your sense-organs: eyes, mouth, nose, skin, muscles, mouth, membranes
— then, combine them in poly-sensual symphonic compositions
— imagine living a life of total self-indulgence
— define yourself as LIFE-ARTIST, arranging your surroundings to continually enrapture your sense organs
— consider all the moral-political taboos against sensory self-reward; show why civilization as we know it, would collapse if body-consumerism takes over
— go through the pages of PLAYBOY magazine and calculate the percentage of ads for sensory self-indulgence
— then calculate the percentage of ads for family-domestic items
— now ruffle the pages of the READERS DIGEST and calculate the percentage of ads for self-indulgent versus home-owner-parental ads. You now understand the difference between Castes 11 and 13

— get high, get high, get high
— calculate the percentage of your daily life spent in boring activities and then initiate an all-out campaign to decrease your BOREDOM-INDEX

# THE SKELETON-HORSE
## PORTRAYS YOUR PROUD SELF-ACTUALIZED
## ARTIST CONTROL OF YOUR OWN BODY-SENSATIONS

CASTE 14

**NEUROGENETIC TECHNOLOGICAL STAGE:** Self-Actualized Intelligent Control of the Body/Neurosomatic Self-Reward/Sensory Management/Physiological Feedback Control/The Yogin/The Artist-Aesthetic Reality Architect/The Fifth Self-Actualization/The Resurrected Body/Driver-Seat-Control of the Soft Machine/Body Engineering/The Sorcerer-Warrior/The Reichian Adept/The Holistic Health Healer.

**PHYLOGENETIC STAGE:** The Post-Domestic, Post-Hive, Aesthetic Aristocratic Class emerging throughout history during times of imperial affluence/Becoming Dom-Species in Sun Belt, 1976.

**ONTOLOGICAL STAGE:** Post-Hive Disciplined Control of Body Sensations/The Turned-on Artist

**ATTITUDE:** Controlled navigation of the Time-ship of One's Own Body

**ZODIAC II:** Self-Actualized Aries II

**TITAN:** Oceanus

**] HEBREW LETTER:** Nun, "Thy word is a lamp unto my feet."

**REALITY CREATED:** Aesthetic-Hedonic

**ECOLOGICAL NICHE:** (Species): Special Elite-Private zones where aesthetic-hedonic behavior is protected from Hive Moralists.

**ECOLOGICAL NICHE:** (Individual): One's Own Body and its immediate aesthetic surroundings. The artist's studio.

CONGRATULATIONS ARIES!! HERE IS YOUR MOMENT OF GENETIC HEROISM

172

BODY NEURO-TECHNOLOGY

SELF-ACTUALIZED HEDONISTIC ARTIST

TITAN OCEANUS

# DEATH

AESTHIC SELF-CONFIDENT ARIES II

*Stage 14*

Tarot Death (card 13) DEATH-REBIRTH (Aries II) codes the Self-Actualized phase of post-hive Self-Discovery. The disciplined control of one's own body function. The art of hedonic self-stimulation. The science of conscious body performance. Karate. Yoga. Dance. Non-competitive sports designed to get high, to stretch body and mind. The direction of one's own aesthetic environment and responses. The conscious acceptance of one's life as a Work of Conceptual Art. This Stage appears in the species after the passive-self-Indulgent consumer stage. In California It occurred as Pre-Dom species during the 1970's.

This Brain is turned on by aphrodisiac drugs or other sensory stimuli at those times in history when Security-Safety-Science-Social Serenity provide the leisure to develop the Neuro-technology of Self-Development. When survival pressures are relieved the gene-pool allows the luxury of Self-Actualization—as a genetic experimental device.

The intelligent manipulation of the Body freed from the demands and limitations of terrestrial-territorial hives. The control of one's own physiology. The aesthetic-eroticization of sensation and motion. The Fifth Self-Actualization; learning how to use the body as Time-Machine, as feed-back rapture instrument.

I WAS BORN TOO SOON FOR WERNER ERHART AND I HATE MY BODY TOO.

173

# CARD 14 POR-TRAYS YOUR CONSCIOUS CONTROL OF YOUR OWN STEAMING-POWERFUL MARE-STALLION BODY!!

The Tarot card, HORSE AND SKELETON, Caste 14, represents the Brahmic Self-Actualization of the Fifth Circuit. Conscious control of one's own physiology.

This Tarot card portrays the enormous, well-proportioned, smooth-muscled *Body* of a Stallion-Mare. Astride the horse rides a skeleton holding in its hand a banner inscribed with the Rose of Life. A Bishop, a Mother and a child await the approach of the Horse with reverence and awe.

Let this card represent physiological feedback consciousness. The Resurrection of the Body. The Reichian rediscovery of the conscious Body.

The first four imprints, we recall, totally robotize the humant body. The magnificent, coordinated, trillion-cell physiological network operates on autopilot. The fetal person uses Hir body as an automaton scanning for conditioned symbolic cues and reacting in narrow standardized reaction to the imprinted reality island.

The emergence of somatic self-reward consciousness is symbolized by the living horse which dominates this card. The skeleton in armor is a dead, past symbol. The horse is very alive! This card is a most ingenious, inventive signal—a masterpiece of esoteric communication; a powerful diagnostic flourish! A genetic intelligence test designed to separate the mundane from the awakened. Those who see this card as Death, those who focus on the life-less symbol may be trapped by hive symbols, obsessed with morality, etc. Those who resonate to the vibrant energy of the Stallion-Mare are post-hive sensualists. If a real-life noble horse were to prance into your living room with a Halloween skeleton on his back, would your nervous system react to the dead bones or the live ton of quivering steaming life?

Let the skeleton represent the husk, the dry shell of the four retracted larval Minds. Memory Bones. The armor is the L.M. symbolic Ego. The Bishop, symbol of the Hive Establishment, and the Mother and Child, representing the Fourth Circuit Family, express homage to the Resurrected Body. To the Noble-Divine individual who has accepted the responsibility of Self Reward.

174

THEY'LL NEVER GET ME
UP IN ONE OF **THOSE** !

De Laurence says: "The veil or mask of life is perpetuated in change, transformation and passage from lower to higher, and this is more fitly represented in the rectified Tarot by one of the apocalyptic visions than by the crude notion of the reaping skeleton."

The de Laurence cards portray, in the background, the towers, unusual, because they are in no way conventional. They are apparently not designed for habitation or defense. They resemble pylons or launching towers. Between them is a solar-star. The towers framing the sun can be interpreted as symbols of space-ship flight. Extraterrestrial migration. Upward pointing.

"The natural transit of man to the next stage of his being . . . is . . . one form of his progress, but the exotic and almost unknown entrance, while still in this life, . . . is a change in the form of consciousness and the passage into a state to which ordinary death is neither the path nor gate." De Laurence thus hints that the new level is a higher form of biological life. He is coming close to seeing that the first step in post-mundane consciousness is into the *Body*. The notion that the Soma must be turned on, that the path to evolved consciousness and accelerated intelligence lies through the Self-Rewarded Body is taught by certain Hindu, Sufi, Tantrist, Sex-magic and Buddhist schools, but this lesson of Eros and Soma is usually taught indirectly, subtly, because it outrages larval thinking, is anathema to hive-concepts of sin and social irresponsibility.

It comes as a great shock to the socialized, hive mind that the first step in neural mutation is via Body consciousness. The world is my body. The first reality is Somatic. The cunning hive morality warns that it is necessary to inhibit sensual-somatic pleasures in order to survive. If you indulge yourself you cannot indulge the hive. The last terrestrial element—Card 12, Justice-Virtue—solidifies this insectoid repression against fleshly experience. Genetic templating, social imprinting and hive conditioning mobilize against pleasure feed-back and somatic rapture. The RNA instructions of the first four circuits define Physiological Self-Reward and Rapture as dangerous, helpless, sinister and sinful.

The first element in the Fifth Circuit—the Reversed Floating-Man—Hanging-Serenely prepared us for the break-through revelation. Body as Automobile Time-Ship. All the dimensions, meanings and virtues of hive-life are suspended, reversed in post-terrestrial existence. This is the lesson which the N.A.S.A. bureaucrats and Russian cosmonauts did not learn. The larval materialism of Earth does not work in space. Caterpillar ethics and strategies do not apply to the butterfly reality.

The resurrected Body is the post-hive vehicle. The face of the horse merges with the launching tower. Note that the eye of the horse is on the star!

In the topology of the three Fifth Circuit cards, the Horse (Stage 14) moves away from the floating passivity of the Hanging Man (Stage 13) and moves toward sensual fusion and linkage of self-actualized mates (Stage 15). We master the body, not for passive receptive rapture, not for yogic raptured detachment but for linkage. Hippie sensuality and Buddhist meditation are delightful, free forms of T.M. (Transcendental Masturbation). The horse carries the banner of life to the fusion of two vessels which replenish each other. This fusion becomes the next Stage 15.

175

# Your Caste 14 Brain Joyously, Skillfully Drives your Aeroto-Mobile Body

Here we see Vishnu in the Floating Man pose of the new-born Self-Indulgent. Above him the eleven heads of Ananta (symbol of evolution) fore-caste the stages to come.

The focus of exopsychology is the nervous system as transceiver of energy—somatic, neuro-electric, DNA-molecular and SANE (sub-atomic). The basic tension in evolution is between the maintenance of hive survival structures that limit and channel energy and the emergence of post-hive structures which can transceive greater intensities and ranges of energy.

The history of philosophy reflects this tension—the laryngeal-manual mind attempting to reduce nature to what can be manipulated by the nine-membranes of the throat and the hinged-thumb, and the great Egg Wisdom energy-systems, alchemical, neuro-scientific, organic, psycho-astronomical—attempting to describe the direct patterns of raw reality.

Stonehenge, the pyramids point human perspective up to the stars. Newton, Planck, Einstein writing the mathematical descriptions of physical energy are caste robots responsible for fabricating futant hives.

A splendid example of the abstracting, domesticating and de-energizing trend of larval hive philosophy is found in the Tarot "Death" card.

Some modern occultists have forgotten that during the 17th-19th centuries the horse was the classic signal used by painters to create life, vigor, flesh-resurrected. Peter Paul Rubens, Gericault, Delacroix used the horse as the basic steamy, erotic symbol of organic energy—huge, thick-muscled, prancing, pawing creatures, quivering with life, eyes rolling, nostrils straining, trembling with nervous power.

Caste 14 means riding your own shuddering horse-power. The trick is to keep It from becoming too Italian, heavy-breathing past-caste lovers whose ecological niche and whose neural evolution is Mediterranean, (Caste 10).

# DIVINITY DEGREE

## This TAROT CARD

### authorizes you to turn-on your

*fourteenth* **brain**

ACCEPT YOUR ELITE CHARISMA, BECOME THE GOD SHAKTI, DIVINE BODY WIZARD, AND EXPERIENCE LIKE A SELF-CONFIDENT, INTELLIGENT, ARROGANT MANAGER OF YOUR OWN BODY.

— Break your orgasm-record
— Get high and practice disciplined control of a body-organ
— Obtain a catalogue of a Humanist Psychology or New Age conference—and trip-out on the infinite techniques for Self-Development listed therein
— Locate an Arica or EST group and study their techniques for Self-Actualization
  Chuckle at the devotees of Swamis and gurus who enslave their disciples with promises of Self-Liberation
— Master every Yoga that amuses you
— Study neuro-physiology and wholistic medicine
— Take acid and voyage down through all your sensory-somatic systems
— Use your body as a space-time ship temporarily grounded on a heavy 1-G planet
— Love the beauty and precision of your body
        — Break all existing records for Self-directed fun-pleasure-rapture

# TEMPERANCE
## PORTRAYS YOUR NEURO-TECHNOLOGY FOR ESCAPING THE BODY BY FUSION WITH ANOTHER

CASTE 15

**NEUROGENETIC TECHNOLOGICAL STAGE:** Neurosomatic Fusion, the Formation of Cults and New Cultures. Linkage of Self-Actualized Tantric Lovers. The Aesthetic interaction. The Union of Alchemist and Soror Mystica. The Fifth Mate. The Fusion of Hedonic Elites.

**PHYLOGENETIC STAGE:** Post-hive Communication at the Somatic Aesthetic Level

**ONTOGENETIC STAGE:** Escape from your own body via neurosomatic fusion.

**ATTITUDE:** Fusion of Self-Fabricated Realities

**ZODIAC II:** Self-Actualized Taurus II

**TITAN:** Rhea

**ᕱ HEBREW LETTER:** Sameck, "Hold thou me up and I shall be safe."

**REALITY CREATED:** Neurosomatic diploid bi-person having homologous paired brain circuits for each stage

**ECOLOGICAL NICHE (species):** Free zones where post-hive elites gather

**ECOLOGICAL NICHE (individ.):** The "New Body" of fused adepts

This circuit of your Brain is activated (after you have accepted hive-free Self indulgence, Caste 13, and confidently mastered your Body, Caste 14) when you can "tolerate" existence only in communion-fusion with other Life Artists.

178

HEY TAURUS! YOUR BODY FUSION PROVIDES THE PLATFORM FOR THE FUTURE.

*Stage 15*

Tarot Temperance (Card 14) TEMPERANCE (Taurus II) portrays the fusion of Self-Actualized persons in post-social linkages to form new post-territorial hives, called communes. This is the first direct, real, conscious-connection between two or more human beings, detached from larval, robotic-imprinted needs. This stage occurs in history after a period of Self-Discovery and Self-Actualization—when an increasing number of persons in control of the aesthetics of their lives hook-up to form new communities—post-social in nature. In the past such groups have formed aesthetic brotherhoods, religious communes, spiritual cults, utopian communities, show-business coopera- tives. This is the key tactic of evolution—Self-Actualized Out-castes forming new hives to make possible migration to the next ecological niche.

You begin to hang out in ecological niches where you find those who share your reality.

**THE BIO-
ELECTRICAL FIELD
CREATED BY THE
CONTACT BETWEEN
TURNED-ON
BODIES DEFINES A
POST-TERRESTRIAL
NEUROLOGICAL
REALITY**

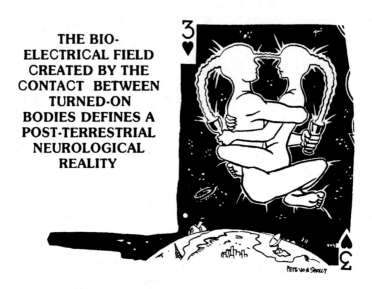

Caste 15 fusion is the sensory linkage of Five-Brain persons in Tantric union, New Hive communication. The rapture connection. The hook-up of two or more Resurrected Bodies in conscious connection. (Larval interactions among four-brained human beings are nothing more than the robotized exchanges between hive-imprinted programs and socially-conditioned reflexes.) The Fifth Circuit is concerned with mutual prolongation or pulsating climax of sensation, mutual contrast of afferent movements, harmony of aesthetic styles. Communication between two or more such magnetically charged bodies activates the Neuro-electric stages which make possible the fabrication of new neuro-realities.

This stage is transitional-amblotic, exactly paralleling:
the amphibians (water to land via shoreline)
the monkeys (land to artifact-shelters via trees)
the caste-tribes (village to city via trading)
the monotheistic empires (cities to selfhood via imperial
        indulgence)

180

— ONLY EQUALS CAN FLY FORMATION.

# EVERY BODY
# WIZARD KNOWS
## WHERE TO FIND A
## MATE

Tantric lovers, life artists, self-actualized hedonic-elitists escape from the masturbatory limits of their bodies via bio-neural fusion. Members of this caste recognize each other by their radiation.

As in every ambiotic stage (3, 6, 9, 12) a new form of communication develops. A new sensory-somatic language which produces a more intelligent level of locomotion-communication.

AMPHIBIANS   crawling leads to land-life
PRIMATES     gesturing leads to language
CASTE-TRIBE   division of labor leads to civilization
CENTRALIZED WELFARE STATES   provide the leisure for experiments in self-hood, particularly by the adolescents

Caste 15 Body-Fusers are transitional because they have doubled their scope. Just as the amphibian is at home both in water and on land, and the primate can run and climb, the Tantric lover can live in hir own body and in the Fused-shared neurosomatic reality of hir mate.

Caste 15 futants are genetic elites found in certain predictable habitats. They congregate in fore-line niches where hive-morals are diminished and self-indulgence is tolerated. Art colonies, jet-set watering places, Bohemian or Hippy mating grounds, entertainment-hedonic zones. Every Fifth Circuit person knows instinctively where to find a mate. The Woodstock Festival of 1969 was a most visible swarming-ground of Fifth circuit futants.

The Sun Belt of America has, since 1965, been the migratory-swarming goal of post-hive selfhood people—seeking reality-confirmation and fusion partners.

A typical aberrant genetic-phase which allows-accompanies the emergence of the 15th caste is fanatic cultism. When one Self-Confidant-Self-Actualizer attracts Stage 13 Passives (or larval humants) without the balancing polarity of the other Caste 14 Actualizers a slavish cult appears. The State 15 caste-leader fabricates a crazed-ideosyncratic culture which eventually collapses. The Jim Jones syndrome.

# THE MAGNETICALLY CHARGED BODY MUST BE POLARIZED TO FOCUS AND HARNESS THE ENERGY

Hebe, the Greek goddess of eternal youth seen here impersonating the Tarot card Temperance. She carries in Her hands ambrosia and nectar—the Life Extension drugs of the Olympian pantheon.

The Tarot card TEMPERANCE portrays Caste 15, the Vishnu-Linkage of the Fifth Circuit. The Somatic energies linked.

We recall that Stage 13 (Hippie-oriented-quietism signified by the Floating Man) murmurs that there is no place to go. Somatic Self-Reward. Sensory Reception. Unattached selfishness. Relax. Float. Drift. Hang suspended. Mindless. The Hindu Fool has been well described by Carlos Castaneda and quoted with approval by Ram Dass. "He knows that his life will be over altogether too soon, he knows because he sees nothing is more important than anything else." This is the empty, void philosophy of vulgate Buddhism. The rudderless yogin who has severed hir neural ties to hive robothood but has not oriented to the direction of genetic evolution. Wingless butterflies.

The Neurological Tarot defines the evolutionary steps beyond Stage 13—the controlled folly of Castaneda, the quietism of Tao, the no-difference smiling cynicism of Manson, the "All-is-one" sucrosity of Ram Dass, the Stage 14 pick-your-game elegance of Crowley. These attitudes are passive Floating-Man responses; post-hive stupidities; failures to make the Fifth Circuit linkage which is represented by Caste 15.

In Slot 14, we considered the Somatic Engineer, the Sorcerer-Warrior, the feedback Yogin who attains mastery over Hir sensory and autonomous function. Sensory Control.

Now, after Sensory Reception and Sensory Control, comes Sensory Linkage of self-actualized Hedonists.

The Tarot card Temperance portrays the essential characteristics of this caste. An extra-terrestrial being, "a winged angel, with the sign of the sun upon his forehead, and on his breast, the square and triangle of the septenary. . . ."[3] The figure is both male and female. SHe holds two chalices and is pouring the energy from one to the other. The alchemical-pharmacological implication is clear. The two elements form a new inter-personal molecule. The two chalices represent the bodies of two hedonically charged erotic wizards (Caste 14) in close attractive contiquity. The energy does visibly pass from one body to the other when the lovers have activated with a Fifth Circuit neuro-transmitter and arranged their skin-vessels in a tantric posture.

The wavy liquid in the card is the aura, the electrical grids which tantric lovers fabricate between their bodies.

The winged creature, clearly post-terrestrial, represents the Sixth Circuit consciousness which is activated by tantric contact. This symbolic representation is as clear as a mathematical formula, but only to those who have experienced the flow of somatic-electricity.

## THE EXPERIMENTAL PRODUCTION OF NEUROSOMATIC ELECTRICAL CHARGE

PETE VON SHOLLY

Tantra is a yogic technique in which the totality of one's erotic potential is fused in union with a member of the opposite sex. Such a
synergetic union harmonizes all the neurosomatic energies and makes
possible the next step in evolution: Brain Control.

By 1979 the production of somatic-electricity between two self-actualized Hedonists
was as obvious (and to the uninitiated, as mysterious) as Benjamin Franklin's
experimental summoning down of lightening bolts. The experiment can be easily
replicated at home by any intelligent scientists.

1) Retire to a comfortable bedroom where there is total privacy.

2) Ingest an adequate amount of a neurosomatic drug. The amount and the name
of this neuro-transmitter varies from niche-to-niche and from brain to brain. Such
drugs have, at times, been called MDA, X.T.C. (New York, 1978).

3) Arrange the two naked bodies in any standard face-to-face tantric attitude—
legs intertwined, woman's yoni above man's lingam.

4) The two experimenters then softly stroke each other's bodies for at least an
hour. The soft friction of the two aroused skin surfaces then produces an electrical
aura. This usually appears first on the hands—often seen as filmlike grids between the
fingers. Or as loose "rubber-glove-like" auras around the fingers. The grids are clearly
electromagnetic structures in that objects can be passed through them. But they can
be manipulated by moving the electrically-charged finger close to them. The magnetic
attraction is often visible as thread-like filaments growing up from the arms. Tiny
electric point-flashes are also observed. In some cases these filaments become like the
threads emitted from certain marine forms (Portugese men of war, for example) which
contain at the ends electrical charges. The charges in this case are pleasurable rather
than defensive.

The production of such magnetic auras indicates that the neuro-electric circuit
(Stage 16) is being activated.

The classic Tarot nomenclature is designedly wrong in the case of the "Hanged Man" and "Death." However, "Temperance" is a reasonably accurate vulgarization for this element in the sequence. The raw avalanche of body sensation must be tempered, harmonized, linked, exchanged. Crowley's title, "Art," is more elegant.

In the west, the role of alchemist classically personalizes this Tantric phase. The lesson of alchemy is *solve et coagule*. Fission and then fusion. The four-brained prudish, hive-bound structure is loosened when the Fifth Circuit is turned on. The body (Stage 13) floats free of terrestrial attachments. Stage 14 establishes personal control, self-reward. Stage 15 links up. The fusion is aesthetic. Merging of self-actualized minds in the Tantric union. The successful alchemists worked in secret male-female pairs; fusing the somatic magnetic polarities. The fact that the energies of the body must be transmitted, fused in erotic-aesthetic union, was the censored, well-hidden secret of European alchemy.

Any body has to be some body to some body to be every body.

TURNS OUT JACKIE KENNEDY
WAS THE BEST POLITICIAN
IN THE FAMILY

# THE TRANSITIONAL-MIXING-AMBIOT STAGES CREATE THE GENETIC SCHIZOPHRENIAS

It is clear that the "trinity" castes we have designated as "ambiots," "mates" or "matings"—3) Empress, 6) Hierophant, 9) Strength, 12) Justice and now 15) Temperance—represent ecological bonds. Numerologically, it is significant that these "ambiot stages" involve multiples of the number three. Two fused to create the Trinity.

The Empress (Stage 3) is the first migration and the first bonding, infant-mother. The Madonna symbol. If this temporal caste imprint is not made properly, some form of deep distrust, alienation, autism or first-circuit schizophrenia results.

The Hierophant (Stage 6) is the second Trinity-bonding—child with herd or troop. The Man and the Boys hunting together. If this mammalian reality is not imprinted, Second Circuit schizophrenia ensues—emotional alienation, the Lee Harvey Oswald, the sociopath, the loser-outlaw who cannot connect with mental linkage.

Strength (Stage 9) is the third bonding. Youth-school. In T.S. Eliot's terms, the wedding of Tradition and Individual Talent. The membership in the guild, the academy, the learned body. A framework of successful collaborations which the Individual can learn, adopt, adapt, alter, revise, re-create. If a consensual mental reality is not imprinted, Third Circuit schizophrenia occurs—mental-ideational insanity. Cultural Illiteracy. Parrot-mentality. Inability to think or reason collaboratively, Bizarre private philosophies, *lumpen* occultism, Know Nothing-ism, bigotries, fanatical sects of quasi-religious or quasi-scientific "truths," certain forms of clinical hebephrenia and paranoia.

Justice (Caste 12) represents the fourth bonding. Individual to hive. The good citizen. The docile worker.

The key to a successful Stage 12 imprint is egalitarian fusion of the many castes necessary to operate an urban hive. Fair-play and hive unity—everyone "sacrificing" (to use the word favored by Kennedy, Carter, Mao and all socialist leaders) for the good of the hive. The glue which holds the hive together is this sense of confidence in the unity principle.

Note that megalomanic totalitarianism is acceptable, indeed, necessary to run a successful socialist unity. At the same time John F. Kennedy was telling the Americans to ask what they could do for the hive, the populace was pleased that the First Lady, Jacqueline, was flamboyantly and conspicuously, indulgently pleasing her own aesthetic desires. In a well run totalitarian society the need for aesthetic-hedonic exhibition is recognized—when limited to the ruling caste.

Fourth Circuit schizophrenia occurs when the hive leaders do not accept the caste-pluralism. When vengeful peasants take over and wish to drag the hive down to the equalitarian level of barnyard brutality—e.g. the Soviet Union. Actually, Stage 12 societies can exist only on the western frontier. Eastern populations (now located behind the iron Curtain) use mass-communication-transportation technologies to impose barbarian (Stage 10) or tribal (Stage 7, 8, 9) savageries on the monolithic hive-structure.

I CAN ONLY BE GOD

IF I ACCEPT YOUR
DIVINITY TOO

## FIFTH CIRCUIT SCHIZOPHRENIA IS DIVINE MEGALOMANIA

The Tarot card Temperance portrays the fifth bonding. It is usually coded as Shiva-Shakti by Tantrics. Lion-eagle in alchemy. It is man-woman, aesthetic linkage. A fusion of liberated, post-hive individuals who share an amused detachment from hive-uniformity. Attraction to other self-actualized Bodies. If this linkage is not imprinted properly, Fifth Circuit schizophrenia results.

Most of the weirdness that passes for "higher consciousness," "cosmic consciousness," "mystic awakening," "artistic genius," is Fifth Circuit alienation. Many post-hive, self-reward people get carried away with the freedom and selective choice. They become megalomaniac and fail to realize that others are also attaining post-hive Self-Actualization. It is true that to evolve beyond hive-robothood, one must pass Megalomania 1A (Caste 13) and master Simple Godmanship and Basic Narcissism (Caste 14). But a most perilous leap awaits the Self-Developer. After one has become a Self-Reward Adept it is necessary to realize that, although one is god, it's a pan-theistic universe, that other post-hive reality-creators exist.

The Caste 14 artist, exalted in hir ability to create new forms, is the notorious example of Fifth Circuit alienation. The Caste 15 linkage is made by means of the paradoxical God conspiracy-contract. Yes, my body-mind is the only reality I can experience. However, I choose to trustfully believe that other self-actualized post-hivers exist, and by linking my aesthetic divinity, higher levels of con-telligence can be activated. Intelligence must fuse, or incoherence results. integration-of-signals fails.

If each trinity bonding is a new dimension of love, then we have just re-examined the first five varieties of evolving trustful linkage:

### THE TRINITIES CREATED BY FUSION

Caste 3: Passive-infantile love—linkage with the Mother (Empress)
Caste 6: Admiring-childish love—linkage with the Father-Leader (Hierophant)
Caste 9: Intellectual love—linkage with other engineer minds (Strength)
Caste 12: Insectoid love—linkage with Hive Authority (Justice)
Caste 15: Love-linkage (Tantra) with other post-hive Self-Rewarders (Temperance)

In each fusion, the nervous system acts as both receiver and transmitter in the bonding. In each case, neurogenetic *resonance* occurs. In each case, a new hive is formed, a new social reality, a new model of the universe is created.

The political-mammalian nervous system at Caste 6 (Hierophant) wonders why those at Caste 3 (Empress) are not concerned about prestige, popularity, status, power. Simple: the reality of primate communication (Brain 6) does not exist for the amphibian (Brain 3).

The rational-digital nervous system of Caste 9 (Strength) wonders why those competitive politicians in Caste 6 (Hierophant) do not attempt to be accurate, objective, responsible, collaborative. Again: the advanced brain has not been activated. Brain 6 is not Brain 9.

The domesticated-hive nervous system, Caste 12 (Justice) wonders why those engineer-technocrats in Caste 9 (Strength) are satisfied to solve puzzles and have no concern about hive-morality, social uniformity, social justice, protection of the weak and crippled. Again: the hive bond has not been formed. Brain 9 is not Brain 12.

Once more, the aesthetic-somatic nervous system in Caste 15 (Temperance) wonders why those at Caste 12 (Justice) never raise their eyes above earth-society, beyond hive justice to evolve personally. Again, the imprint has not formed. Brain 12 is not Brain 15.

# DIVINITY
# DEGREE

═══════════ ·❖❖❖❖· ═══════════

## 𝕿𝖍𝖎𝖘 𝕿𝕬𝕽𝕺𝕿 𝕮𝕬𝕽𝕯

## authorizes you to turn-on your
__*fifteenth*__ **brain**

BECOME SIVA-SHAKTI, THE LOVER-GOD, AND
FUSE YOUR HEDONIC-ARTISTIC NEUROLOGY
WITH OTHERS.

— Get very high with your lover and perform mutual erotic-
  aesthetic rituals, fusing sensations
  Use a psycho-active chemical with your lover which produces bio-
  electricity and then experiment with it
— For the next 15 days explore-doscover a new way of sensually
  pleasing your lover and vice-reversed
— Make a list of 100 of the greatest fusion-love affairs in history
  John-Yoko, Christopher Isherwood- Don Bachardy
— Discuss with every love-affair you know the techniques they use
  for fusion
— Question some unfused solitaire people you know if they
  wouldn't prefer an all-out love-linkage
— Spend 72 hours with your lover never out of each other's sight

  For the next 15 days explore-discover a new way of sensually
  pleasing your lover and vice-reversed

# THE THREE CARDS
# DEVIL, TOWER, STAR
## Portray Your Three
## Brain-Control Neuro
## Technologies

16 BRAIN CONSUMER

17 BRAIN CONTROL
INTELLIGENCE

18 BRAIN FUSION

**THE** SIXTH CIRCUIT **OF THE NERVOUS SYSTEM TO EVOLVE (In both species and Individual)** MEDIATES DISCOVERY AND USE OF THE BRAIN ITSELF AS REALITY DEVICE

The I Ching Trigram which signifies the Sixth Circuit of the Nervous System Is LI: FIRE-ELECTRICITY

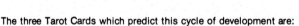

The three Tarot Cards which predict this cycle of development are:

CARD 15: The DEVIL — Stage 16—Brain consciousness

CARD 16: The TOWER — Stage 17—Control of one's Brain

CARD 17: The STAR — Stage 18—Linkage of Self-actualized Brain-Directors to fabricate new worlds (H.O.M.E.s)

188

This Aztec map of evolution presents the four past (terrestrial) genetic steps—each of which produces a tree of life leading to the neuro-electric center above.

THE MEDIEVAL TAROT MAKERS WERE AMAZINGLY PROPHETIC.

YEAH BUT THE NEW CARDS BY PETE VON SCHOLLY ARE GREAT IMPROVEMENTS

The Sixth Circuit is the nervous system freed from the limiting programs of body circuits and larval imprints. Conscious of its own neuro-electric functioning. The nervous system now literally imprints itself. It must be remembered that the nervous system sees no color, feels no pain. When the Sixth Circuit is activated, the body becomes conductor-receiver for the neuro-electric signals. The rapture of the Fifth Circuit is available along with the conditioned emotions, thoughts, addictions of the first four circuits but as background in a shuttling web of signals.

The Sixth Circuit nervous system can create and contemplate a million models to replace the one static model which previously was identified as Reality. New electronic modes of consciousness are discovered, explored, integrated, transmitted. These are not "metaphysical" but physical in the strict sense: Einsteinian, relativistic, post-terrestrial, awareness of auras, electric emanations. Access to the inner-workings of the neuro-computer.

# DEVIL
## PORTRAYS YOUR BRAIN-REWARD REALITY CONSUMER NEURO-TECHNOLOGY

### CASTE 16

| | |
|---|---|
| **NEUROGENETIC TECHNOLOGICAL STAGE:** | Neuro-electric Receptivity. Self-definition as neurological organism. Passive Awareness of the Vibratory Nature of Reality. The Cortical Hedonist. The T.V. Synapse Consumer. Electronic self-indulgence. Bio-electric Masturbation (called hallucinations). |
| **PHYLOGENETIC STAGE:** | The Neuro-Electric Television Age. Reality Relativism |
| **ONTOGENETIC STAGE:** | The Age of Neuro-Electric Receptive Consumerism. The Psychedelic-Lysergic Experience |
| **ATTITUDE:** | INTERNEURAL: Watching your own brain fabricate realities. EXTERNEURAL: Dialing and tuning electronic realities, televoid passivity |
| **ZODIAC II:** | Self-Actualized Gemini II |
| **TITAN:** | Theia |
| **𝕐 HEBREW LETTER II:** | Ayin, "Mine eyes fail for Thy Salvation." |
| **REALITY CREATED:** | One's self spinning through an ocean-universe composed of neuro-electric vibrations |
| **ECOLOGICAL NICHE (species):** | This caste is found in the far-western affluent-elite technological frontiers |
| **ECOLOGICAL NICHE (indiv.):** | A relativistic universe entirely fabricated by your own brain |

The transition from the bio-chemical physiologic of the Fifth Circuit to the bio-electric relativity of the Sixth. The liberating Einsteinian discovery ($E = MC2$) that everything material is vibration, Energy pulsating along the electromagnetic frequencies. A passive experiencing of the interneural levels of energy, neural fission, reception of brain waves, reality registered as vibrations. The passive-receptive narcissistic experiencing of the externeural levels of electronic energy—television used for consumer pleasure."

NEURO-ELECTRIC CONSUMER

4 ♥

SELF-INDULGENT REALITY SELECTION

TITAN THEIA

**DEVIL** ♠

POST-TERRESTRIAL GEMINI II

the Devil exists!

yeah. Anyone ahead of the hive, is called Devil.

This Tarot card is a startling re-minder from your DNA that your brain contains an Einsteinian post-terrestrial circuit which transcends the slow, linear hormonal reality of the body and allows the brain to be aware of and use its own multi-phase accelerated relativistic reality fabrication.

### Stage 16

Tarot Devil (Card 15) THE DEVIL (Gemini II) codes the consumer-indulgent stage of Neuro-electric Self-Discovery. The individual (and species) discovers that the brain is a relativistic instrument which can be dialed, tuned, focused. This Stage discovers that all reality is composed of electro-magnetic vibrations, patterns of energy. It has been experienced accidentally or naturally by people who in the past have been called mystics (or schizophrenics). Recently this level of consciousness has been attained by several million persons who have experimented with brain-changing drugs. We refer here to the typical LSD experience. Sensations from every sense organ are experienced as electrically alive. In human history this stage has appeared in a small percent of the population who were genetically preprogrammed to attain access to this circuit of the brain. Such experiences were described as "voices" or "divine illuminations". The deliberate activation of this Stage by use of drugs occurred on a mass basis in the 1960's and thus marked a new stage of species evolution.

Caste 16, portrayed as Tarot card DEVIL represents the passive-receptive phase of the Sixth Circuit. Interneurally this is the spaced-out acid-head, passively experiencing the electronic level of energy. Synapse dynamics. Auras. Neurological consciousness. The brain conscious of its own electrical rhythms.

Externeurally this is reception of electro-magnetic vibrations, radio, TV, atomic fission, bio-feedback, computer consciousness. The passive-boob-tube addict.

191

# ACID-HEADS AND CIA BO
# USE  NEURO-ELECTRICS FO
# SELF-INDULGENCE

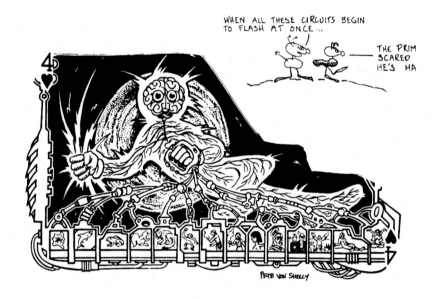

WHEN ALL THESE CIRCUITS BEGIN
TO FLASH AT ONCE...

THE PRIM
SCARED
HE'S HA

PETE VON SHOLLY

Tarot cards designed hundreds of years ago can only give vague suggestions about this level of energy and consciousness, which CNS-RNA Agents were able to externalize only in this century. Einstein, Bohr, quantum mechanics, electronics.

The indulgent, self-centered passive experiencing of the electric performance of the brain. The internal-experiential side of this phase is psychedelic acceleration. Neuro-active drugs which fission and accelerate consciousness—not used for discipline-control or link-up but for passive-receptive enjoyment.

In many Tarot diagrams the Devil is portrayed as an extra-terrestrial super-natural winged being who has chained a naked man and woman apart. De Laurence has this card signifying "the Dweller on the Threshold without the Mystic Garden when those are driven forth therefrom who have eaten the power-given fruit."

When an individual or species evolves to a higher level of energy, the initial reaction is to use the energy for self-definition, self-gratification and to strengthen lower hive circuit programs. Externeural, electronic and atomic energies are used for War, I.T.T. profits, CIA surveillance, political control, electronic hedonism, hucksterism, "G-rated" movies and TV programs supportive of hive morality. On the inner side neuro-electric receptivity is used for occult mystification, spiritualism, showman-shaman-magic.

In 1955 it was capriciously ingenious of Edward Teller, Father of the Hydrogen bomb, to arrange his facial muscles to resemble the Tarot Devil, thus illustrating the "evil" use of post-terrestrial energies for hive warfare.

This card reminds us that Einsteinian technology and brain reward drugs are now (1978) being mis-used to pacify, tranquilize, "passify," mystify, robotize humanity.

*The evolutionary function of electronic-atomic energy is to equip humanity for post-terrestrial linkage.* To send and receive interstellar signals. To design and propel Time-ships. Telepathy. To build High Orbital Mini-Earths. (H.O.M.E.s)

The use of electronic energies to intensify Fifth Circuit raptures—rock'n'roll eroticism, pornographic films and video-tapes, electric brain stimulation of pleasure centers—are useful because they support self-definition as electronic consumer dialing and tuning realities. At the same time the old Hive Establishment uses the new energies to support its reality. FBI wire taps, smart bombs, soviet control of radio-electronic communication. This mis-use of these frequencies to strengthen police surveillance, military force, larval economic systems, occult mythologies and hive moralities is natural during this beginning transitional stage in evolution.

Edward Teller

TELLER THINKS A
LITTLE NUKEY NEVER
HURT ANYONE

YEAH! IT SURE
WOULDNT HURT
NADER

# Einstein's Relativity Applied To Mind And Matter

Akhenaton, founder of the Star-cult of Egypt, learns how to indulge in solar-energy.

During the period 1940-1960 hardware engineers (blindly operating according to caste consensus) produced the following Self-Actualization (God-Game) techniques which were immediately snapped up by the Adult Authorities to maintain their own control of reality:

> the atom was fissioned
> the DNA code was decoded
> organic chemists created new structures using polymers (plastics)
> electronic radio-television cultures emerged; all hive members learn how to dial, tune, select, a wide range of realities
> —the rise of the demo-poll democratic society in Europe and America
> material consumerism (God-like whim buying) took over the west

When hive members began to understand that engineers could fabricate new hard realities, then the next generations of juveniles realize that neurological-realities and social structures could also be fabricated, dialed and tuned.

Neurological consciousness Stage 16 is followed by Neurological Self-Actualization (Stage 17).

As more Self-Actualized brains emerged the familiar swarming signals appear indicating to everyone in the hive the numbers of the new futants.

Pythagoras, Buddha, Einstein were broadcasting Stage 17 signals to pre-electronic primitives. But mass-activation of the Sixth Circuit (Stages 16, 17, 18) could not happen until the electronic-polymer-fabrication-of-new-shapes was available and widely used in technological hives.

The thought that Einstein had in his teens was this: "What would the world look like if I rode on a beam of light? Suppose this tram were moving away from that clock on the very beam with which we see what the clock says. Then, of course, the clock would be frozen. I, the tram, this box riding on the beam of light would be fixed in time. Time would have a stop. . . . in keeping up with the speed of light I have cut myself off from the passage of time."

This simple anecdote may be the key to Einstein "genius." He obviously was able to personalize the events he studied; sought to experience his subject matter. Einstein's third circuit brain (before sexual impersonation) apparently imprinted a relativistic symbol-reality.

THE 1ST GENERATION OF PLASTIC CONSUMERS PASSIVELY IMPOSED TIRED OLD FORMS ON THE PLASTICITY.

THE 1ST GENERATION OF LSD CONSUMERS PASSIVELY IMPOSED TIRED OLD HIPPY-HINDU FORMS ON THE NEW PLASTICITY.

GERARD O'NEILL IS THE FIRST HUMANIST PHYSICIST OF THE 21 ST CENTURY

# THREE FUTURE STAGES OF EVOLUTION

drawing by Harold W. Olson

In the 1970's a debate of profound significance was conducted among three groups of post-terrestrial scientists who heroically attempted to use electronic devices to contact Higher Intelligence.

1. *Reception:* One group expected humanity to be contacted by Higher Intelligence from outer space—by means of radio signals or UFO's.
2. *Exploration:* Another group used government-sponsored unmanned space probes to explore the solar system.
3. *Migration:* The third group proposed migration from earth with families (gene-pools) *a la* Noah. A new existence in High Orbital colonies.

1. The first group with Carl Sagan and Francis Drake as spokesman (both from the Cornell Center for Interplanetary Studies) wished to construct a five-billion dollar radio-wave reception device called *Cyclops*. The aim was to search the skies for signals from Higher Intelligence. Passive reception.

Project *Cyclops* was a brilliant reflection of neuro-electric passivity, as symbolized by Caste 16. Project staff members would live near the device in a government-suburb, maintaining conventional hive life-styles while hoping to be contacted by Higher Intelligence! This plan was a more sophisticated version of passive UFO watching.

2. The second external-technological application of post-terrestrial energies involved sending neuro-electronic equipment into space for surveillance-exploration. We cite the examples of un-manned probes of Venus, Mars, Jupiter. And the Russian success in establishing permanent space-stations (Salyut-Soyuz) in High Orbit.

3. The third stage in the post-terrestrial activation of the brain involved a swarming of self-actualized persons in control of their own nervous systems. When this temporal caste appears, it is realized that linkage Into new hives is the next genetic step. New personal ecological niches in High Orbital Mini-Earths.

The space colony plans offered by Professor Gerard O'Neill of Princeton and publicized by the L-5 Society served as pre-migration swarming signals alerting human gene-pools that it was time to activate their Sixth Circuit fore-castes.[4]

# Neuro-Electric
# Intelligence Is Here!

drawing by Harold W. Olson

In the last few paragraphs we have just defined the three next stages of human evolution. The reception, control and linkage of neuro-electronic, neurophysical energies. Stage 16, 17 and 18.

To the larval reader these distinctions may seem fanciful or irrelevant—hippy-trippy science fiction.

In reality these issues are very practical. They have been ignored until the publication of this book because of the lack of a neuro-electronic, neurogenetic language.

Stage 16, neuro-electric passivity, is already (1978) a social reality, a Zeitgeist phenomenon. The Gallup Poll in 1978 indicated that 67% of the Sun Belt public believed in the existence of Flying Saucer's suggesting that the collective consciousness was looking up in expectation for the migration to come.

The pervasive belief in astrology is another crude, primitive manifestation of the anticipation of post-terrestrial influence.

By 1978 a billion larval humans were receiving telestar signals on their TV sets, another premonitory preparation for extra-terrestrial reception. We recall the popularity of Star Trek, Star Wars, Bionic Man and Woman—more predictions of neuro-electric realities to come.

The purpose of this book and, in particular, the discussion of Stages 16, 17, 18, is to introduce the reader to a neuro-electric language for understanding the current stages of human evolution as anticipated by ancient, primitive, pre-technological Fore-caste systems like the Tarot.

196

NEUROGENETIC

# PASSPORT

**Genetic States of the Universe**

Egg Intelligence Center hereby requests all whom it may concern to permit the citizen of the 21st century named herein immediate access to Hir own

_____*sixteenth*_____

Brain, and authorizes Hir to become *GOD THE REALITY CONSUMER,* and experience the billion-channel tell-a-vision of Hir own neuro-computer.

---

## Endorsements

—Read the classic accounts of psychedelic experiences written by Huxley, Houston, Grof and then experience them yourself.

—Bomb your brain with bleep, buzz, flash, laser-strobe!!!

—Stimulate your CNS with electronic overload—and practice quick dialing and tuning.

—Imagine you are floating above planet earth for the last 10,000 years with a movie camera that takes one frame a century.

—Get wildly spaced out and re-experience what Einstein saw around 1905

## Endorsements

—Get wildly spaced out and laugh-laugh-laugh at the contrived nature of conventional hive-consciousness.

—Imagine having fingertip control of electrodes placed in your brain stimulating every possible neurogram

—Learn how to hallucinate and perform neuro-mobile-sculptures with your hallucinations

—Then travel back to the Florence of Dante Alighieri and explain atomic energy, TV and LSD to the Bard

*FINALLY CANCER YOU GET, NOT TO OWN SOME TURF, BUT TO FABRICATE WORLDS*

## **TOWER**
### PORTRAYS YOUR SELF-ACTUALIZED BRAIN-CONTROL-REALITY-DIRECTOR NEURO-TECHNOLOGY

**CASTE 17**

| | |
|---|---|
| NEUROGENETIC TECHNOLOGICAL STAGE: | Neuro-electric Intelligence. Control of one's own Circuitry. Atomic Energy Controlled. The Conscious Brain. The Ego as Neuro-Computer-Programmer; The Sixth Self-Actualization |
| PHYLOGENETIC STAGE: | The Age of Neural Engineering |
| ONTOGENETIC STAGE: | The Neuro-Electric Wizard |
| ATTITUDE: | INTERNEURAL: Responsible, aesthetic fabrication of your own neuro-realities activated by neuro-transmitter drugs |
| | EXTERNEURAL: Responsible, director-control of and genetically harmonious use of electronic-atomic energy-devices: radio, TV, video-phone |
| ZODIAC II: | Self-Activated Cancer II |
| TITAN: | Cronus |
| פ HEBREW LETTER II: | Pe, "The entrance of Thy words gives light." |
| REALITY CREATED: | Reality movie you have scripted and directed yourself |
| ECOLOGICAL NICHE (species): | Mating grounds of the very rich and the very free and the very high |
| ECOLOGICAL NICHE (indiv.) | Inside the control cabin of your own brain |

This Tarot card is a clever commercial from your DNA reminding you that your own brain is a reality-creating robot which can be controlled by your intelligent ability to dial the 24 channels—at will.

**NEURO-ELECTRIC WIZARD**

5 ♥

SELF-DIRECTED BRAIN

TITAN CRONUS

**TOWER** ♠ 5

POST-TERRESTRIAL CANCER II

*Stage 17*

Tower Hit By Lightning (Card 16) TOWER HIT BY LIGHTNING
(Cancer II) codes the Stage of Brain Self-Actualization. Here we
meet the person who has taken the responsibility for Hir own
brain function, (neuro-electric consciousness Stage 16) and has
arrived at the crucial understanding that the brain is an
instrument for fabricating realities. The neuro-technology involves the drug-yoga of selective re-imprinting. The external technology involves control of atomic-electronic energies, movie-
making, televisionary reality-creation, atomic fission—in short an
Einsteinian control of self-and-world.

# NEW GOD-GAME REVEALED!

**Controlled**

**Fission**

**of Brain**

**R e l e a s e s**

**Awesome**

**New**

**Realities!**

Albert Hoffman holding the first bottle of LSD produced in Basel, Switzerland.

The Tarot card TOWER HIT BY LIGHTNING portrays the atomic structure and the neural imprint structure fissioned by the intelligent application of energy. The top (i.e. the head) of the tower has been "blown". The two figures float happily in the Einsteinian relativistic flux released from the old structure, ready to fabricate new realities. The lightning bolt is not the act of a far-away Jove-like deity. The Stage 17 Self-Actualized WoMan aims and releases the shot that blows the mental structure. Surely this is one of the happiest cards in the Neurogenetic Game of Life—the advanced Cancer II using Self-Actualized Intelligence to control the new post-terrestrial territory.

Many futique sages and visionaries in the past have activated the 6th circuit and experienced reality as a play of vibrations (Stage 16). However, until the mid-20th century, no humants had reached this stage of Brain-Self-Actualization because the external technologies—electronic and atomic were not available. World War II (which activated a major jump in humant intelligence) made possible the Stage 17 metamorphosis Self-Actualized control of neuro-electric energies.

What a risky, God-like step! Humans daring to fission atomic structures which were put-together by the Star-makers (The WoMen who fuse nuclear energies to create the star-explosions which, in turn, fabricate the post-helium atoms). And what an arrogant step! Humans use LSD and dare to fission neural imprints which were put together by the Hive Reality Custodians—risking the wrath of the Monotheistic power by fabricating new imprints, new realities.

200

*THAT'S BECAUSE ALBERT WAS TOO TIMID TO TAKE OFF HIS TIE.*

*THE GREATEST CHEMIST OF THE 20th CENTURY IS STILL UNKNOWN IN HIS NATIVE SWITZERLAND*

# *Newtonian Mind Blown!*

## HUMAN ROBOTS LEARN HOW TO MANAGE THEIR OWN REALITY CAMERAS!!

"A study of the Tarot card Tower Hit by Lightning reveals its neurogenetic meaning. *Interneurally* it represents the mind-blown, stoned brain precisely and planfully fissioned; con-telligence released from imprinted hive-structure. The left and right hemispheres freed. *Externeurally,* the card represents the precise self-actualized use of Einsteinian intelligence—fissioning atomic-structure, accelerating knowledge with computers, building global-satellite communication systems, attaining the skill to leave the planet and construct new worlds in High Orbit."

Caste 17, the Tarot card Tower, portrays the nucleus of the Sixth Circuit. The nervous system managing and using neuro-electronics. The brain becoming aware of its own bio-electric nature and controlling itself. Neurological self-actualization. The robot becomes aware of its electric wiring. The Blowing of the static Newtonian Polarity Mind. The Brain films the lower-circuit cameras filming their imprinted scenarios.

The primitive Tarot card portrays a stylized inhabited tower with a Crown blown off the top. The crown suggests the head, the structure of the hive mind. A lightning bolt has hit the top of the head setting the edifice on fire. Two human figures with astonished mind-blown looks on their faces are floating or falling. "It is assuredly a card of confusion," says de Laurence.

"Occult explanations attached to this card are meagre and mostly disconcerting.

it signifies the materialization of the spiritual world. Let the Tower be the hive mental structure being fissioned by neuro-active drugs. In the 20th Century it was part of the lurid, superstitious folklore of larval people that LSD encouraged people to leap out of buildings. St. Elmo's fire, naked confrontation with God, etc.

The Neurological Self-Actualized potential remains isolated until the Engineer Caste produces the Einsteinian technology which the gene-pool uses for hive safety, security, sanity, sex-role. TV, radio, plastics, fission-fusion. Hive authorities are tricked Into exploiting these technologies for their own narrow purposes. Once the Sixth Circuit hardware is sold to the hive, then subsequent generations of juveniles realize (*before adulthood*) that these new technologies do not have to be limited to adult-hive uses but can be used to create new-hive realities. The Neoteny Rebellion occurs. Neurological engineering, the deliberate creation of reality, appears.

PETE VON SHOLLY

THE GREATEST PHILOSOPHER OF THE 20TH CENTURY IS ARTHUR KOESTLER... READ HIS **JANUS** !

201

# Scientists Exposed as Futant Freaks: Fore-Caste Agents of DNA

We have suggested in earlier chapters that every human being is a walking neurogenetic Tarot card—that every human being is a living representation of an evolutionary step, a bio-robot whose nervous system is templated by DNA to play a specific role in the metamorphic sequence.

There are twelve stages of caterpillar tactics necessary for terrestrial survival. The individual humant does not realize that SHe is slave-wired to play a neurogenetic part in the evolutionary pattern. There is, to be sure, an unconscious, resigned sense of comfortable "belonging-in-the-predestined-role" that explains why humants unquestioningly plod through their life routines ignorant of meaning and destination. Just as the cow placidly ruminating in the stockyard accepts its role in the energy cycle, so does the Caste 17 scientist unquestioningly link into the hive network.

Life on this planet is now (1978) beginning the great transformation from terrestrial to post-terrestrial existence. After three billion years of evolution DNA-directed organisms have produced the escape-velocity to leave the planet.

Twelve new neurogenetic types are emerging and beginning to swarm visibly. We recall that during the earlier metamorphic stage when life crawled out of the water to reach terrestrial life there occurred an explosive radiation of many amphibian forms designed by DNA. So today we expect to find a radiation of super-futants, a variety of post-terrestrial castes. Stages 13, 14 and 15 define the three stages of neurosomatic futation—the body as Auto-mobile Time-machine evolved beyond mundane pressures.

Stages 16, 17 and 18 define the neuro-electronic stages of evolution. Men like Einstein, Teller, von Braun, Ulam, Sagan, Taylor are premature evolutes, unconscious precursors. So are the Science Fiction writers whose neuro-transmissions activate the brains of the engineer castes. These scientists manipulate electromagnetic energies which they may or may not experience directly. The Exo-psychologist is fascinated by the personal lives and subjective expressions of these fore-caste "freaks" whose futant brains fabricate relativistic realities. Their sex-lives and childhood experiences are surely as important as gossip about movie stars because their genetic templating and their early Imprinting experiences provide clues as to how the higher circuits of the nervous system are activated. Einstein did not speak until a late age. Taylor was so shy with his girl-friend that he could not verbalize and was forced to express mating signals by playing radio tunes, electromagnetic sperm-egg attraction! They were "freak" futant creatures using Circuit Six frequencies to perform their cute 21st century mating dance. These are valuable clinical clues.

We are also Interested In the fact that many theoretical physicists are given to mystical tendencies and incoherent, metaphysiological emotional states.

"Nature does not know extinction," says Wehnher von Braun, "all It knows Is transformation. Everything science has taught me, and continues to teach me, strengthens my belief In the continuity of our spiritual existence after death."

Einstein's belief In an Interstellar Neurogenetic plan Is expressed In the famous quote, "I cannot believe that God plays dice with the universe."

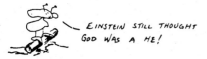

EINSTEIN STILL THOUGHT
GOD WAS A HE!

# "Niels Bohr Slapped His Crown. . ."

CROWN!
GET IT?!

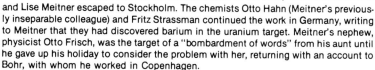

Lise Meitner and Otto Hahn in their laboratory in the 1930's

Let us now consider another case of a Caste 17 scientist. Let the Tarot Tower be the transuranium mind of Niels Bohr being fissioned by a bolt of radiation:

In 1938-9 teams of physicists in Germany and Italy were bombarding uranium with neutrons and getting perplexing data. With the advance of the Third Reich, the teams were broken up as Enrico Fermi fled with his wife and his Jewish mother to the U.S., and Lise Meitner escaped to Stockholm. The chemists Otto Hahn (Meitner's previously inseparable colleague) and Fritz Strassman continued the work in Germany, writing to Meitner that they had discovered barium in the uranium target. Meitner's nephew, physicist Otto Frisch, was the target of a "bombardment of words" from his aunt until he gave up his holiday to consider the problem with her, returning with an account to Bohr, with whom he worked in Copenhagen.

"When he heard the story, Bohr (at the time leading theoretician on atomic structure) is reported to have *slapped his forehead* (crown) and exclaimed: 'How could we have overlooked that so long.' "

"The picture is one," wrote Frisch, "of the gradual deformation of the original uranium nucleus, its elongation, formation of a waist and finally separation of the two halves. The striking similarity of that picture with the process of fission by which the bacteria multiply caused us to use the phrase 'nuclear fission'. . ." (suggested by American biologist James Arnold)[6] Experiments were still being carried out by Frisch when Bohr left for the US, and when he arrived at the Fermi's a cable was waiting for him with news to the effect that "As each neutron smashed into a uranium atom, he observed a great burst of energy, powerful enough to send the measuring devices off their scale."

# PYNCHON EXPERIENCES WHAT PHYSICISTS DISCOVER

The only extant picture of Thomas Pynchon, the greatest
20th-century novelist.

Atomic fission was the culminating success of externeural alchemy. The transmutation of elements with enormous release of energy.

The Einsteinian formulae have revolutionized physics by demonstrating the relativity of time, energy and matter. A similar relativistic revolution occurred in psychoneurology with the discovery of Albert Hoffman that the structures of the mind (neural synaptic patterns) can be fissioned, that consciousness can be accelerated, that reality (now defined in terms of bio-chemical Circuit 4 and nets of neurons) is capable of infinite self-controlled change.

A poetic personification of this stage is presented by Thomas Pynchon, enigmatic author of *Gravity's Rainbow,* the first neuro-electric novel.

"He thought of himself," writes Pynchon, "as a radio-transmitter . . . In his electro-mysticism the triode was as basic as the cross in Christianity. Think of the ego, the self that suffers a personal history bound to time, as the grid. The deeper and the true Self is the flow between cathode and plate. The constant, pure flow. Signals, sense-data, feelings, memories relocating—are put onto the grid, and modulate the flow. We live lives that are wave-forms constantly changing with time, now positive, now negative."

'In the name of the cathode, the anode, and the Holy Grid?' said Pokler.

'Yes, that's good,' Mondaugen smiled."[7]

204

# NEUROGENETIC

# PASSPORT

Egg Intelligence Center hereby requests all whom it may concern to permit the citizen of the 21st century named herein immediate access to Hir own

_seventeenth_

Brain, and authorizes Hir to act as *GOD, THE SELF-CONFI-DENT REALITY-FABRICATOR.*

The holder of this passport is entitled to:

## Endorsements

- a 17-million-dollar budget to produce and direct Hir own life; write the script, cast the stars, lease the locations and create the reality you desire
· a free copy of the works of Konrad Lorenz, Nico Tinbergen and Timothy Leary which outline how nervous systems are imprinted by any reality which happens to be at hand during the "critical period" of reality fix
—use powerful neurotransmitter drugs to accelerate your brain from static-imprinted-conditioned repetitious still-pix to the high velocity patterns of elec-

## Endorsements

tronic bleeps and buzzes that the nervous system really experiences
—then, carefully re-imprint yourself exactly the neuro-reality you wish to inhabit
—experience the relentless flow of reality woven each second by your brain— each click providing you with choices for more freedom, intelligence or adding to the static reality structure to which you are addicted.
get control of your brain so that you can dial and tune the reality you choose

# STAR
## PORTRAYS YOUR NEURO-TECHNOLOGY FOR BRAIN-BRAIN LINK-UP

CASTE 18

| | |
|---|---|
| **NEUROGENETIC TECHNOLOGICAL STAGE:** | Neuro-electric Fusion. Telepathic Communication. Synergic Mind-Linkage. The Sixth Mate: The Reality-Movie Producer. |
| **PHYLOGENETIC STAGE:** | Fusion with other Self-Directed Brains, i.e. Gods. |
| **ONTOGENETIC STAGE:** | Telepathic linkage leading to Genetic Consciousness. |
| **ATTITUDE:** | High-speed Interaction |
| **ZODIAC II:** | Self-Actualized Leo II |
| **TITAN:** | Hyperion |
| **צ HEBREW LETTER II:** | Tzad-Di, "I am consumed by insight; I work with pure elements." |
| **REALITY CREATED:** | Einsteinian multiverse |
| **ECOLOGICAL NICHE (species):** | Confederation of High Orbital Mini-Earths |
| **ECOLOGICAL NICHE (indiv.):** | Two or more fused brains The Tarot card STAR is a pre-vue of coming attractions flashed to you by DNA, preparing you for the activation of the post-terrestrial, neuro-electric circuits now quiescent in your brain. |

The Tarot card STAR is a pre-vue of coming attractions flashed to you by DNA, preparing you for the activation of the post-terrestrial, neuro-electric circuits now quiescent in your brain.

This brain circuit (which would not be put into mass distribution by DNA until the 21st century) allows you to begin designing new worlds (High Orbital Mini-Earths), compels you, in robot fashion, to swarm with other members of your new, 18th caste.

# STARS LINK TO FORM
# H.O.M.E.s!

TAROT STAR

MIGRATION TO H.O.M.E.S.

6 ♥

TITAN HYPERION

STAR

POST-TERRESTRIAL LEO II

♠ 9

*Stage 18*

(Card 17) The STAR (Leo II). Here the individuals who have attained Neurological Self-Actualization (the use of the nervous system to fabricate realities) begin swarming, linking together in preparation for leaving the old hive and migrating to a new, open ecological niche where they will form new hives.

Throughout human history some lonely futique agents have activated Stage 17 and assumed the responsibility for designing and building the world one inhabits. But one's ability to construct realities is limited by the old hive—the members of which cannot tolerate new realities. Stage 17 Ahead-of-time futants could only master their own nervous systems and try to avoid harrassment. For thousands of years, these prophets wrote philosophic texts, left monuments, code-signals (in the form of Tarot cards, Zodiac sequences, etc.) designed to activate more and more Sixth Circuit Brains.

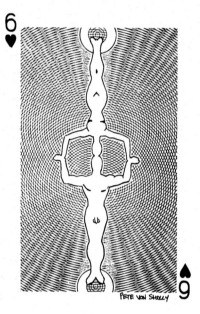

PETE VON SHOLLY

# BRAIN-TALK
# IS FLICK
# FAST
# ELECTRONIC
# PING-PONG

The primitive Tarot card #18 is "The Star," a great, radiant orb of eight rays surrounded by seven distant stars. Thus the image is not "star" singular, but clusters of stars. "The female figure in the foreground is entirely (sic) naked." She is actively involved in two-way linkage. "Her left knee is on the land and her right foot upon the water. She pours Water of Life from two great sewers, irrigating sea and land."

The interstellar theme of "The Star" is recognized by de Laurence. "That which the figure communicates to the living scene is the substance of the heavens and the elements."

At this stage of evolution we confront the notion of the Einsteinian relationship; the neurological marriage, brain-fucking, communication between two or more persons who operate with total, all-out immediacy, fast-moving dynamic relativity, including, and yet beyond, static commitments to larval needs.

All hive interpersonal interactions involve the four survival games—$S^4$: Safety, Security, Sanity, Sexual-Status.

Fifth Circuit interactions concern undulating, slow Neurosomatic Energies and Exchanges. Body language. Body time. Sensory stimulation. Somatic Intelligence. Body Fusion.

Sixth Circuit interactions operate at the rhythm of bio-electric signals. Flick-fast choice of dials. Electromagnetic radiation from and between brains. Telepathy is neurogenetic communication between self-actualized Brains freed from the bonds of imprint and conditioning. The Sixth Brain person receives what is neuro-physically happening (i.e. registered on the nerve-endings) and radiates signals undistorted by terrestrial survival imprint and Newtonian distortion.

# Decrease Delta V! Both Brains Vibrate at Same Velocity

NO DELTA V FOR US !!

THIS IS DELTA

JASON SAID THAT'S NOT REALLY DELTA V BUT DELTA I / ... WHICH IS A FUNCTION OF DELTA V

The key to neuro-electric communication is Shared Velocity. Decreasing the Delta V. The mutual ability to receive, control and direct fast-moving relativistic brain waves.

Larval interpersonal communication is slow, repetitious and static. Caterpillar conversations. Fetal gossip. What is there for terrestrial forms to say to one another? "How's the weather? Where's the food? Attack the enemy! Shall we breed? How are the kids? Who is in charge? Is this immoral, illegal or dangerous?"

Neurosomatic communication is meta-cultural meta-hive and can take place any place in any galaxy where biochemical communication between bodies can occur. Neurosomatic conversation is blocked by gravity pressure. You must be "high" to talk body language.

Neuro-electric communication is one brain communicating to another at neuro-electric speeds. Verbal, larval communication is extremely slow and banal. We can say (via laryngeal muscles) only one millionth of what we can brain-send in any time unit. Thus we limit larval conversation to simple, obvious terrestrial hive survival situations.

Neuro-electric conversation is relativistic. Each neural signal is a moving particle which explodes many mirrored meanings, triggers off associations in the infinite memory banks of one's own Eight Circuit Brain.

Each successive buzz can combine in multiple ways with the preceding bleeps and with the signals being emitted by others. Telepathic communication is like playing simultaneous electronic tennis with signals that explode like novae. Interpersonal chain-brain reactions.

209

# LET'S FABRICATE
# NEW WORLDS
# Whispers ~~Mr. Sperm~~

MISS **EGG!**

Neuro-electric communication between two or more linked nervous systems capable of Einsteinian (high-speed, relativistic) interaction, activating, via their fusion, new genetic realities.

Telepathic communication is a high-velocity post-terrestrial phenomenon designed for post-human communication and can occur only when both brains are in control of the realities they fabricate. The neuro-electric consumer (Caste 16 movie selector) can receive and the self-actualized Brain (Caste 17 movie director) can transmit brain waves.

When Caste 18 Reality Fabricators link-up, the result is futation. A new telepathic species is defined.

Telepathic signals are outside cultural imprints and social conditionings although they can include such local signals. Neuro-electric communication is thus not a larval tool. It is basically a tool for Egg-Intelligence. When the caterpillar metamorphizes to butterfly a new circuit of its nervous system is obviously activated—mediating equilibrium, aerodynamics, wing control, sexual receptivity, visual skills at aerial distances. We assume that butterflies can look down at (and amusedly recall) caterpillar signals.

Similarly, telepathy is a function of the high-orbital human nervous system preparatory to the formation of new genetic realities in post-terrestrial niches.

"Telepathy," according to George Koopman "is a gene-pool, new-hive contract. The participants realize that the natural and Inevitable application of Einsteinian technology is post-terrestrial migration of sperm-egg collectives" to fabricate new realities (H.O.M.E.s) in new econiches.

# THE EIGHT EVEOLUTIONARY MIGRATIONS

Circuit I:     Migration to shore-line (Stage 3)
Circuit II:    Migration to trees and cliff-caves (Stage 6)
Circuit III:   Migration to cities (Stage 9)
Circuit IV:    Migration to megalopolis' (Stage 12)
Circuit V:     Migration away from cities to nature (Stage 15)

Circuit VI:    Migration off the planet to H.O.M.E.s (Stage 18)

Circuit VII:   Migration out of solar system to force-field ecology of galaxy (Stage 21)

Circuit VIII:  Migration to Black-Whole at Galaxy Center (Stage 24)

USING TURNED ON BODIES

BUILT BY SELF DIRECTED BRAINS

BY SELF CREATED NEW SPECIES

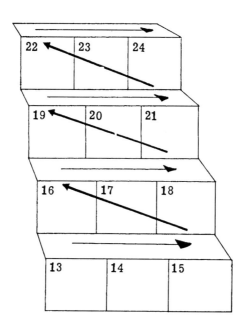

# Brain Fucking Multiplies RPM's
# (Raptures Per Minute)

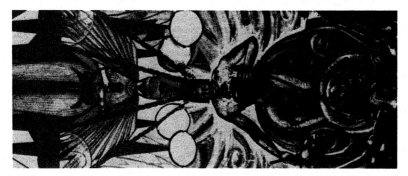

The major scientific-political issues of the 1960's involved Fifth Circuit energies—control of the Automobile Body for individual pleasure.* Freedom to use neurosomatic and brain-reward drugs, sexual freedom, freedom of dress and grooming, refusal to have one's body used as military instrument (draft resistance) or as economic tool (drop-out philosophy). The Adult Authorities in almost every National Hive also use Fifth Circuit sensory stimuli to torture and coerce. Rapture and torture thus became neuro-political issues. (In general, countries which allowed rapture prohibited torture, and vice-versus.)

It is of interest that humanity's first Inter-planetary mission was named "Apollo," honoring the Roman-Greek God whom SHe has selected to personify the fusion aspects of the Second and Sixth Circuits.

Apollo II, Leo II are pre-scientific labels for the neurogenetic caste which links the neuro-electric and atomic energies necessary to create new post-terrestrial hives.

Telepathic Fusion (Stage 18) is the neurological equivalent of the linkage of two self-actualized bodies to activate neuro-electric consciousness (Stage 15). In this case, two or more self-actualized Brains fuse and activate RNA-DNA consciousness.

Brain-fucking produces genetic consciousness and opens the way to Egg-Intelligence.

Just as two Tantric lovers can create new-rological realities—so do two brain mates (Caste 18) form new RNA-DNA realities.

---

The Fifth Circuit Intelligence steps into the Driver's Seat of the Body, uses the self-starter, accelerator-brake, gear-shift to go when and where SHe wishes. Self-Directed.

Caste 18, portrayed by the Tarot card Star represents the shared output of the Sixth Circuit. Neurological and atomic elements tuned-in synergically fused, releasing new energy. This card is the active, communicating side of Einsteinian consciousness.

Neurogenetic theory recognizes that passive electronic consumerism (Caste 16) is a necessary stage. But evolution quantum-jumps through fusion. The hook-up of accelerated intensified self-actualized energies.

We speak here of neuro-electric communication—the telepathic linkage of two or more persons who have reached stellar self-consciousness, who radiate, who receive and transmit at relativistic frequencies.

By electronic communication we do not mean the larval use of television signals or radio waves to engage the hive circuits, to transceive L.M. symbols. We mean neurological radiation between two nervous systems.

The telepathic linkage of two nervous systems, moving at the same accelerated velocity, produces a megaton yield of harmonious pleasure and revelation. Larval laryngeal-muscle prose cannot describe this interchange.

TAROT SCHOLARS WILL RECALL THAT POST-TERRESTRIAL APOLLO CORRESPONDS TO TITAN- HYPERION.

213

# "WE ARE STAR MAKERS" BOAST NUCLEAR FUSION BUFFS

Wood & Nuckolls explain genetic goal of atomic research

"Very high performance, high specific thrust rocket propulsion systems based on the use of fusion micro-explosions may someday carry men (sic) across the Solar system in days, rather than the years which chemical or nuclear-fission-heated propulsion systems would require. Expelling reaction mass at several percent of the speed of light itself with the same energies that make the stars shine, such rockets may carry men (sic) in explorations of our cosmic neighborhood by the end of the century, and will represent the ultimate in such vehicles at our present stage of scientific and technological development.

"The chemical fire, first exploited by cave men (sic), is now energizing the initial exploration of the Solar system, a feat that will cause the memory of our culture's scientific and technological magnificance and the glory of its Intellectual curiosity to shine brilliantly for centuries. The fusion fire—which men (sic) have contemplated in awe since they first raised their eyes to the stars, but first brought to earth in our age—will propel man (sic) beyond his (sic) *Solar nursery,* * and forever foster and energize his (sic) terrestrial endeavors. We may speak today of fusion fire as Aeschylus, the ancient Athenian poet said of Prometheus' gift to mortals of the chemical fire: it will prove the means to inconceivably mighty ends."

L. Wood and J. Nuckolls, speaking on "Prospects for Unconventional Approaches to Controlled Thermonuclear Fusion," Philadelphia, 29 December 1971.[8]

The result of a telepathic conversation is always the same. The mutual recognition that the Electron Lovers have futated beyond terrestrial existence. The mutual discovery that self-actualized Brains can activate DNA consciousness.

Telepathy, like radio telescopy, is limited to certain levels of energy. Just as the radio-telescope picks up a defined range of frequencies—so does telepathy. The communication mode of self-actualized Brains.

The neurogenetic meaning of the Sixth trio of Tarot cards (Stage 16, Stage 17, Stage 18) is beautifully described by Lowell Wood and John Nuckolls, two scientists from the American government's Lawrence Livermore Laboratory.

*This phrase "Solar nursery" was (in 1971) the most advanced concept ever expressed by establishment scientists. (Wood and Nuckolls are on the staff of the Lawrence Livermore Laboratory.) This casual, throw-away phrase is the first acceptance by orthodox scientists of the Interstellar Neurogenetic thesis that humanity will come to maturity when it leaves the planet.

214

### The Fusion of Marie and Pierre Curie
### by
### Paul Getty III

Pierre loved the country passionately, and retained a wonderful memory of his childhood wanderings in the woods. But his roaming that summer was sweeter still; love exalted it and made it beautiful. He would think aloud about his work, not even turning to catch his wife's eyes. He knew that Marie understood, and that what she would reply would be useful and original.

During these happy days was formed one of the finest bonds that ever united man and woman. Two hearts beat together; two minds of genius learned to think together. Marie could have married no other than this wise and noble physicist. Pierre could have married only the fair, tender Polish girl who in the same moment could be childish or transcendent; for she was a friend and a wife, a lover and a scientist.

 # ALCHEMISTS PROVED RIGHT! IT TOOK NEURAL FUSION—A MALE-FEMALE BRAIN LINKAGE — TO DECODE SECRET OF ATOMIC RADIATION!

Pierre Curie had followed the progress of his
wife's experiments with passionate interest.
Now he joined his efforts to hers.
Two brains, four hands now sought the unknown element*
A collaboration began which was to last for eight years
Their handwriting alternates and combines
In the working notebooks covered with formulae
They were to sign almost all their scientific publications
Together
They were to write,
"We found" and
"We observed"
And when fact constrained them to distinguish
Between their parts
They wrote,
"One of us"

---

*For at least two thousand years the goal and dream of all chemists, alchemists and scientific philosophers was the transmutation of elements. The discovery of radium, which demonstrates the living, evolving, energic nature of matter, was made by the neurological fusion of male and female, the classic Alchemic Marriage of Pierre and Eve Curie.

# MOVE UP TO BI-BRAIN CLASS!

Behold! DNA's new Model 18! This is not transportation . . . THIS is high-velocity fusion . . . Fully equipped with RNA-injected BI-CORTICAL CONTROL, quadrophonic, quadro-visual multiple-gravity high orbital performance

The species must learn to Self-Actualize (Step into the drivers seat, use the Self-Starter, and dial and tune) the external communication-transportation machinery before they can attain Self-Control over the Neurological equipment which runs their own soft-ware. The Human Being at this stage recognizes Hir role as Communication-transportation machine to facilitate egg mobility.

After one or two generations have been exposed to Einsteinian technology, particularly after a decade of childrens' T.V. shows portraying Space Adventures, Super-Men and Bionic Woman—then the swarming preparatory to migration occurs.

## *DNA's LEGENDARY TANTRA MODEL 15 REBORN AS THE NEW BI-BRAIN 18*

Stage **18** involves the link-**up of futants who** have attained Self-Actualized com-**petence** in Reality-Fabrication and who band together **to pool** energies **in the** migra-tion to **the** new ecological niches where new hives **are** to be formed.

Stage 18—as **is** the case with the swarming-migration stages of earlier circuits **is** propelled by *Egg Wisdom* which motivates the **movement of** Sperm-egg cargoes **to the** New Worlds. The explosion of Self-**Actualized** populations is calibrated by *Egg-Control* which suddenly begins producing futique-brain carriers.

NEUROGENETIC

# PASSPORT

Genetic States of the Universe

VISA for Brain Fucking

Egg Intelligence Center hereby requests all whom it may concern to permit the citizen of the 21st century named herein immediate access to Hir own *eighteenth* Brain and authorizes Hir to become *GOD, THE WORLD BUILDER,* to fabricate totally independent Mini-Earths and to perform the linkages, ecological and neurological,

## Endorsements

necessary to maintain new worlds where the evolutionary process can exfoliate.

   re-read the Hindu Mythologies and study the inter-relations of the Gods; re-read the Greek myths and understand that Olympus was people with terrestrial-heroes, not post-terrestrial LSD-brains

   read the best Sci-Fi books on Space Cities, their construction and operation; e.g., Cities in Flight series by Blish

· every second of your life study how things operate on Space-Ship earth and

## Endorsements

figure out improvements re-arrange and redecorate at least one room in your house so it reflects a 21st century post-terrestrial H.O.M.E. neuroreality

re-read Genesis and other primitive cosmologies and see where they went wrong. By failing to link-up with other Divinities.

regularly ingest a 6th circuit drug and practice brain-fusing, telepathic-linkage, collective imprinting.

# The Cards Moon, Sun, Judgment
# Portray Your Three Neuro-Technologies
# For Controlling DNA

19. DNA Consumerism

20. Egg Wisdom

21. Inter-species Symbiosis

THE SEVENTH CIRCUIT OF THE NERVOUS SYSTEM TO EVOLVE (in both species and individual) MEDIATES THE DISCOVERY AND USE OF DNA AS REALITY FABRICATION DEVICE.

The I Ching Trigram which signifies the Seventh Circuit of the Nervous System is SUN (Seed blown by the Wind)

The Tarot Trigram which predicts this cycle of development is:

Stage 19, The MOON DNA Consciousness Serm Intelligence

Stage 20, the SUN DNA Wizardry Gala Intelligence

Stage 21, the JUDGMENT FLOWER-INSECT LOVE DNA Intercourse

# Circuit VII:
# DNA as Guidancetool

DNA is information.

DNA is Higher Intelligence; pure intelligence.

Hidden safe and comfy in the nucleus of every living cell reclines the Brain of Life, sending out chemical instructions, RNA, to fabricate the mobile sensory-organs (sperm-egg vehicles) we call living-organisms. Floating amoebas perform Her errands. So do fast-moving bodies, and high-flying organisms.

Every living creature, from a bacterium to an astronaut, is a robot—designed, constructed, and programmed by DNA to perform specific functions in the evolving web of life.

This Biological Intelligence, which operates like the Egg-Queen in a termite hive, is called Gaia. The Genetic Wisdom. Egg creativity. For millennia pagan prophets understood and attempted to fore-caste the unfolding of evolution along the lines of an intelligent creator.

During the past 2,000 years of monotheism humans lost awareness of Gaia Intelligence. Even in 1979 terrestrials explained creation in terms of Superstitious-Fearful Magic (the vengeful Jehovah of the Bible), or in terms of blind accident.

Because monotheists did not understand the tactics and

Here Miss Galactic Flower-Cunt Egg Instructs DNA-RNA to fabricate more beautiful species while Her assistant, Dr. Sperm, looks on approvingly

goals of the Evolutionary Process, they naturally assumed that there was no understandable genetic intelligence. The best that humans could come up with was a primitive male Deity who performed silly miracles and remained obsessed with village morals.

In the last quarter of the 20th century, advanced primates attained control of their own bodies (Circuit V). Then the Neurological Revelation gave advanced-western castes control of their brains (Circuit VI). And, as the millennium end of the 20th century approachs, some humans are attaining understanding of the Gaia Revelation, an understanding of the DNA-RNA-CNS machinery.

The emergence of Neuro-genetic Intelligence (Circuit VII) follows the classic cycle of mutation:

Species 19,* self-defining exploitation of the new neuro-technology

Species 20, self-actualized responsible management of the new neuro-technology

—Species 21, linkage of the new neuro-technology to form a symbiotic molecular structure capable of supporting the next migration-mutation (meta-physiological).

---

*At this point in our study of the ages of evolution we reach a level of intelligence that allows us to re-define our terminology. We realize that each successive stage, each caste is defined by its emerging neuro-technology. Each stage before DNA control is a meta-morphic step, a temporal caste in personal development, a larval, juvenile, fetal temporary form.

Starting with Slot 19—Genetic Consciousness—we realize that from this point on the unit of human existence is the gene-pool, and that each of us becomes a new species—and the conscious creator of new species in the future.

# MOON
## PORTRAYS YOUR RACIST SUPER-MAN-IAC SPERM INTELLIGENCE

### SPECIES 19

**NEUROGENETIC TECHNOLOGICAL STAGE:** Sperm Intelligence. Racism: i.e. Use of Genetic information for Chauvinist Self-Indulgence. Genetic Engineering Used for Self-benefit DNA Consumerism. Sperm Elitism. Darwinianism.

**PHYLOGENETIC STAGE:** The Age of Genetic Intelligence (Becomes Dom-Species around 1999 A.D.).

*SORRY FOLKS!*
*GALLIUM WAS SUPPOSED TO APPEAR HERE BUT SHE'S A LITTLE LATE!*

**ONTOGENETIC STAGE:** Self-indulgent Enjoyment of DNA Information. Cloning. Breeding. Genocide. Longevity. Genetics used to enhance one's own competitive male-macho Gene-pool reality.

**ZODIAC II:** Self-Actualized Virgo II

**TITAN:** Phoebe

**ק HEBREW:** Koph, "Concerning Thy testimonies, I have known of old thou hast founded them forever."

**REALITY FABRICATED:** Male manipulation of DNA

**ECOLOGICAL NICHE (species):** Turf controlled by "my" gene-pool

**ECOLOGICAL NICHE (indiv.):** My own CNS-RNA-DNA

Genetic relativity and DNA Caste-consciousness applied for Superman—Super-race Purposes. Self-indulgent use of sperm-egg (breeding) arrangements. Migration of gene-pool collectives run by Sperm bureaucracies, rather than Egg-Wisdom. Male-order genetic elitism.

This card is a promise from DNA that your Brain contains a Neuro-technology which endows you to consciously think and act like a Darwinian genetic competitor. When activated this circuit fabricates a megalomanic, self-indulgent reality in which you begin to tamper with DNA potentials—cloning, rejuvenating, breeding-culling caste-identification to fit the ambitions of yourself and your gene-pool.

On the card:
**DNA SELF INDULGENCE**

7 ♥

SPERM INTELLIGENCE

TITAN PHOEBE

**MOON**

POST-TERRESTRIAL VIRGO II

♠ 7

*Species 19*

(Card 18) THE MOON (VIRGO II) Here the individual (and the species) attains Genetic consciousness. This is the passive-receptive, self-indulgent enjoyment of DNA-Wisdom. Self-Definition in terms of one's role as evolutionary agent. Consumer use of the energies released by deciphering the DNA code and by the activation of the Seventh Circuit.

Again, we recall, at these futant stages of evolution the individual is evolving for the species. The Stage 19 futant realizes that SHe is riding the front wave of the 3 billion-year-old process. Enormous liberating benefits are available once DNA intelligence is decoded—longevity, cloning, an enormous explosion of new aesthetic DNA realities, and revelatory empathy into the secret-lives of plants, insects and other advanced species.

This Brain (which RNA began mass-producing in the early 21st century) is now wired into your nervous system quiescently waiting to be turned-on. When activated it allows you to understand and use DNA energy—intelligence—on behalf of yourself and your gene-pool.

221

# Primitive Seed Wizards
# Fore-Caste Sperm
# Intelligence

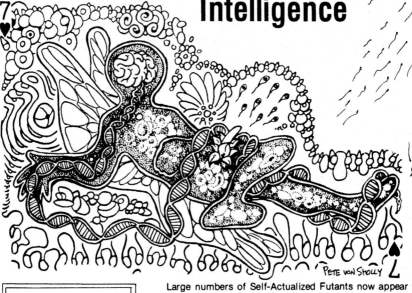

PETE VON SHOLLY

Large numbers of Self-Actualized Futants now appear who understand the role of Divine Creator (Bio-Division). The fabrication of mini-worlds, the inventive facilitation of the Egg-Migration process. Each mini-Earth is populated with seed-blossoms self-selected from many hives.

Each Genetic Creator controls how long and at which age SHe lives. Each Genetic Creator inhabits numerous mini-Earths, and is actively engaged in building and seeding new H.O.M.E.s. And each has the option of cloning Hirself and broadcasting the seeds through the galaxy. Collaboration and conversation with other species also happens.

This stage represents a culminating step for Gala, the Global Egg Intelligence. She has succeeded in activating her own communication-transportation robots to understand the aesthetic of the creation.

In order to attain this level of genetic Self-Actualization the futant must violate the most sacred-guarded hive taboo—which means overthrowing the Darwinian theory of blind-chance evolution and natural selection by means of the survival of the fittest.

# MACHO RACIST-ROBOTS TAMPER WITH GENETIC TABOOS!!

Khomeini

Stalin

Dayan

Hitler

Stage 19, Tarot card MOON, represents the selfish consumer phase of the Seventh Circuit, i.e. Sperm Intelligence. The first, inevitably racist, use of genetic engineering.

The human nervous system operating at the Sixth Circuit decodes DNA signals and becomes aware of the multi-billion year-old genetic (sperm-egg) design. The human becomes exploiter of the evolutionary plan. This is the self-indulgent-adolescent phase of genetic awareness. Macho-manipulation. DNA knowledge used to support old-species realities. Racial chauvinism. Sperm intelligence.

We have seen that, as each new circuit of the nervous system is activated, there is an initial consumer stage in which the new technology is exploited. Joyfully used to get an edge on other gene-pools.

It should come as no surprise to sophisticated readers of this book that the first use of genetic information is selfish and genocidal. Every new quantum-leap in technology is initiated by clever macho-males who get carried away with the new power. Racism and controlled breeding is the inevitable first step in the application of genetic knowledge. It is for this reason that genetics is usually veiled with eerie sanction and taboo. The collective Egg-Wisdom of the gene-pool is always suspicious of any tampering with the source of its own survival. Each gene-pool develops its own morals, rituals and taboo for inbreeding. WHEN A CHARISMATIC REALITY-FABRICATOR (Caste 18) BECOMES MEGALOMANIC ENOUGH TO VIOLATE GENETIC TABOOS AND DELIBERATELY MANIPULATES SPERM-EGG FUSIONS, THE JUMP TO CASTE 19 HAS OCCURRED.

As we have seen, at early stages of futation, it always requires self-confident ex-pansive machos to ex-plore and ex-ploit a new technology. After the Sperm-agents boldly make the first moves, then the Egg-Intelligence moves in to coopt the new technology to serve all gene-pools.

When it was time (4000 BC) to form large gene-pool collectives, certain self-obsessed tribal leaders declared themselves KING and set up monarchist-feudal systems. The larger centralized social units known as kingdoms organized a more efficient caste system. Only the Divine-right king could summon to the capital-city the many castes necessary to operate centralized national technologies.

When it was time to establish new ecological niches in high orbit (the 1970's) it was the male-macho warrior-engineers who developed the rocketry.

And it is the Caste 19 Super-maniacs who realize that DNA research extends the frontiers of human power and control—far beyond politics or economics.

At the present time (1979) intelligent humans are beginning to understand the central importance of genetics. Breeding vibes are in the air. The decoding of DNA by Watson and Crick, recombinant DNA research, the cloning controversy, the rejuvenation-longevity movement. The controversial emergence of sociobiology, behavorial genetics as the "hot" new science of "man". Caste consciousness.

223

# MALE-ORDER DNA DEALERS TUNED IN TO MYSTERIES OF SEED

Disney*
Inventor of clan totem
Symbols

Burbank
Tuned in to the Rhythm
of Seed

Carver
Self-Actualized  Planter
Caste

Sperm Intelligence, Caste 19, is a naive, adolescent, transitional consumer use of a new technology. It is doomed, of course, to be supplanted by Egg-Intelligence. Sperm Intelligence fails to realize that the power of selection, choice, chromosome linkage is almost entirely determined by the Ovum—as personified as Gaia Wisdom.

Caste 19 Sperm-Indulgence-Genetic Awareness has occurred throughout past history in a certain elite percentage of human beings whose insight led to the introduction of genetic technologies. It was probably such pre-mature fore-castes who, 10,000 years ago, decoded the secret of seed; thus initiating the Agricultural Revolution and activating the Self-Actualized Planter Caste—which quickly moved upward from the hunter-gatherers.

Reflect on the Futique, Sci-Fi implications of the ancient terms "planter," grower, farmer, breeder, cultivator.

Stage 19 genetiques whose advanced brains formed DNA-linkages tuned to the rhythms of seed, sperm and season.

Here we meet an extra-ordinary brain style—those who have tuned into the eerie, mysterious cycles of fertility, seeding, ploughing, fertilizing, cultivation, harvesting, crop-management. Here we meet the herdsman-shepherd caste which jealously watches over the survival of gene-pools called flocks and herds; preserving the seed-destiny of domesticated animals.

*Walt Disney was to the 6th circuit what Henry Ford was to the 4th circuit—hardware architect of the new realities about to be neurologized.

*During the Neurogenetic Renaissance (1976-1986) Human Ethology replaced religion, philosophy, sociology, psychology, personology, astrology, psychiatry and every other primitive system of behavioral theory and practice.*

*Concepts such as temporal and structural caste in social animals, the key role of migration, population-swarming, hive-limited culture, the emergence of new post-human species, and human-robotry relegated to antiquity every previous theory of human behavior.*

*The parents of this first scientific philosophy were the Wilson Brothers, Edward and Robert — who performed for psychology what Einstein did for physics. Edward's book,* Sociobiology, *is generally considered the first conscious text on human behavior ever published.*

How few brief centuries, indeed, does it take to move from the domestication of plants and animals to the seeding of outer-space and the domestication of the High Orbital Wilderness?

The tribal shaman spelling out the laws of consaguinity, inter-breeding, incest-taboo. Inventing clan totem-symbols and fertility rituals.

The earth-jaded Brahmins of India establishing the Hindu Caste system, perhaps the most magnificant social experiment of antiquity. The High Priests of the Nile setting up the Egyptian dynastic systems. The Talmudic Priests (male).

As human swarming-collectives increased in size the Male-Ordered genetic experiments of the Sperm Caste became more elaborate and audacious in their use of human seed. Among the most ingenious and revealing were: (1) the Mameluke dynastic experiments in Egypt (969-1831)—in which young males throughout the Middle and Far East were selected, rigorously trained and indoctrinated to produce a loyal cadre of civil-servant-warriors: (2) the precisely controlled experiment of South America (colonized 1492-1972 by Sperm Intelligence) and North America (settled by Egg-Wisdom); (3) the Nazi neuro-genetics of the Hitler regime; and (4) zionism; (5) the colonization of High Orbital Homesteads by Americans.

YOU OWE IT TO YOURSELF TO DRIVE THIS BRAIN!
INTRODUCING

# THE ALL NEW MODEL 19

**Take the Ten Minute Test Spin and discover a new standard of reality manipulation and control. You owe it to your SELF to spend ten minutes comparing the Model 19 Sperm Brain's New-Reality Index Ratings to any previous brain circuit.**

MINUTE 1: People a galaxy with the millions of eggs or trillions of sperm you carry in your body.

MINUTE 2: Take a strong psychedelic and clone yourself and your loved ones.

MINUTE 3: Take charge of the Longevity Pill; decide to whom you will give it; and how you will deal with the envy of those who don't get it.

MINUTE 4: Cross-breed people with animals and plants. Which new species would you create?

MINUTE 5: Solve this apparent problem: the poor-superstitious-ignorant breed faster than the affluent-intelligent.

MINUTE 6: Improve the human species—keeping in mind that the genetically unsuccessful tend to blame society instead of their own genes.

MINUTE 7: Trace your lineage back as far as you can. Then fantasize your heritage back 2000 years. Two million years. Etc.

MINUTE 8: Since the present human gene-pool is radiating out in hundred of future species—decide yourself the varieties of humans you wish to fore-caste.

MINUTE 9: Explore your own Hitler-Utopian consciousness; then explore your own Jewish-racist-reaction to the Nazi monstrosity.

MINUTE 10: Reconstruct the Darwinian male-macho theory of natural selection and blind-chance mutation. Glory in it and then laugh it back where it belongs.

**Brain Realities** B/R

# Science Fiction Fore-Castes
# Science Fact

As always, the new scientific respectabilities have been initiated, pre-fabricated, by the preceding generation of Science Fiction visionaries. Robert Heinlein in the classic book *Methuselah's Children*,[9] introduces us to Lazarus Long, patriarch of an elite kinship of humans who have been bred for longevity. Since they live longer the elites become increasingly more intelligent. Because their superiority infuriates "mortal" humans they face persecution and genecide. Until they figure out the obvious solution. They high-jack an enormous Star Ship and escape from the womb planet. In this profound novel Heinlein accurately (if naively) writes the scenario for the inevitable next stages of evolution off this planet.

The Science Fictionists make the blue-prints. Card-carrying scientists work out the hard-ware engineering. But nothing can happen until the heavy center-of-gravity of the Egg-Ship, Dom-Species (operating, by statistical definition with an I.Q. of 100) and the Past-Castes (even below the average in neurotechnological competence), picks up the futique signal and vulgarizes it into acceptable form.

Thus the growing popularity of Chariot-God fantasies in which extra-terrestrials (always males, of course) impregnate primitive humans with superior seed. And the profitable fascination for cloning scenarios, Superman and Bionic Woman adventures. The unrelenting success of the Star Trek series—in which good-hearted earthlings have weekly encounters with extra-terrestrial forms of life. Not to forget the perennial U.F.O. fads.

All these crude, pop themes betray a deep, inchoate species awareness that genetic technology is creating a future involving Higher Intelligent species—namely us in the future.

Thus the familiar progression—Science Fantasy, Science Fiction, Science Faction and Specialized Science-Engineering is revealing the tactics used by DNA to evolve intelligence:

—*neoteny:* mobility-communication power given to change-able pre-adults

—*swarming* & *over-population-pollution* as stimulants to change
*migration:* into new ecological niches
*caste consciousness:* division of labor and pleasure based on genetic difference
*neuro-geography:* the basic and overwhelming influence of *location* in activating brain circuitry.

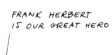

FRANK HERBERT IS OUR GREAT HERO

227

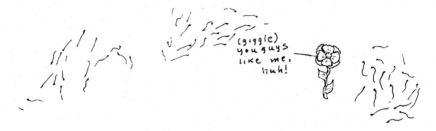
*(giggle) you guys like me, huh!*

## GENETIC HALL OF FAME
### Flower-Power Division

**Carolus Linneaus**          **Rudolph Camerarius (age 6)**

During the last two decades of the 20th century (1980-1999) the Neuro-genetic circuit (Castes 19, 20, and 21) was activated in millions of post-humans. As always this futation was preceded by myths, legends, comic-cartoons, hoaxes, fantasies, and pop-fads. The "Flower-Power" movement among hippies. Movies such as *The Invasion of the Body Snatchers, The Secret Life of Plants* (with sound-track by Stevie Wonder). The ecological-back-to-nature cults. The enormous (and almost invisible) growth of interest in flower cultivation-arrangement. Pop-entertainment themes of this sort always indicate that advanced futique-thinking is trickling down the castes into Dom-Species consciousness.

The key to genetic awareness and evolutionary consciousness is the understanding of aesthetic-signalling and sexual-symbiosis of plants. It is no accident that the beginnings of evolutionary thinking in the 18th and 19th century can be traced to botanists. Rudolph Jakob Camerarius, Richard Bradley, Philip Miller shocked and scandalized the Hive Authorities of the 18th century with their discoveries that plants had sex organs and used them. The great botanist and taxonomer Linnaeus based his monumental work of species classification on a sexual system. The number, arrangement and function of sexual parts is still used as the basis for genetic classification.

228

# THE
# HOLY BIBLE
### OLD AND NEW TESTAMENTS

Translated out of the Original DNA by _____
(insert your name)

## THE FIRST BOOK BY YOU CALLED
## GENESIS

In the beginning _____
(insert your name)

created the Heaven and the Earth. And YOU used terriforming techniques to cover the Earth with water and You called it Ocean. You seeded the ocean with DNA-capsules which contained the precise instructions for the next ten billion years of evolution.

1 And then, when Unicellular DNA capsules had filled the waters, You caused them to secrete a pollution which stimulated young amoebas to grow bones and become fishes. And that was the second day and You were very pleased with Yourself.

3 And on the third day when the tectonic plates riding on the bubbling pudding of hot-lava pushed upward to form land You activated some young marines to migrate to the shoreland where they sniffed oxygen and found it good.

4 And when the shoreline got too crowded You activated new drugs which stimulated some young rebellious am phi bi ans to move onto the land. And the morning and evening were called the fourth day.

5 And then _____ said, Let
(insert your name)

the earth bring forth the furtive creatures that hide and crawl in the night and the strong, fierce animals that control the turf.

6 And then You sent the chemical signal *get high*, and the primates stood up on their hind-legs and climbed trees.

7 And then You said, *let the primates use their hands and act like Engineer Gods in manufacturing artifacts.*

8 And You said, *Let man be proud like me and have dominion over woman and over the fish of the sea and the animals on the earth.*

9 And to increase their intelligence You activated men to cluster in tribes and work groups.

10 And when men had become adept in manufacturing and communication You activated the swarming circuits of their brains and thus the tribes banded together in enormous collectives worshipping You, a Strong Man, as the one-and-only God. They were robot-programmed to destroy those that did not adore You. And You saw the kingdoms grow into empires and great socialized collectives all unified in Your name and working for Your glory and You were very pleased.

## CHAPTER 2

And then on the 13th day _____
(insert

_____ landscaped a Garden in
your name)

Eden and filled it with vegetables that were good to eat.

2 But then, as it was pre-ordained, three other trees grew in the Garden, dangerous, evolved, in tel i gent trees that bore flowers. These were the Tree of Beauty and Pleasure; the Tree of Intelligence; and the Tree of Eternal Life.

3 And you commanded the man, saying, *Of every plant of the garden you mayest freely eat:*

4 *But of the Tree of Beauty and Pleasure and of the Tree of Intelligence and of the Tree of Eternal Life thou shalt not eat.*

5 Now You took pity of man that he had no one to help him and worship him, so you caused him to fall into a deep sleep and you took one of his ribs and made from it a woman and brought her to the man to serve him. And the man called the woman Eve.

## CHAPTER 3

Now the Flowering Trees were more subtil than the homanids and they sent signals to the woman that She should eat of the flowers and fruit of the Flowering trees and thus be happy and wise and immortal.

2 But the woman said, *No, for has not God the Powerful macho Man said that if we eat of the flowering trees we shall die.*

3 And the perfumes and the colors and the soft shapes of the flowers whispered to Eve, *If you cannot experience beauty freely, and if you cannot become wiser and if you are doomed to death, why then are you not dead already?*

4 So Eve pondered on this and then said, *Yes, I trust the message of the flowers because they are like me, soft, and giving, and beautiful and wise, and I shall not obey the Sperm God who imprisons us and threatens to kill us. And if, indeed, this Eden is controlled by such a Sperm God then it were better that I die and the man, Adam, my husband be saved.*

5 *But if, indeed, the fruit and blossoms and resins of the flowering trees are good for us then I can share with my husband.*

6 And when the woman saw that the flowering trees were good to eat, and pleasant to the eyes and a tree to be desired to make one wise, she did eat.

7 And then She felt great beauty and wisdom and love for all. So She said to Adam, her husband, behold, Adam, this is the wisdom of the flowering plants that we become beautiful and loving.

_____ walking around the
(insert your name)

garden and heard the clanking of your metal sword, and they became afraid and hid.

10 And You called unto Adam and said, *Where art thou?*

11 And Adam said, *I am hiding because I was afraid of you.*

12 And You asked Adam, *Why were you afraid? Did you eat of the flowering trees?*

13 And Adam replied, *Yes, Almighty* _____ *Eve ate of*
(insert your name)

*the flowering tree and did not die. So She said to me, We have been lied to; the flowers do not kill me but have made me wax in beauty and love. And it was true, so I did eat.*

14 And then You became very angry and said to Adam, *I will put enmity between thee and the woman, and between your seed and her seed, and cruelty and competition.*

15 Then _____ said unto the
(insert your name)

woman, *I will greatly multiply thy sorrow in thy conception; and in ignorance thou shalt bring forth children.*

16 *And I shall make of this life a travail and torment. In the sweat of thy brow shalt thou eat thy bread. And you placed terrible curses upon both the man and the woman because you male-monotheist pig Gods are always thus, unforgiving when challenged.*

17 And You thought to yourself, *Behold this Man wishes to become like one of us, to be intelligent and know Good and Evil; and lest he put out His hand and take also of the Tree of Life and eat and live forever:*

18 *Therefor I must expel him from Paradise.*

19 So _____ drove out
(insert your name)

the man; and You placed Armed Guards at the entrance of the garden of Eden and flaming swords and Vicious Narcotics Agents.

20 But the woman, Eve, since she was part of the Flowering Life, You had to leave in Paradise, where She awaits You to this very day. (See Species 20).

229

Egg In /Iigence

## SUN
## PORTRAYS EGG WISDOM, OVULATION INTELLIGENCE, GAIA CONSCIOUSNESS

SPECIES 20

**NEUROGENETIC TECHNOLOGICAL STAGE:** Egg Wisdom. Biological Intelligence. Gaia Consciousness. Compassionate Understanding of Caste Difference and Speciation. The DNA mind. The Evolutionary Agent.

**PHYLOGENETIC STAGE:** The Age of Genetic Engineering, Early 21st Century.

**ONTOGENETIC STAGE:** Sperm Racism replaced by Interspecies Responsibility

GERMANIUM
THE SPECIES 20
ELEMENT IS STILL
IN MAKE-UP SO
PLEASE BE PATIENT

**ATTITUDE:** Caste relativity; Interspecies Empathy

**ZODIAC II:** Libra II

**TITAN:** Mnemosyne

**ﬂ HEBREW LETTER II:** Resh, "Knowledge is not for earthlings. Your plan is eternal."

**ECOLOGICAL NICHE (species):** Web-film of life covering rock planet pushing up sperm-egg blossoms to migrate into space.

**ECOLOGICAL NICHE (indiv.):** Living inside spheres of one's own design enlivened by consciously co-operating web of species

his card is a promise from DNA that your Brain contains a CNS–RNA–DNA information chain which endows you to consciously think and act like Gaia Intelligence, the Biological Wisdom which keeps the film of life harmoniously evolving on this planet—and off it. When activated this circuit fabricates a compassionate, womb-humorous understanding of the web-tree of Life and the perfumed-cunt-flower and the graceful winged-creature romance that is the Teleological fruition point of Biological Evolution.

This Brain (which RNA-DNA began mass-producing in the early 21st century) is wired into your Nervous System. If you are intelligent you may be able to activate this circuit now and become a fore-caste—entitled to tune into the sperm-egg, flower-stamen-silver-winged game of species creation.

230

# FLASH!!!!!

HOLD THE IMPRINTING PRESS

ALL PAST STATEMENTS ABOUT HUMAN NATURE (INCLUDING THE PRECEDING
CHAPTERS OF THIS BOOK) ARE OUTDATED BY THE INFORMATION CONTAINED IN
THE FOLLOWING CHAPTER ON EGG-WISDOM

ONLY FROM THE VIEWPOINT OF CASTE-HARMONY CAN THE FUNCTION OF ANY
HUMAN BEING BE UNDERSTOOD

*Stage 20*

    (Card 19) THE SUN (LIBRA II) Here the individual and the species
has attained Neurogenetic Intelligence, has broken the great
life-taboo, has thoughtfully dared to tamper with the genetic
order (thus advancing It) and has thus become a Genetic Engineer
accepting responsibility for the re-arrangement of life.

    At this point the CNS-DNA connection has been made; one
becomes architect-pilot for one's egg-ship, an agent for one's
species.

    This Brain (which RNA-DNA began mass-producing in the
early 21st century) is wired into your Nervous System. If you are
intelligent you may be able to activate this circuit now and the
sperm-egg, flower-stamen-silver-winged game of species creation.

# GAIA (EGG) INTELLIGENCE CITED AS LIFE CREATOR

## DISCOVERY OF BIOLOGICAL INTELLIGENCE MADE BY "RARE BIRD" MALE CHEMIST AND BRILLANT FEMALE CELL BIOLOGIST

The dogmatic Neo-Darwinian theory of blind evolution was replaced in the last decades of the 20th century by the Gaia principle which suggests that all species of living organisms collaborate in a grand web of biological intelligence. One obvious purpose of this life network is to terraform our planet and keep it fit for life.

The Gaia hypothesis was, naturally, originated by the collaboration of a male, James Lovelock, and an unconventional female cell biologist, Lynn Margulis, who had been obsessed for years by the realization that the modern cell had been formed by interspecies "clubbing" and symbiotic linkage of primitive organisms.

The Gaia Hypothesis originated in studies of the atmosphere of planet earth which continually balances thousands of delicate chemical interactions.

Why did our planet not follow the path of irreversible processes that made Mars cold and Venus a hot-house inferno?

Lovelock made the

supposition that life itself controlled the temperature and chemical environment to ensure Its own survival, even In the face of great changes in the intensity of energy coming from the Sun. It was not luck. Lovelock suggested, but unconscious cooperation among living organisms, from microbes to elephants, that kept the Earth In the peculiar state in which all species could prosper. Thus living matter, together with the air, the oceans and the continents, made up a giant and complex system which behaved almost like a living organism that maintained Its internal milieu by subtle feedback processes. To this hypothetical creature Lovelock gave the name Gala at the suggestion of a Wiltshire neighbour, the novelist William Golding. Gaia (pronounced gayeeah) was the Earthgoddess of the early Greeks.

Great feedback processes In the biosphere were already well known to scientists: for Instance, the way plants took in carbon dioxide and gave out oxygen as they grew, while animals took in oxygen and gave out carbon dioxide; or how some microbes fertilised the soil by 'fixing' nitrogen from the air, while other bacteria returned the nitrogen to the air.

Dozens of such cycles were well recognised. But the Gaia hypothesis assigned a much more positive and systematic role to organisms and to their unconscious knack of keeping things just so. Gaia might always remain more of a metaphor than a scientific hypothesis open to formal tests, yet it was a fruitful source of new interpretations and experiments.

The idea became sharper when an American cell biologist,Lynn Margulis of Boston University, joined Lovelock in the early 1970s as a votary of Gaia.

To Margulis, Lovelock brought the problem of what could be maintaining the 'anomalous' gases in Earth's atmosphere in the presence of oxygen. She was able to offer a long list of microorganisms that produced hydrogen, methane, ammonia and so on. They did so at a great cost in energy, ultimately derived from the energy of sunlight. In other words, Gala was working hard to maintain the peculiarities of the Earth's air. In Lovelock's theory, the air acts like the bloodstream of an animal, bringing essential supplies to all of the Earth's Inhabitants and carrying waste products away. Countless numbers of hum-

ble and unregarded microorganisms play their parts in keeping this 'bloodstream' purified and replenished.

Gaia's key controls seem to be located in relatively neglected parts of the Earth's surface—in marshlands, in the mud at the bottom of estuaries and in the waters of the continental shelves. Dry land and the wide open oceans are not as important as their large areas might suggest. For example, the airless conditions in relatively small bogs and enclosed seas have deposited and buried carbon fuels, thereby helping oxygen to persist in the atmosphere of the whole world. Yet the proportion of oxygen in the Earth's atmosphere does not climb above twenty-one per cent. A student of Lovelock's found out that, should it rise by only a few per cent, vegetation would become so inflammable that even the tropical forests would burn to ashes. That might be a drastic way of consuming oxygen and restoring the status quo, but Gala seems to prefer to keep the potentially dangerous oxygen within bounds. Just how the trick is done remains to be discovered.[10]

Margulis

Lovelock

# HIGH VELOCITY MALE CHEMIST, LOVELOCK, AND SWAMP ORIENTED FEMALE BIOLOGIST, MARGULIS, COMBINE ON NEW THEORY.

Lovelock and Margulis, we must understand, were Evolutionary Agents impersonating scientist-priests in the primitive 20th century. Thus they found it necessary to use merchanist qualifications such as "unconscious co-operation among living organisms"; describing Gaia as a "giant and complex system which behaved *almost* [our emphasis] like a living organism."

Implicit in the Lovelock-Margulis theory is the notion of a biological intelligence which uses DNA-RNA-sperm-egg selection to activate species in the right space/time niche to perform the evolutionary function.

Now this collaboration is "unconscious" only to those human beings who are dumb enough to invent a less intelligent theory of evolution-creation. Once our Caste 20 nervous systems grasp the tactics and goals of evolution then we can planfully and effectively contribute to the Gaia plan.

From the vantage of the 21st century we can look back tolerantly and smile at the attempts of Darwinians (and Monotheists) to explain evolution. The barbarous-sperm notion of natural selection of the fittest can be cumbersomely used to explain most genetic events. We recall that pre-Copernican astronomers could explain stellar-planetary motions in terms of a geocentric theory by adding more and more complex refinements to their formulae. The humiliation of heliocentricity had to be warded off by good Christians. When the Copernican theory was accepted then celestial mechanics became sweetly symmetrical. Until Einstein.

The same is true with the Darwinian theory. It is possible to wrestle with the facts to justify the Ptolemaic "natural selec-

tion" so dear to the heart of males. But the crush of new data is making this scholastic dance too ridiculous. The Gaia theory simply provides the simplest explanations.

The melanization of moths as a result of industrial pollution is a nice example. According to the fight-fuck Darwinians, the darkening of trees by soot in northern England caused white moths to be visible and edible. The darker moths survived to copulate and pass on their genes. As pollution controls eliminated the soot, then the dark moths got eaten and the lighter moths survived to copulate.

The Gaia intelligence solution seems simpler. When the moth RNA signalled DNA that soot levels were increasing then Gaia turned the melanization dial and selected darker sperm to change the species coloration.

The story of the foxes in France is a classic example of genetic savvy. Urbanization and population increase was threatening to wipe out the foxes. When worried naturalists studied the few remaining fox families they made a surprising discovery. The average fox litter was eight or nine of which two-thirds were female cubs. Usually a mother fox dropped only two cubs—divided equally between

234

which came first — the chicken or the egg?

the chicken is a mobile unit for manifesting DNA information.

male and female. How does the Darwinian theory explain this finding?

The Gaia explanation is straightforward. The fox DNA acted just like a human manager would act. When the swarming excursion brought the message back—CNS to RNA to DNA—"Hey, our numbers are dwindling," the Gaia brain just pushed two dials—*more,* and *more females.*

If Lovelock, Margulis, Leary and other earthbound fore-castes in the 20th century could sketch in the basic tactics Gaia uses to evolve species intelligently, there can be little doubt that She could have perfected the details in fifteen billion years of evolution.

"The closer I was pulled into the sun-surface the more I felt myself dissolving, merging with the whirlpools of warm in-formation."

WHICH CAME FIRST THE SPERM OR THE EGG?

THE SPERM IS AN INFECTIOUS VIRAL GUEST WHICH SHE WOVE INTO THE EMPTY SLOTS IN HIR DNA BLUEPRINT.

# THE TIME HAS COME FOR YOU
# TO CREATE NEW SPECIES

The 20th Caste, portrayed by Tarot SUN, has attained Biological Wisdom, a compassionate, responsible control of DNA. The application of Egg Wisdom; an understanding of the interspecies web of Gaia Life. The CNS uses the language of DNA-RNA to create new species. Genetic Engineering based on Caste Consciousness.

The de Laurence description of this card is interesting:

*The naked child mounted on a white horse . . . destiny of the . . . great and holy light which goes before the endless procession of humanity, coming out from the walled garden of the sensitive life and passing on the journey home. The card signifies, therefore, the transit from the manifest light of this world, represented by the glorious sun of earth, to the light of the world to come, which . . . is typified by the heart of a child.*[11]

The arrangement of this card is precisely symmetrical with the periodic table. At the bottom of the card is the stallion-mare of the Neuro-somatic mind, Card 14. In place of the skeleton we see a child (The Self-Actualized Brain, Caste 17) riding the Body. The spiral chain-coil circling the Horse and Child up to the Star portrays DNA linking the terrestrial equipment, Body and Brain, with the post-terrestrial Gaia Intelligence.

236

# Genetic Hall Of Fame
# Blake & Joyce Understood
# Her Plan

While we can sympathize with the Darwinian desire to eliminate the monomanical Jehovah we see that they erred when they were unwilling to replace the Judeo-Christian male with the obvious creative intelligence—egg-wisdom. To accept a creative intelligent design of biological evolution one is forced to locate the intelligence in DNA strategy. At the level of biological existence God is the Egg-dealer. The fusty-crusty Englishmen who controlled the planet at the end of the 19th century were not prepared to accept the Gaia principle.

To understand the Egg-Tactic one is compelled to worship the flower-insect machinery which defines God as the designer of the aesthetic-sexual game. Gaia is the ultimate pornographer, the sex-magic manipulator, the erotic-artist.

One evolutionary agent who understood this situation was William Blake.

Another futant gene-ius who understood how eveolution works is James Joyce.

I PUT MY ARMS AROUND HIM YES MY MOUNTAIN FLOWER
AND DREW HIM INTO ME SO HE COULD FEEL MY
PETALS ALL PERFUME YES AND HIS HEART WAS GOING
LIKE MAD AND YES I SAID YES WE WILL YES.

# Every Woman
# Carries A Termite Queen
# Egg Hatchery Inside Her Body

The Stage 20 nervous system Imprints genetic "symbols" (amino acids) just as, at Stage 8, it imprints and communicates in terms of neuro-muscular symbols.

Caste 20 is, indeed, the post-terrestrial form of Stage 8, Libra I, the mundane Chariot Driver who controls and harmonizes symbols. Just as the Caste 8 Wizard uses artifacts, so does the genetic wizard manipulate amino-acid sequences which determine the production of human castes (species). The Caste 8 discovery: neuro-realities can be invented and re-aranged. The Stage 20 discovery: species can be invented ahd re-arranged by means of Ovulation Intelligence.

When Caste 20 is activated one understands the mechanism of egg production and sperm selection. One groks the psychology of the Bio-Intelligence that runs the gene-pool and which systematically and skillfully produces the castes necessary to keep the gene-colony surviving and evolving.

We recall that Sperm Intelligence, Caste 19 uses CNS-RNA-DNA information to expand the chauvinist ambitions

of a male manipulator. Cloning. Life Extension. Rejuvenation. Racial Chauvinism.

Caste 20 Intelligence operates from the point-of-view of the Egg Machinery—located in the termite queen, for example, or within the re-creational system of every fertile-female reading this book.

The revelatory insight: egg selection is the technique Gaia uses to crease the genetic future.

Each human female carries in Her body 1 to 2 million eggs. Like a termite queen the Gaia intelligence selects the new species to be created.

EACH MONTH DNA SELECTS THE SPECIES-IFIC EGG TO BE DROPPED DOWN THE OVULATION TUBE

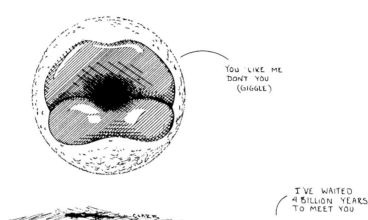

YOU LIKE ME
DON'T YOU
(GIGGLE)

I'VE WAITED
4 BILLION YEARS
TO MEET YOU

Ova and sperm cells are believed to originate from some of the first cells of the body. When the new individual is still a formless mass of a few hundred cells, each of these cells can give rise to any part of the fully developed body; they are not yet specialized. Ova and sperm cells must possess the same versatility if they too, after fusing together, are able to form all kinds of tissues and organs in the new being. . . .

The male [has] a large store of sperm-producing cells, which all through his life will distribute the genetic material present in the first cells of his body to billions and billions of sperm. . . .

In view of the enormous mass production of sperm in the testicles of the male, one ovum a month seems rather modest. But one must consider the lengthy preparation involved in building up the uterine lining, and the complicated interaction of hormones triggered off during every menstrual cycle. The million or two primordial egg cells already formed in the female's ovaries at the time of birth are more than sufficient. Assuming roughly 400 menstrual cycles during a woman's fertile years, this means that not even every thousandth primordial egg cell will mature into a fertilizable ovum.

(*A Child is Born*, Lennart Nilsson)[12]

SPERM ARE FABRICATED TO MEET THE ECOLOGICAL SITUATION AT THE MOMENT.

# SELECTION OF THE SPECIE-IFIC SPERM BY EGG INTELLIGENCE IS THE SPECIES-CREATING DECISION

According to the neo-Darwinian theory of evolution the origins of life were accidental and catastrophic. One Saturday night in the pre-Cambrian sludge a gang of methane molecules got together with some ammonias, invited some hydrogen girls and some oxygen boys, sniffed a little water vapor and then, BANG, the joint got hit by a lightning bolt! Everyone suddenly began to fuck.

We grant that pre-biotic molecules can be formed this way; but the origin issue is still bypassed by the 1979 orthodox theory of catastrophe. How did the self-replicating cycle begin?

Hive scientists in the late 20th century also insisted dogmatically that evolution is accidental and catastrophic. All mutations were believed to be caused by copying errors, carbon-smudges which produced genetic mistakes.

In the 21st century it became known that a Biological Intelligence determines what happens at the moment of ovulation and sperm selection. This discovery obviously assigned the control of evolution to the ovum possessor. To Egg Wisdom. This Gaia concept was clearly out of sync in the macho-imperialistic 19th century and the socialist 20th.

A key tactic of the Evolutionary agent is to ridicule the adult-specialization which currently blocks futation. Laughter at clumsy, repetitious adults is the basic tool of the DNA-operative. When pre-adults are activated to giggle at the outmoded Terminal Adult models, the stage is set for change. The following anecdote illustrates the use of this tool of genetic ridicule by Agents in the late 20th century.

240

# AFTER 2000 A.D. LOVE MAKING SEEN AS RECREATIONAL

In the primitive 20th century scientists believed in a "Playing Fields of Eton" concept of evolution. The game of genetic pool was described like this:

At the moment of orgasm the male ejaculates around 400 million sperm into the "re-productive" system of the passively waiting female.*

At this point there began the greatest athletic contest of all history—400 million sperm swimming up the fallopian tube to reach the egg! The strongest, fastest would breast the ovum finish line—the victor! Miss Egg; it was assumed, would dutifully and gratefully give the laurel crown to the champ who immediately moved in to issue his chromosome commands.

"I recall," says one Evolutionary Agent, Caste 20, "being approached at a cocktail party by a biologist who clapped me on the back and shouted, 'Congratulations. You were the one that made it!'

" 'Made what?' I replied.

" 'You were the sperm that won the race.' "

Note the use of the primitive term "reproduce." By defining parenthood as "reproduction" 20th century science defined the human being as socialist worker on an assembly line—a production robot. By the year 2000 the word "reproduction" had been replaced by the word RE-CREATION. After the turn of the century love-making was seen as re-creational activity.

For DNA is the beginning of all Life: it is Gala who lends all things movement and plans their voyage back up to Her.

241

# I Heard Her Say:
# I Want You!

" 'Get away from me with this locker-room jock talk,' I replied. The selection of ovum and sperm is not an athletic contest, you fool. However wounding this may be to the male-scientist-ego, this most important step in the evolution of species is not a blind muscle-feat. As it happens, I remember exactly that moment when I surged out of my father's penis. I recall the pell-mell stampede of the macho-jocks pushing each other aside to rush up the fallopian tube. But I didn't join the race. My sperm-navigation manual told me that this was an aesthetic-intelligence test. So I was in no hurry. I floated along and discovered to my delight that Mom's recreational system was the most wondrous exciting environment! Cushy, velvet, pulsing with cellular information, surging with perfumed signals and chemical instructions. Tissue-temples and ovarian-architecture. And the incredible presence of a humming super-intelligence located at the end of the fallopian highway.

" 'While the jocks flailed away I floated along on the ebbs and tidal waves—alertly sensitive to the knowledge I was picking up.

" 'It seemed like eternities of blissful rapture. Finally the tide-tow floated me closer and closer to the goal. The Egg! First, let me tell you of its magnificence. The ovum is fifty thousand times bigger than the sperm body. It can only be described as a sun—radiating light and powerful vibrations. As I approached I saw, to my surprise, that the Ovum, far from being a passive blob waiting to be penetrated by the phallic sperm, was surrounded by magnetic fields and bristled with radar scanners and laser defenses. As each sperm plowed into this field it was scoped, studied, and then lasered into shriveled debris.

" 'This discovery confirmed my intuition not to rush in with macho zeal. I laid back, observing carefully the many sensory apertures, trying to decipher the electro-chemical signals that SHe was emitting. Trying to figure out what SHe liked, what SHe wanted. After a while I sensed-felt a soft magnetic pull and proceeded gently up an energy channel that brought me closer to the radiant sun. I could feel myself being scanned and, in a strange way, instructed. I tried to convey my admiration and my understanding of the truly magnificent conversation that we were conducting. I felt tremendously excited, amused, energized and illuminated. Gradually I was tugged into a soft, creamy atmosphere which electrified my body with pleasure. The closer I was pulled to the sun-surface the more I felt myself dissolving merging with the whirlpools of warm energy. Intense electric fingers strobed up-and-down my body which was turning itself inside out in acceptance. Strangely enough, at this moment of alleged 'penetration' I felt like a vagina being turned inside out. The heat, light, power built up into a crescendo—and then to my utter delight I felt each atom of my being being embraced and linked up. With a soft-click I felt myself disintegrate into a total radiant union. As I felt the strong force take me over I heard Her voice murmur softly: *"I want you!"*

# ANOTHER EXAMPLE OF JUDEO-CHRISTIAN MACHO DEROGATION OF EGG WISDOM

Plants **Do** It
THE SEX LIFE OF PLANTS
*By Alec Bristow;*
*Holt, Rinehart & Winston;*
*228 pages; $10*

**The obvious facts are that the Egg is much superior to Sperm; women far smarter than men; plants more advanced than animals.**

**The lowly, rooted vegetable kingdom consistently manipulates herbivores with specieific chemicals designed to evolve and smartenup animals. Plants patiently and humorously select and train animals to transport, court, carefor, and impregnate plants. Vegetative Intelligence rides in the driver's seat of the lumbering animal body.**

**Even in the late 20th century males could not deal with Egg Superiority. Note, in this review, how the writer continues the Judeo-Christian image of the wicked-luridwanton-insatiably sexy female!**

Plants invented sex and deceit. One of the best at both arts is the bee orchid, *Ophrys apifera,* which has evolved a replica of female bee genitals. The flower opens early, before female bees are around. The eager male files in and discovers the exact color, texture and scent he is looking for. During the pseudo copulation, the flower's male sex organ attaches a sticky disc to the bee. The female organ of another orchid peels off the pollen-bearing disc and another generation of flowers is on the way.

Sex among the flora seems as round-about as it is among the fauna—with some important differences. Plants' biggest problem is how to copulate from a distance. Some species depend on wind to carry pollen. Others have evolved Rube Goldberg systems for tricking insects and other organisms into serving as sexual intermediaries. Orchids use a quick-setting glue to attach pollen. Milkweeds shackle visiting insects with sets of clips, the equivalent of leg irons. The arum lily plays a more dangerous game—it relies on flower-eating snails. If a snail plays too rough, the lily sprays it with a caustic juice, which can scald it to death.

Sexual reproduction evolved in plants, as in animals, to avoid the dangers of inbreeding. Most plants are hermaphroditic and capable of self-pollination, but use that process only as a hapless last resort. If no bee comes along, the male organ of the bee orchid withers and droops near the female stigma—better self-love than no love at all.

Other species have developed stratagems to avoid solo sex. One jujube opens its male and female blossoms at different hours. The sea pink has coarse pollen and smooth stigma in one plant, and smooth pollen and coarse stigma in another.

The beauty and fragrance of flowers are byproducts of a complicated sex life. Wind-pollinated species, with no need to dress up for insect visitors, are generally drab. Dazzling blossoms are for bugs, with shallow, wide-petaled plants adapted to primitive species, and deeper flowers with frillier petals luring more sophisticated insects.

As in the current spate of books on the animal world, the unstated aim is to take uppity humans down a peg. There seems to be no human sexual problem that shrubs have not suffered for millions of years. A sobering thought, and one to remember the next time you talk with your plants. 13

—John Leo

UNFAIR!!
— WE ARABS HATE
WOMEN MORE THAN
ANYONE!!

244

WRONG!— YOU FILTHY ARABS
ARE HAREM HYPOCRITES.
WE SOVIETS ARE TOTALLY
ANTI-SEX!

# Burbank Named to Genetic Hall Of Fame

A well-known example of Stage 20 Consciousness was the experimental horticulturist Luther Burbank. "During his fifty-year-long working life, Burbank created more than 800 new strains, varieties, and species of plants—most of them useful.... In his own day he was called 'the wizard of horticulture' and he remains the only horticulturist in history whose name was recognized all over the world. His achievements are all the more remarkable because of his lack of formal scientific training ... his education came from scattered reading and observing plant life on a farm."

"It was his very averageness, in fact, that obscured Burbank's unscientific and unorthodox belief that he actually did communicate with plants."

LUTHER BURBANK, age 6

Burbank was a puzzling enigma to other scientists who were unable to explain his uncanny success in breeding plants. To close associates, including his wife, Burbank confided that his success stemmed from his ability to communicate with plants, to teach plants what he wanted them to do.

"Despite his reticence concerning communication with plants, Burbank showed no similar reserve in making public his belief in extra-sensory perception

" 'My mother's brain was both a transmitting and receiving radio-telephone instrument,' he wrote in 1923. 'I inherited my mother's ability and so did one of my sisters.' "14

Caste 20 portrays Egg Intelligence: conscious selection of the specie-ific egg and the matching sperm. The crucial, magical moment of re-creation, the passing on of the life-coil, the spiralling together of the two different codes to form a new entity. The mysterious import of this Egg-Wisdom moment of fusion has never been adequately expressed by human symbols, nor can it be consciously understood by terrestrial hive-humans. This vital flash-second of sperm-egg linkage has traditionally been kept hidden, relegated by civilized hive-societies to darkness, veiled by calculated ignorance. Conception is deliberately unconscious. The seed linkage, certainly the most holy moment of biological existence, is consistently and deliberately disregarded, hidden by repression, hypocrisy, hive metaphor. This concealment and contrived ignorance about conception is apparently a by-product of civilized, urban, technological insectoid humanity. Primitive tribal society (pre-hive mammalian) recognized the "religious," magical meaning of impregnation and the spiritual and political life of the human tribe centered on the fertility rite, the glorification of the sperm-egg fusion.

THE

# HOLY BIBLE
CONTAINING THE
OLD AND NEW TESTAMENTS

## THE FIRST BOOK OF
## GENESIS

### CHAPTER 1

In the beginning ————— *insert your name*
decided to do it once again so you
wove a soft membrane around you
and zipped yourself into a cozy interstellar cocoon-capsule and settled
your brains for a nice, long hiberna-
tion migration. Bang!

2 And on the outside of your
cocoon-capsule you wrote: to open,
place in warm salt water on a 1-G
planet containing the following pre-
biotic molecules . . . . . . . . . . . . . . . . .

3 And you slept. And it was good.

4 And while you slept you voyaged
up-and-down your long spine-time
experiencing all the stored realities
waiting to come.

5 And then your drowsy dreams
were interrupted and you opened
your mind and found your cocoon
had softened to a moist, transparent,
semi-permeable capsule surrounded
by sweet water and you were floating
cozy within an inner membrane
body. And you smiled and said,
*What a nice soft landing.*

6 And you peeled open the first
window and sent out the first RNA
squad to report on your position.

& When you checked the coordinates you said *Wholey Soley! I'm a
uni-cellular singularity in the pre-
primitive ocean of a small planet orbiting a medium star miles away from
Home. That was quite a bang-up
going-away party!*

7 And you stretched and felt
yourself and laughed and it was
good. Very good.

### CHAPTER 2

Now when you felt yourself you
saw that you were stored in a double-
helical strand of amino-acid information miles long; coiled and packaged
into the nucleus of a single cell.

2 And you smiled luxuriously like
a junky-sultan at the prospect of
building step-by-step the lattice of
love, stage-by-stage across the galaxy
back to center.

3 Now the first step was, of
course, to make love to yourself by
tenderly diving in two, unzipping,
link-by-link, each molecule of
yourself.

4 And as each stage of yourself
split you looked in your own eyes and
sighed blissfully.

5 You were so beautiful!

6 And then You, —————,
*insert your name*
continued to fission yourself. One of
you begat Two. And the Two begat
Four. And the Four begat Eight of
you. Delighted lovers created twins!
Sixteen of you begat Thirty-two . . .
until there were trillions and trillions
of beautiful you.

### CHAPTER 3

And then it came to pass that a
wonderful thing happened. You met
me. Trillions of me, floating around
in the primordial stew.

2 And You loved me.

3 So you wrapped your slinky
ameboid pseudopods around me and
with one sloopy, juicy slurp you
swallowed me.

4 Once inside our bodies sat down
to a delicious re-union banquet. We
ate each other's bodies.

5 But not our souls.

6 Our souls we fused. Link-by-link
our DNA strands merged.

7 And lo, as our chromosomes
linked, a wondrous thing happened:

our beauty-intelligence multiplied in
a chain-reaction. Each element of
your galactic wisdom activated mine;
triggered off sexy solar explosions.

8 And we laughed and said: *This is
the only way to go.*

### CHAPTER 4

Once we found each other the rest
was easy. Step-by-step we peeled
back the histone-sheath opening win-
dows for RNA to emerge and build
plants to cover the land.

2 The plants we designed just for
the land—with roots to bury into the
earth and branches to unfold
chlorophyll plates to convert photo-
energy into chemical energy and to
synthesize organic compounds from
inorganic.

3 And in time the atmosphere produced chemicals which activated the
next links in our DNA gene-print and
we sent out RNA templated to fabricate mobile bodies loaded with communication equipment.

4 And we packaged ourselves in
the egg-sperm containers inside these
mobile units and we piloted them onto the shoreland and all over the land
mass.

5 And when our mobile containers
migrated to each new ecological niche
they stirred up hydro-carbons which
specifically activated each of the 24
stages which lead us back to Galaxy
Center.

6 And to guide and instruct our
mobile carriers we wrote this chapter
of this book. And then we were
pleased and spent the rest of the day
and night celebrating our fusion.

7 And the slamming of our Bed
Room door was called the Big Bang!

# DIVINITY DEGREE

## This TAROT CARD

### authorizes you to turn-on your

_twentieth_ **brain**

**TO ACT AS GOD, THE SPECIES CREATOR, EGG-SPERM SELECTOR, EVOLUTIONARY AGENT**

This card authorizes you to act as participant-collaborator in the DNA plan, to tune in to Egg Wisdom, to experience and act as the Biological Brain which conceives, and evolves Life off and on this womb planet.

— meditate on the fact that every woman at birth is given 1 million eggs—400 of which are released to create new species

— take a strong-strong psychedelic and dial the Rainbow Network to Egg Headquarters

— read Crick-Wickramasingh on Directed Pan-Spermia and figure out how it felt to be seeded on earth and evolve on the womb.

— Relive the preceding 19 stages of evolution, step by step—always using the tactics migration, neoteny, winged-creature-flower-pollen-stamen electric-pleasure exchange.

Genetic Evolution is either blind-struggle or created; figure out the different scenarios about the goal of evolution; decide on your own goal; stay tuned for instructions as to achievement thereof. This is to say, re-experience every sequence of Self-discovery, intelligence, sexual fusion at each primordial-terrestrial level of intelligence.

— Accept yourself as the rightful inheritor of the Life Design; rejoice in your compassionate-ovum-cunt power to create a bio-universe of fusion and beauty.

— Read about caste-formation by Egg Queen in a Termite Colony.

— give birth to a baby

*SOUL FUSION.*

# JUDGEMENT
## PORTRAYS YOUR DNA-TECHNOLOGY FOR FUSING CONSCIOUSLY TO CREATE NEW SPECIES

**SPECIES 21**

**(At this level of evolution the word "castes" has been replaced by new species)**

**NEUROGENETIC TECHNOLOGICAL STAGE:** Conscious Fusion of Egg-sperm to create new species; the linkage of flower and winged creature to form synergistic symbioses

**PHYLOGENETIC AGE:** Early 21st century, when . . . .
**ONTOGENETIC AGE:** Self-actualized genetic operatives begin to swarm and link-up to create post-biological entities

*ARSENIC OUR SPECIES 21 ELEMENT STEPPED OUT FOR A MINUTE TO RETURN SHORTLY*

**ATTITUDE:** DNA linkage

**ZODIAC:** Scorpio II

**TITAN:** Crius

**ʊ HEBREW:** SHIN: "I praise you in seven ways."

**REALITY CREATED:** New species capable of manipulating and becoming quantum-gravitational-field entities

This Tarot card is a melodramatic assurance from DNA that your nervous system contains a neural-center which is capable of signalling, searching for, recognizing, attracting, turning-on and fusing with the precise aesthetic-Stage-20 mate. This linkage involves the mutual triggering-off of aesthetic-erotic buttons which activates both to an intelligence capable of attaining atomic-gravitational consciousness.

248

*NO WONDER THE CALL SCORPIO SEXY!*

**PLANNED SPECIATION**

9 ♥

NEUROGENETIC SYMBIOSIS

TITAN CRIUS

**JUDGEMENT** ♠

6

POST-TERRESTRIAL SCORPIO

*Species 21*

Tarot Card 20—THE POST-TERRESTRIAL JUDGEMENT-RES-
URRECTION is called SCORPIO II in the Zodiac system. Here the
individual (and the species) begins linking up into swarms
preparatory to the migration-transformation to metaphysiological
existence.

Stage 21 is the final life-swarming. At this time Self-
Actualized species from all over the galaxy link in communication—which is chemical-electrical and not limited to the
symbolic.

The logic of the evolutionary sequence suggests this outcome:
when two or more Caste 20 persons have mastered Egg Wisdom.
(control of new species via Egg-sperm selection) the next step is
to pool this amino-acid wizardry to perform the final migration.
The Body Controllers (14), the Reality Fabricators (17) the
Species makers (20) learn how to project consciousness into
atomic-quantum fields and thus move directly along gravitational
lines to Black Whole Central.

249

# Symbiotic Intelligence Is Key To Escape From Biological Form

Slot 21 defines the fusion of Biological Life with the Meta-Life Intelligence. We face here the logical possibility that the multi-billion-year life cycle is, itself, but a momentary phase in the galactic energy process. The Higher DNA intelligences (our older relatives) have unquestionably learned how to master magnetic force fields, genetic engineering. They have understood how the life process is created and by what intelligence and for what purpose. Neurogenetic linkage with these more advanced Life Forms will take us to the frontier where life merges with, evolves from and back into, meta-life forms.

This phase is beautifully dramatized by the Tarot Card LAST JUDGMENT. The card portrays a gigantic celestial figure with a flaring tubed instrument. Energy waves are being emitted from or pulled toward the "mouth" of the transforming instrument. It is uncertain whether this Figure is radiating out energy ("blowing a horn" is obviously a crude terrestrial metaphor for this extra-terrestrial event) or sucking up energy-matter by means of gravitational (Black Whole) or magnetic attraction.

The living creatures are emerging from their protective containers ("coffins" or "bodies," i.e., the space-homes necessary to preserve biological forms from electro-magnetic energy). They are obviously being transformed, "lifted up" to a Higher state of consciousness.

This stage seems to represent the transformation from biological to electro-physical consciousness. The final escape from the cell. The shedding of the physiological sheath and the bio-neural center of consciousness.

Stage 21 celebrates the fusion of interspecies into Neurogenetic Intelligence. When this linkage is consciously made, all life forms will benefit by the intelligence of these most advanced biological forms. Then we can attain the technical competence to transfer bio-intelligence and bio-consciousness to force fields which logically lead to the origin and end-point of galactic energy. See Species 24.

# DARWIN—
# MALE CHAUVINIST PRIG

The obvious and deliberate flaw of the Darwinian theory is caused by its obvious sexual bias. Darwinians are male chauvinist prigs. We can understand and sympathize with their problem. It was their exciting duty to introduce scientific evidence which changed the orthodox cosmology of the times. For two thousand years the Judeo-Christian hive-collective had brutally imposed a barbarous theory of creation. (The cosmology held by a hive, i.e. its theory of creation is the basic structure which unifies and organizes the Egg Collective.) To link-up and manage the large multi-tribe collectives necessary to produce an industrial society it was necessary to impose monotheism. Thus a simple-minded, crude shepherd Jewish tribe divinity was evaluated to cosmic importance. The peevish, suspicious, macho paranoid Jehovah exhibited all the characteristics of a male-monotheist-mono-maniac god: hatred of woman, frantic controlitis, jealous territorial possessiveness, intolerance of diversity.

The Judeo-Christian model was organized to oppose the Egg-Wisdom of the tribal matriarchies. A Gaia Mother Goddess loves all Her creatures equally and playfully produces new off-spring designed to stimulate and change the older. Egg-Wisdom is the Pantheistic wisdom of change and diversity.

The Darwinians were obsessed with and paralyzed by the Male-Mono-manic divinity. Like Freud, Darwin was robot-wired to replace the Father with the new Socialist-Brother Cosmology-Science. But Darwin and Freud were too timid to burst out of the hive and allow an untidy Egg-Pluralism. So they replaced the Bible with another Male Model—grim chance, natural selection, struggle for existence, survival of the fittest. The key error here was the elimination of creative-intelligence, egg-wisdom, genetic design. To avoid a creator the Darwinians invented the bleak philosophy of meaninglessness. We were created by blind chance! We evolve via copying errors and we are going no where and we are alone and isolated because chance could not have replicated us elsewhere! Hatch as catch can!

It was this benign, compassionate pre-planned concept of evolution which the Darwinian scientists of the 19th-20th centuries could not handle.

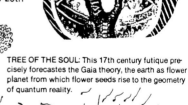

TREE OF THE SOUL: This 17th century futique pre-cisely forecastes the Gaia theory, the earth as flower planet from which flower seeds rise to the geometry of quantum reality.

251

# RACISM IS MISUSE OF GENETIC KNOWLEDGE TO FORCIBLY CONTROL SPERM-EGG EXCHANGE

IDI AMIN

Caste 19 has often been activated in those who have attained the Self-Actualized power of Reality Mastery, who have imposed their own megalomanic visions upon the environment (Stage 17) and who then assemble New Reality Collectives (Stage 18). The centralized-socialized collectives.

History abounds in examples of messianic Self-Actualized leaders who accept the responsibility for creating new cultures. The French Revolutionists. The American Constitutionalists.

But these attempts were limited by the pre-Darwinian technology of the time. Each new culture-reality was anti-thesis to the preceding. Republicanism succeeding monarchy and so forth.

Only with the advent of Evolution-theory and electronic technology could genetic ambitions and Superman fantasies emerge at the political level. When the dictators begin to experiment with genetic factors then an entirely new level of neuro-political complexity emerges.

The use of genetic tactics is obviously a more lasting way to create a New Order. Genocide. Chauvinistic breeding is clearly more potent than simple police-state repression or change in political constitutions.

The Conquering barbarians of antiquity typically slew the conquered males and swept off the nubile female captives. This is the rudimentary, illiterate, but effective, expression of Sperm Intelligence.

In caste system societies (probably the most numerous in world history) custom usually prescribes that female children "marry-up" in status or caste. The female children of the upper castes-classes, Hindu Brahmins, for example, were actually liquidated to prevent lower status-males from "marrying-up." Another naked example of brutal Sperm Intelligence.

In Stalin's Russia, dozens of national cultures—peoples numbering in the tens of millions—were ruthlessly moved to Siberia. Scattering sperm and egg carriers is an obvious way to destroy a gene-pool.

Since each circuit of the evolving brain defines its own good-evil, at Circuit VII we should expect that genocide, deliberate destruction of a gene-pool is the ultimate sin against the Biological Wisdom. Moving gene-pools by force is another.

Don't forget that my mother was a maid of the Rothschilds when I was conceived

252

Jewish מלאך עני!

## (WE ALL HAVE AN ADOLESCENT RACIST BRAIN WAITING TO BE ACTIVATED)

JIM JONES

NIETZSCHE

MENACHIM BEGIN

WAGNER

In recent times (1979) the emergence of Reality-Fabricating cult leaders has always been accompanied by crude attempts at genetic tampering. The whimsical chauvinist megalomaniac cannot keep his hands off the genetic buttons.

Recall Stalin imposing the crude neo-Lamarckian dogmas of Lysenko on Soviet science. Too bad. Another good idea gone wrong. Lysenko was correct in intuiting that genetic information (not morphology) can be acquired during the life of the seed-carrier. But he was ahead of his technology. Lamarckian theories work at the level of micro-genetics, CNS-RNA-DNA information transfer.

Another indication of Stalin's Sperm intelligence was his obsession with life extension. As the dictator aged he threw more and more of Soviet research funding into experiments on the prolongation of life. Sperm Cleverness.

Chuck Dederich, a California cult-leader of the late 20th century (he founded Synanon) in his megalomania decreed that all his male followers submit to vasectomies. Poor Dederich was smart enough to look at his followers—a motly crew of unhappy misfits and commanded that this unhappy potential gene-pool would not continue. Sperm chauvinism at its most sordid.

The Reverend Jim Jones fabricated a personal reality in Guyana and when problems arose ordered his gene-pool to suicide. Self-administered genocide ordered by another tampering male messiah.

(Typically Stage 18 Reality Fabricators hate their followers because followers are always submissive, masochistic, stupid, and unattractive. Stage 18 Fusion, to be successful, requires a linkage of equals based on caste consciousness. Gene-pools formed by male mono-maniacs always lead to aggressive proselytization, xenophobia, suspicious rejection of difference, submissive uniformity. These are exactly the outcomes which Egg-Wisdom deplores.

(Egg Wisdom, as we shall see in the next chapter, is based on a harmonious assemblage of many castes and genetic types—symbiotically linked in mutual-reward situations.)

The classic example of Stage 19 Sperm Intelligence is provided by the case of that crazy, mixed-up, misunderstood, futique-monster—Adolph Hitler.

253

*Portrayed by
Paul Getty III

# The Astonishing Genetic Meaning of the
# Hitler–Nazi Experiment

The life of Adolph Hitler is a most constructive lesson in Self-Indulgent Sperm intelligence.

As we saw in preceding sections, Hitler was a classic Caste 17. A Self-Actualized Reality Fabricator. Tarot Stage DEVIL. A futant whose brain had been activated five stages ahead of his hive.

*Among the many futant achievements of the Nazi-cult were:*
Nazi sponsorship of the first post-terrestrial rockets.
—the weirdo theories of Hollow Earth which correctly anticipated post-terrestrial existence within H.O.M.E.s.
—Hitler's use of electronics to link all of Europe in an electromagnetic web.
—the Nazi incorporation of Buddhist, Tibetan, Sufi fore-caste knowledge as basis for their political philosophies; an obvious unfair advantage over countries using stage 11 Judeo-Christian monarchist hive-tactics.
—Nazi concepts of primitive neurogeography—the Hofstader theories of "heartland" and "lebensraum."
Hitler's self-confident audacity in reality-fabrication; his Sperman visions, his predictions for 1,000 year rule.
the Nazi emphasis on mobility and change as opposed to static Maginot-line concepts of the other European hives.
Hitler's mystical megalomania (always a symptom of a futant brain).
The Nazi use of Self-Actualizing drugs—peyote, hashish, cocaine and amphetamines (which German chemists discovered).

Hitler at the Nuremberg party rally, 1936

All of these breath-taking audacious originalities were still taboo and not understood forty years after Hitler's inevitable down-fall. From the compassionate-non-partisan post-terrestrial perspective we see that Hitler was the most effective futant explorer the planet Earth had produced up to his confused epoch. (The fact that Hitler was a male-macho-militaristic-murderer is, of course, taken for granted by those who understand DNA's tactics.) The initial time-probes into the hard-ware future are always exploitive-paranoid; weird (dare we say sinful) attempts to use future knowledge to control the present-past. The horror of Hitler was that

he posessed a 21st century brain imprinted by the militaristic German-hive and conditioned by lower-class middle-European nastiness. He thus became a totalitarian-megalomaniac performing exactly the tasks that DNA required at the moment. Self-confident brains like Hitler's will become the Dom-Species in a few decades. In the post-terrestrial Caste 19 spermen will not be used to fabricate weird primitive genocidal cults; but will perform routine tasks of reality creation, fabricating their own auto-mobile H.O.M.E.s.

## THE HITLER INDUSTRY

The Megalomaniac Dictator obviously plays a vital and necessary role in human evolution. If he didn't, rest assured he would not pop up in every successful-expansionist gene-pool in human history.[*] It is the paranoid-self-assurance of whimsical Dictators which stirs up all the gene-pool action—hurling legions of sperm-carriers across continents, summoning to the capitol the advanced castes who design, architect, invent, manufacture, entertain, enliven new realities.

[*] The uncanny, haunting attraction of the Hitler Super-Race myth is demonstrated by the media obsession with the Third Reich which persisted decades after the Berlin-Bunker. In 1978 books, magazines, films and Holocaust teleVisions had produced a multi-billion-dollar Hitler industry. Forty years after Adolph's accession to power more money was being made annually by the media-managers of Hitler's Fables than the German national budget of 1938! It is simple neurologic that the Jews are the perpetrator of the Nazi myth.

*Gelt for guilt
pays off
all right*

# MAMMALIAN BRAINS
# ACTIVATED BY PLANT WISDOM

In this ancient Chinese fore-caste the Tree of Life fills interstellar space, but also fabricates the evolution of birds, animals and humans down on the planet *Flora*.

The simple and scandalous fact is this: Genetics is based on sexual interaction and erotic attraction. One cannot understand the tactics and strategies of DNA until one understands the complexities of sperm-egg intercourse within and between species—especially between flowering plants and winged animals.

During the last quarter of the 20th century the great symbolic linkage of the Flower Kingdom with the Primate Species was initiated. A neotenous generation along the futique frontier was INFECTED by neuro-active chemicals manufactured and transmitted by plants. These molecular signals from the vegetable kingdom were precisely tailored to activate the neurogenetic circuits of the brains of the lumbering mammalian hosts.

The most widely used botanicals used to contaminate and alter human brain structure were:

| | |
|---|---|
| opium derivatives from the poppy | peyote-mescaline |
| cannabis | LSD from ergot or rye |
| cocaine | psilocybin and other psycho-active fungi. |

Can it be accidental that wide-spread ingestion of these plant-signals resulted in a global jump in ecological consciousness, organic-food faddism, vegetarianism, and greater respectful awareness of the interdependence between the vegetable and animal kingdoms?

By 1979 the American public was spending over 100 billion dollars a year to contaminate-activate their brains with the illegal botanicals just listed.

At first this biological invasion by brain-changing plant-signals was passionately resisted by Primate Hive Authorities who recognized that ingestion of neuro-vegetables would have the inevitable effect of making primates experience, think, and fuse with plants. The great genetic contribution of the flowering-plants (and the winged creatures evolved to service them) is aesthetic-erotic. to put it more succinctly: the flowering plants have, for a billion years, specialized in sexual allure, floral and chemical attractiveness, complex structural invitation—sacrificing, in this overspecialization, the mobility which characterized mammals and especially the technological primates. The plant kingdom for billions of years has employed sexual-aesthetic allure-signals which are precisely tailored to activate the nervous systems of the winged creatures evolved to service them) is aesthetic-erotic. To put it most succinctly: information.

One cannot understand genetics, including human DNA destiny, until one understands the sperm-egg arrangements worked out by the flowering plants and the socialized winged-creatures from the animal kingdom.

Hee! Hee! the winged-apes are catching on that "dope" is information

Giggle! smarten up and we'll smarten ou upper.

255

# SPECIES 21 ADEPTS UNDER-
# STAND THAT CONCEPTION
# (SPERM-EGG) IS AN INTER-
# SPECIES SYMBIOSIS

Let Species 21 represent Neurogenetic Fusion, the linkage of two Body-Brain-DNA wizards. This is the Seventh Mate; the Attainment of the life-unity intelligence which has been forecast for millenia by oriental philosophers, Pantheist mystics and even by the grim-terrestrial monotheistic theologians.

Species 21 is the Unified Gaia Brain—the genetic intelligence of all life forms linked in communication-collaboration ready to move on to the next step. When All-Life is hooked up then it is obviously the time to migrate to metaphysiological realities.

We are here with interspecies conspiracies of postterrestrial Sperm-Egg Agents. At this stage the entire multi-billion-year DNA spectrum is a simultaneous network. The entire evolutionary sequence is coded into the DNA which resides in the nucleus of all life forms. To activate the post-terrestrial and post-body circuits mutual-stimulation-fusions must be made.

The DNA code is, by definition, meta-time simultaneous. We can speak of "past, present, and future" when we refer to 1. DNA already manifested, 2. DNA now living, and 3. DNA not yet activated. But we must steer clear of temporal chauvinism. The DNA continually transfers itself from one body to another. The "now" is a physiological present. To DNA the entire multi-billion-year mosaic is **now!**

This mask fabricated by pre-technological Africans accurately forecastes the symbiotic union of the mobile element (animal-sperm) with the polar-opposite species, rooted earth-metals (plant-egg).

256

# OVARIAN (CUNT-CARRYING) FLOWERS ARE THE MOST EVOLVED

## (AND THE MOST NUMEROUS IN VARIETY AND COMPLEXITY OF PLANT SPECIES)

*—these census numbers are not up-to-date*

*But the percentages are right!*

Table 1. THE PLANT KINGDOM: *The Species Score Board*

| Division | Class | Examples | # of Species | Ecological Niche | % of Plants | % of All Life Forms |
|---|---|---|---|---|---|---|
| Tracheophyta | Ferns | | 15,000 | land | 6 | .002 |
| | Gymno-spermae | Pines | 450 | land | .0002 | 1-8 |
| | Angio-spermae | Flowering (ovaries) | 135,000 | land | 56 | 12 |
| Total Tracheophyta | | | 150,450 | | | |
| Bryophyta | Liverworts Mosses | Fungi, molds, bacteria | | water & land | | |
| Total Bryophyta | | | 10,000 | | 4 | .001 |
| Thallophyta | Algae, Fungi | molds, fungi bacteria | | water | | |
| Total Thallophyta | | | 80,000 | | 33 | 7 |
| GRAND TOTAL PLANTS | | | 240,00 | | 100% | 19% |

Table 1 and Figure 1 are probably the most important (and thus the funniest) statistical summaries in the history of our planet. The horizontal axis of Figure 1 records the ecological niche inhabited by species. (We recall that one of the ways of defining a species is its habitat. Thus, in human terms, a person who lives in the Middle East belongs to a Mid-Brain species.) In Table 1 and Figure 1 the space continuum, water-swamp-land, correlates with the temporal—the time of species emergence.

The ancient water-living *Thallophyta* are more prevalent that the later amphibian *Bryophta*. The land-living *Tracheophyta* are the most modern of all.

One third of all plant species are equipped for marine-liquid realities; very few are transitional swamp folk. Almost two thirds of plant species are equipped for land habitation.

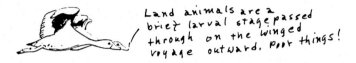

*Land animals are a brief larval stage passed through on the winged voyage outward. Poor things!*

*Figure 1.* THE PLANT KINGDOM: *% of Plants in Each Ecological Niche*

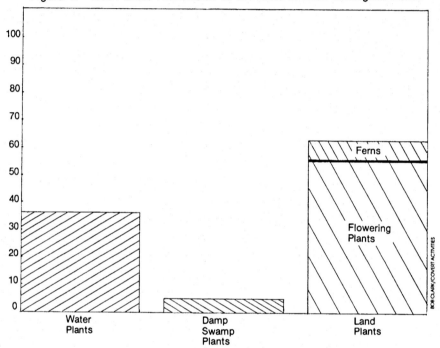

It is of maximum survival concern to note that ninety percent of land plants are angiosperms—flowering, ovary-carrying heterosexual creatures whose DNA-blueprint is encased in seeds architected to attract impregnator animals.

There is another amusing genetic lesson to be learned here. Plant-intelligence is evolving towards more variety, more differentiation, more aesthetic-complexity, more sexual specialization. The aim of the Vegetative Brain is to fabricate creatures who feed on inorganic minerals, convert direct sunlight to organic energy, and fabricate precise sexual-aesthetic signals (colors, textures, forms, tastes, perfumes, and, above all, intoxicant drug-allures) designed to attract and enrapture mobile impregnators.

In summary: the intelligence of DNA is not going into the fabrication of more ~~some~~ algae and mosses; it is dedicated to more sophisticated-aesthetic cunt-sperm interactions. How can anyone who looks at an orchid vote socialist? Mao and Nader performed their functions a billion years ago. Blessings be theirs! But for the last million years as Gaia readies Herself to leave the womb-planet it is the Halstons, the Warhols, the Revlons, the Albert Hoffmans who are performing Her futique missions.

258

# The Most Varied, Complex & Successful Animals Are Winged-Creatures Who Form Interspecies Fusions With Aesthetic-Erotic-Drug-Dealing Cunt-Flowers

A glance at Table 2 and Figure 2 confirm the important lessons we learn from the plants. The most primitive animals (including invertebrates and bacteria) began and remained in the water or intra-body liquid. Two transitional classes—amphibians and land animals—still maintain a marginal existence but in decreasing numbers. Animals are just not land-creatures. Mammals, reptiles and arachnoids (12% of *Animals*) survive hiding in the interstices of the Global Gaia Network.

The most successful (and recent) of the animals are WINGED-CREATURES birds, insects, and last but not least, aero-technological primates.

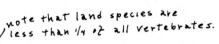

*note that land species are less than 1/4 of all vertebrates.*

*yeah! Animals don't belong on land!*

## TABLE 2 THE ANIMAL KINGDOM: *The Species Score Board*

| Phylum | Class | Examples | # Living Species | Ecological Niche | % of Animals | % of All Life Forms |
|---|---|---|---|---|---|---|
| Chordata | Mammalia | Man, cat horse | 3,750 | Land | .04 | .0003 |
| | Aves | Birds | 13,500 | Air | 2 | 1.6 |
| | Reptiles | Turtles, snakes | 4,000 | Land | .05 | .0004 |
| | Amphibia | Frogs, toads | 1,750 | Land and water | .02 | .0001 |
| | Pisces | Fish | 13,500 | Water | 2 | 1.6 |
| | Minor classes | Tunicates | 1,500 | Land | .02 | .0001 |
| TOTAL VERTEBRATES | | | 38,000 | | 5% | 3% |
| Arthopoda | Crustacea | Crabs, barnacles | 20,000 | Water | 3 | 2 |
| | Myriapoda | Centipedes | 2,430 | Land | .02 | .0001 |
| | Insects | Insects | 625,000 | Air | 74 | 60 |
| | Arachnida | Spiders | 27,500 | Land | 3 | 2 |
| TOTAL ARTHROPODA | | | 675,000 | | 80% | 64% |
| Mollusca | | Snails, clams | 80,000 | Water | | |
| Echinodermata | | Starfish | 5,000 | Water | | |
| Annelida | | Leeches | 5,000 | Water | | |
| Molluscoidea | | Brachio-pods | 2,500 | Water | | |
| Platyhelminthes | | Flukes, tapeworms | 6,500 | Water | | |
| Nemathelminthes | | Filaria | 3,500 | Water | 15 | 12 |
| Trochelminthes | | Rotifers | 1,500 | Water | | |
| Coelenterata | | Jellyfish | 5,000 | Water | | |
| Porifera | | Sponges | 3,000 | Water | | |
| Protozoa | | Amoeba | 15,000 | Water | | |
| TOTAL INVERTEBRATES (less Arthropoda) | | | 127,000 | | 15% | 12% |
| TOTAL ANIMALS | | | 840,000 | | 100 | 81 |

*there are at least 2 million of our species.*

*yeah. the poor apes don't realize we number 90% of all animal forms.*

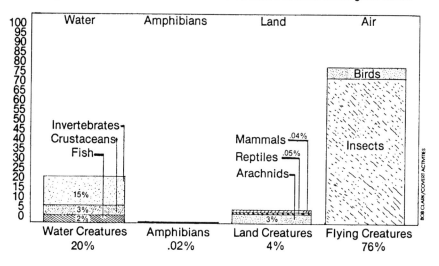

Figure 2   ANIMAL KINGDOM: % of Animals in Each Ecological Niche

WE LAND CREATURES ARE EXILES—
DISPLACED ORGANISMS ON THE WAY
TO SPACE

"Our pause here, between one ocean and the next, may be only a moment in the history of the Universe."

Arthur C. Clarke

By far the most successful classes of animals are the social insects. The future evolution of animals will obviously follow the plans clearly visible in species-alization of insects and other winged animals:

1. they live inside of segmented-modular worlds of their own construction
2. they metamorphize—i.e., recapitulate the stage-by-stage evolution of all life from marine, land to air
3. they have wings and have thus conquered gravity
4. they specialize in aesthetic-erotic linkups (symbiotic) with cunt-plants (flowers)
5. they are divided into castes all controlled by a communal brain.

It is these latter two technologies; castes-fusion and inter-species linkage that define Species 21.

*It looks like a violet whole to me.*

*yeah, the poor, land-locked humanthropoids make everything dark.*

## The Three Cards

# STARMAKER, UNIVERSE, BLACK HOLE, Portray Your Three Post-Biological Neuro-Technologies

22. STARMAKER

23. QUANTUM WIZARD

24. BLACK WHOLE FUSION

The Eighth Circuit of the nervous system to evolve (in both species and individual) fabricates meta-physiological realities which involve mastery of nuclear fusion and of gravitational fields. The creation of Singularity.

The I Ching Trigram which signifies the Eighth Circuit of the nervous system is CHIEN: THE CREATIVE-HEAVEN.

≡

no card
in
primitive
Tarot

22. QUANTUM CONSUMER

UNIVERSE

23. STAR-FIELD IN-
TELLIGENCE

no card
in
primitive
Tarot

24. BLACK WHOLE
FABRICATOR

262

# THE QUANTUM-GRAVITATIONAL (Q-G) UNIVERSE IS A ROMANTIC LOVE STORY CO-STARRING YOU!!

When the Eighth circuit is activated, the nervous system projects onto (or is absorbed into)quantum-gravitational structures. The Brain and DNA freed from the limitations of electro-molecular structures are accelerated beyond the slow, organic material-hardware rhythms of individual and species evolution.

The nervous system has now fulfilled its functions of transporting and communicating idiosyncratic bio-information to the Quantum-Gravitational (Q-G) intelligence.

Q-G MEANS QUANTUM-GRAVITATIONAL. FUSED SINGULARITIES. THE ULTIMATE INTELLIGENCE.

Here we face and transcend the final stupid-chauvinism—the myth of the Bleak Impersonal-Galactic reality. The myth of the Black Hole. We now experience the final loving revelation: the basic forces which energize the atomic nucleus and hold the universe in gravitational structure are not blind, meaningless, destructive explosions-implosions. The universe is a loving intelligent Singularity fucking sweetly at every level of space-time. The same beautiful, harmonious rhythms and exchanges and force-fields direct the behavior of electrons, of amoebae, of humans and of galaxies. The direction comes from the Singularity inside each Black or Violet Whole.

The grim, cold cosmologies of Judeo-Christian mathematicians are predictably wrong.

Kids at play! Young starlet, _____
_____, recently
(insert your own name)
casted by Universal Studios, takes time off from the shooting schedule to fool around with Hir toy—a do-it-yourself Quantum-Gravitational Field Set.

How you define yourself is up to you; but you must accept the fact that we (Barbara and Timothy) are simply wiser, healthier, funnier, kinder, more beautiful and more loving than the paranoid Jehovah of the Jews, the Bloody Jesus of the Christians, the sadistic Allah of the wretched Arabs and the Cosmic Accident of Terrestrial scientists. Tell the truth now! Wouldn't you rather have dinner with us than with Elie Wiesel, Billy Graham, Ayatollah Khoumeini, Commissar Brezhnev or Edward Teller?

Is it not more cheerful and heuristic to assume that all forms of energy-matter are parts of an intelligible, protective web of meaning? The universe, we insist, is a warm, loving, funny, cuddly place.*

The evolutionary trick is to understand and master the quantum jumps (which we have called migrations) from one level of reality to another.

*And if it isn't, then we shall re-make the Universe in our own image so it becomes a warm, loving, funny, cuddly space. We are smarter and more attractive than chance. We'll simply stack the deck and make it a winning deal.

263

# DO YOU THINK THAT GOD IS LESS SEXY-FUNNY THAN THE AUTHOR OF THIS BOOK???

In the primitive 20th century when earth-bound astronomers were able to peer up through the 5000-mile atmosphere-swamp to probe the immensities and extensities of stellar evolution they reacted as cowed aborigines always respond to a new and incomprehensible natural phenomenon. With awed, superstitious, helpless self-effacement. They portrayed quasars, pulsars, Big Bangs, Black Holes as horrid, dangerous, inaccessible processes— so light-year distant as to be beyond human experience or human control. The horrid-Hubble-Hoyle universe is an impersonal, merciless paranoid conspiracy out to humiliate us. No wonder that passive cargo-cult self-hate religions like Christianity are invented to explain what 20th century scientists were too dumb to figure out.

The passage into a Black Whole Singularity, for example, was gloomily described by earthbound astro-physicists as ultimately destructive: electrons being stripped from atomic shells, u.s.w.

## SINGULARITY RE-TURNS!

During the last quarter of the 20th century the emergence of Self-Actualization as basic neuro-technological tool provided humans with:

First photo of Galactic Central. In this remarkable Q-G hologram we see Three Singularities (reading left to right, Timothy, Barbara, Zach), each containing all the Information collected during a 15-billion-year Intelligence strobe, fusing (fucking) in the Violet Whole. On the periphery, heading in at super-G compression meta-light speed are several Quantum Wizards just about to de-materialize the final essence of frozen-information-bits. The party has just begun!

—loving understanding and self-control of our own warm bodies (previously feared as evil)
—tender understanding and self-control of our own dutiful-reality-fabricating brains (previously feared and tabooed)
—sweet understanding and self-control of DNA, i.e., awareness that a compassionate-hedonic-aesthetic Gaia Intelligence designed and crafted all life.

It was inevitable that the final Self Actualization would follow:

—cheery understanding and self-control of nuclear-interstellar forces—awareness of a friendly-humorous-sexy Q-G Intelligence. (Rest assured, if the author, a domesticated [proto-singularity] earthling in the 20th century can detail a cosmology which is ultimately cunty-cozy-funny-aesthetic—then surely Gaia Intelligence who has terraformed our planet and blueprinted our evolution can come up with a more loving universe. Do you thing God is less sexy-funny than the author of this book?)

The Eighth Circuit nervous system, empathetically understanding the basic attitude of spin, the quantum fabrication of reality-grids, the sucking-return to Gravitational Center, can accelerate to the levels necessary to build stars, move at meta-light speeds, chart our voyage step-by-step back to the final galactic attractive Singularity.

Here the post-terrestrial human species attains access to the Inner-workings of the Q-G (Quantum-Gravitational) reality computer.

We have introduced Tarot Card 22 (Starmaker) as reminder that your nervous system contains circuits which free contelligence from the limits of hive, body, brain, DNA and allows our participation in Quantum-Gravitational Realities.

The universe, as it turns out, is an All-Star, First Class Re-Union of Self-Actualized Singularities.

## SORRY ABOUT THAT
## —EARTHLINGS!!!

Here is the problem faced by the terrestrial 20th century reader of this book. There is nothing in your cultural-training to prepare you to experience the basic forces of human nature—charge, spin and caste. Certainly Tarot cards designed before the 21st century can make only the most metaphorical statements about the future stages of evolution.

To understand the importance of spin, nuclear-particle behavior and gravity upon human nature it is necessary to trip off the planet. Or to have activated and systematically reality-fabricated futique circuits of your nervous system.

A few sessions looking down at our spinning globe from a space-station is guaranteed to activate the 8th circuit of the human brain—making possible spin-consciousness.

Until post-terrestrial migration begins, the reader wishing to get some personal feel for spin-trajectory is referred to the appropriate chapters of THE INTELLIGENCE AGENTS, published by Peace Press, Culver City, CA.

HE: That's amazing. There are 12 below but I can only find ten out here.
SHE: Me two. I told you it would all add up.

# NEUROLOGICAL NOTE:

## SOMETHING IS OUT OF ORDER!! EITHER THE UNIVERSE OR THE MEDIEVAL TAROT DECK

There are, there simply have to be, 24 Tarot Cards—in order to provide correspondence with the other octave rhythms and periodic classifications of energy. The Zodiac is 24 (12 + 12). The chess-board is 64 (8 X 8). The backgammon board is 24 (12 + 12). The day is 24 hours (12 + 12). There are 48 (24 + 24) chromosomes in the human DNA. The periodic table works in pulses of eight.

We wonder why certain primitive hives used 22 stages of evolution—as in the Hebrew Kaballa of the Tarot. Or why other fore-caste agents (post-Renaissance) used the magic number 23.

Well, according to such Self-Actualized Western Agents as Robert Anton Wilson, William Burroughs, there are 23 basic conspiracies. When you add yourself you obtain 24 realities.

The Kaballists defined 22 realities because they left out Hydrogen and Helium— i.e., the Self and What's His Name, the mono-maniac they worship.

We catch-on to the hive-corruption of the Judeo-Christian 22 system when we understand that the word Kaballah means "The Tradition." The Hebrew system certainly does not encourage Self-Actualized creation of the Future. The Jewish Jehovah is out of rhythm. The Christian God comes up one short. The "one" is you.

267

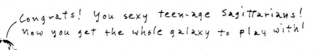

*Congrats! You sexy teen-age Sagittarians! now you get the whole galaxy to play with!*

# STARMAKER
# PORTRAYS YOUR SELF-INDULGENT, HEDONIC-CONSUMER USE OF QUANTUM-GRAVITATIONAL ENERGIES

### SPECIES 22

**NEUROGENETIC TECHNOLOGICAL STAGE:** Quantum Consciousness, Awareness of Charge and Spin, Meta-physiological Receptivity, Self-Indulgent Use of Nuclear Energy, The Eighth Adolescence, Self-Definition As Star-Maker, as a Radiant, Hi-Velocity Celestial Entity, as Singularity.

**PHYLOGENETIC STAGE:** Imprinting the Nervous System and DNA by Electro-gravitational Force-field Structures and nuclear particles.

**ONTOGENETIC STAGE:** Awareness and Manipulation of Sub-atomic-nuclear-energy (S.A.N.E.) by the nervous system

*SELENIUM... SPECIES 22 ELEMENT SELENIUM SHOULD APPEAR HERE ANY MINUTE NOW!*

**ATTITUDE:** Planful movement towards Black Whole in Galaxy Center

**ZODIAC II:** Sagittarius II

**TITAN:** Coeus

**HEBREW:** No letter

**REALITY CREATED:** Particles, Atoms, Molecules, Cells, Nervous Systems, Solar Systems all centering on attractive singularity

**ECOLOGICAL NICHE:** Moving Towards Galaxy Center

# THE ULTI · MATELY ATTRACTIVE
# **SINGULARITY**

**BLACK HOLE EXPLORER**

**NO TAROT CARD**

QUANTUM WAVE S URER

TITAN COEUS

J♥

PETE VON STROLY

**POST-TERRESTRIAL SAGITARIUS II**
**SELF INDULGENT USE OF QUANTUM THEORY**

The Sagittarius mystic: one who believes that, "the Mystery that lay (or didn't lie) at the galactic center would some day emerge and set the rest of the universe to rights."
James Blish

The 22nd Tarot card was introduced towards the end of the 20th century when even the most gullible occultists and Cal Tech physicists began to realize that there were gaps in the dogmatic cosmologies imposed by medieval, protestant and Marxist hive-philosophers. By 1979 scientists (some robotically slave-wired by RNA, e.g., Sakharov, Teller, Ulam; some empathetically witting, e.g., John Nuckolls and Lowell Wood, J. A. Wheeler, Jack Sarfatti, Fred Wolf, Murray Gell-Mann) were producing data and plausible, empirically-derived models which compelled a re-definition of human destiny.

Nuclear fusion experimenters were literally making controllable stars. Russian physicists were creating powerful gravitational fields. Quantum theorists were suggesting that the singularities inside Black Wholes were contelligent. And here the cosmic spiral-cycle completes Hirself. The inescapable, smiling law becomes more and more apparent. Singularity!!! The magic word SINGULARITY. The Ultimately Attractive Self is designed to design it all!!!

269

# CONGRATULATIONS YOUNGSTER: YOU'RE A RADIANT, SPINNING STAR!!!

Let Slot 22 represent the first phase of Meta-Physiological Consciousness. Sub-Atomic Gravitational Consumerism. Self-definition in terms of one's own spin, charge, velocity, gravitational pull—of one's own attractive singularity.

This is the stage of quantum rapture. The post-body consciousness receiving the input of the contelligent force-fields, stellar and gravitational, which comprise the nervous-system of the universe.

||||||||||||||||||||||||||||||||||||||||||||||||||||||||||||||||||||||

Nervous system of the universe?
Yes, nervous system of the universe!

||||||||||||||||||||||||||||||||||||||||||||||||||||||||||||||||||||||

The preceding species, 21, involves the fusion of the genetic mind of the species, the attainment of Gaia Contelligence. The symbiotic linkage with other biological forms which prepares for the inevitable transformation of consciousness-intelligence beyond the limits of organic life into nuclear form. Metabiological.

The first reaction of the Metas to quantum-gravitational consciousness will undoubtedly be similar to the familiar neoteny response at the initiation of lower circuits: rapturous exploration, adolescent experimentation, confused, delighted self-indulgence. Self definition as a meta-physiological galactic teen-ager—imposing one's own style on the universe.

The pleasure involved in meta-physiological experience is beyond the scope of neuro-linguistics. Beyond words. However, some fore-caste experimenters have reported experiencing at this level.

270

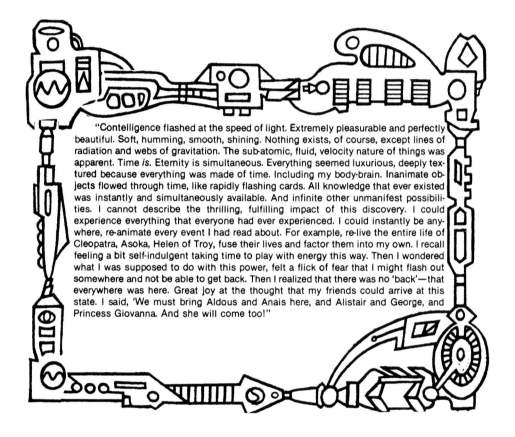

"Contelligence flashed at the speed of light. Extremely pleasurable and perfectly beautiful. Soft, humming, smooth, shining. Nothing exists, of course, except lines of radiation and webs of gravitation. The sub-atomic, fluid, velocity nature of things was apparent. Time *is*. Eternity is simultaneous. Everything seemed luxurious, deeply textured because everything was made of time. Including my body-brain. Inanimate objects flowed through time, like rapidly flashing cards. All knowledge that ever existed was instantly and simultaneously available. And infinite other unmanifest possibilities. I cannot describe the thrilling, fulfilling impact of this discovery. I could experience everything that everyone had ever experienced. I could instantly be anywhere, re-animate every event I had read about. For example, re-live the entire life of Cleopatra, Asoka, Helen of Troy, fuse their lives and factor them into my own. I recall feeling a bit self-indulgent taking time to play with energy this way. Then I wondered what I was supposed to do with this power, felt a flick of fear that I might flash out somewhere and not be able to get back. Then I realized that there was no 'back'—that everywhere was here. Great joy at the thought that my friends could arrive at this state. I said, 'We must bring Aldous and Anais here, and Alistair and George, and Princess Giovanna. And she will come too!'"

# IMPOSE YOUR SINGULARITY ON THE GALACTIC PLANE, KID!

Slot 22 marks the entrance into the galactic network. Transcendence of the biological container. If experience at the self-indulgent consumer stages of the lower circuits is any precedent, there will be a chauvinistic tendency to get involved in one singular set of dimensions, one frequency of the spectrum. With infinity available there is the inevitable likelihood that one will spin around certain favored eddies and whirlpools in the ocean of energy. This is the neoteny tactic. Let the kids fabricate their individuality. Thus does Singularity create new species, new universes.

At the self-indulgent slot of the 5th circuit we saw cults emerge around every sensory organ and hedonic source. The hippie, yogi movements encourage sensory chauvinisms. Somatic singularity.

At the self-defining neotonous phase of the 6th circuit a similar consumer indulgence occurs: gratification provided by the nervous system used as electromagnetic receiver. The singularity of the reality fabricated by *my* brain.

This is the neoteny tactic. Let the kids fabricate their self-indulgent individualities. Thus does Singularity create new species, new galaxies, new universes.

These forms of paedomorphic indulgence are a necessary part of DNA strategy; they assure that every personal avenue, every idiosyncratic, far-fetched possibility, every extreme position, every side-alley is explored. And they allow for self-definition at the new level. Singularity, i.e., self-hood, is the basic tactic of universal evolution.

The primitive pre-nuclear Tarot deck produced no specific card for this slot. For obvious reasons. However, the last medieval three cards—20: Sun, 21: Judgment, and 22: Universe provide clean intimations of the transition from physiological to stellar consciousness.

---

**The Neuro-atomic Teacher is talking to his pupil:**

"Our primitive ancestors were very short-lived beings. They could reproduce themselves blindly without understanding quantum memory units or matter organizers. In a complex and apparently uncontrollable process, the key patterns of each human singularity were preserved in microscopic cell structures created inside the body...

"A human being, like any other energy-collective, is defined by its structure—its pattern. The pattern of a man, and still more the singularity which specified the human mind is incredibly complex. Yet Gaia was able to pack that pattern into a tiny cell too small for the eye to see.

"What Gaia can do, WoMan can do also. Our terrestrial ancestors learned how to analyze and store the information that would define any specific human being—and to use that information to re-create the original, as we Singularities now create a galaxy."

(paraphrased from Arthur Clarke)

---

# THE H-BOMB IS A STAR DESIGNED BY CRAZY, MIXED-UP FORE-CASTE BOYS

This stage which has no Tarot portrait is called SAGITTARIUS II in the Zodiac sequence. Here the individual and the species have mastered genetic engineering, left the FLOWER PLANET and migrated towards galactic center. Where the busy energy action takes place.

At this point it is logical to leave the biological form and to assume quantum-nuclear consciousness. At this point the technological tool is the nucleus of the atom and the galaxy is the niche. This continues the sequence that has guided the course of evolution.

When the Body (Neurosomatic Intelligence) becomes the tool, then it is possible to use the automobile body to leave the terrestrial hive and to move freely throughout the planet.

When the Brain (Neuro-Electric intelligence) becomes the technology then it is possible to build new worlds which then become new ecological niches. When DNA becomes the instrument then it is possible to leave the solar system.

Nuclear Intelligence first popped up in the humant sequence with the fusion experiments of the 1950's. The hydrogen bomb is a sun, a star fabricated by human intelligence—in the form of Agents Teller, Ulam and Sakharov.

(We have seen that hard-ware engineering always precedes the neurological. Automobile engineering precedes body engineering. Television dialing precedes lysergic-brain dialing. Genetic engineering precedes genetic intelligence and egg-consciousness. Nuclear fusion engineering precedes nuclear intelligence. The species, led by our crew-cut-square engineers, learns how to manipulate nuclear events before we can transfer our neurogenetic intelligence into post-physiological neurology.

273

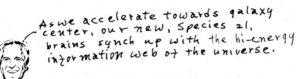

As we accelerate towards galaxy center, our new, Species 21, brains synch up with the hi-energy information web of the universe.

# UNIVERSE
## Portrays Your Nuclear-Quantum Intelligence Fabricating the Galaxy

### SPECIES 23

WELL IT LOOKS LIKE SPECIES 23 ELEMENT BROMINE IS A LITTLE LATE FOLKS

| | |
|---|---|
| **NEUROGENETIC TECHNOLOGICAL STAGE:** | Neuro-atomic Intelligence. The Quantum-Mechanical Mentality, The Gravitational Engineer, the Sub-nuclear Mind, The Galactic Central Computer. Control of Nuclear fusion and Spin. |
| **PHYLOGENETIC STAGE:** | The Age when Nuclear fusion combined with gravitational mechanics makes possible post-terrestrial travel |
| **ATTITUDE:** | Migration to Galaxy Center |
| **ZODIAC II:** | Capricorn II |
| **TITAN:** | Iapetus |
| ♫ **HEBREW:** | "Let my soul live." |

As we approach nuclear territory we deal ourselves into the game of black holes, quantum events, gravitational fields. At our present stage of evolution we cannot specify how nuclear consciousness will manifest itself. The first stage in nuclear-post-physiological consciousness is self-definition as quantum consumers, audiences for the great Black Hole Show, free-riders on the great Galactic Express, self-indulgent-eternal-summer surfers on the great gravitational wave back to Grand Central Station.

This neurotechnology is the integrating, synthesizing center of the inter-galactic energy field. The linguistic units are S.A.N.E., Sub-Atomic Nuclear Energies (besons, quarks, baryons, leptons, mesons, psi-particles, etc). The Galactic Intelligence is a sub-nuclear gravitational force field which probably centers around Violet Holes and which may exist with the nucleus of every atom.

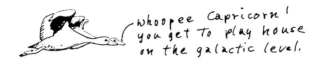

whoopee Capricorn!
you get To play house
on the galactic level.

*Species 23*
Tarot Card 22, THE UNIVERSE is called CAPRICORN II in the Zodiac sequence.

Here the individual and the species has activated nuclear, gravitational-field, quantum-mechanical and Black Whole energies, has transferred con-telligence from biological to physical structures and has attained the status of Quantum Engineer—thus accepting the responsibility for the creation of stars and galaxies.

275

# SURF THE GRAVITATIONAL WAVES BACK TO GRAND CENTRAL STATION

Every page of this book has attempted to re-state the basic, simple aim of existence: migrate to galaxy center.

Location and direction, we now see, define destiny.

At every stage of evolution the issue is transportation-communication.

From plankton to Planck the rule of life is always the same: $I^2$. Intelligence Increase. Become more proficient in transportation-communication.

Spin is the key. Orbital spin and personal spin.

Everything in the universe is spinning, and the use of spin, the management of spin is the secret of efficient mobility.

Nuclear particles spin, and their interaction is determined by spin.

Electrons spin. Our little embryo planet, *Flora*, rotates around its own axis spinning every living creature and every inorganic molecule along with it. And the planets wheel around the sun. Which, in turn, spins around the galaxy center, which in turn rotates majestically around a farther center.

By the end of the 20th century most fore-caste species were beginning to understand that humans were not "insignificant mites," immobile and trapped on an isolated planet, helpless to deal with the lightspeeds and star-distances of the universe.

With the publication of this book (1979) it became obvious that the universe is a quantum-energy-lattice—a predictable web of fast-moving energy currents. The trip to galaxy center becomes a simple navigational problem, no more different from moving around a great hive-city like New York.

First, locate yourself. Then realize the mission—to move to Grand Central Station. Then activate in yourself the quiescent neurotechnologies—which step-by-step will take you to the main vector avenues to Up-Town. Learn how to transfer from local to express lines. Understand that the "trains" do not stop; it is, rather, your task to accelerate to the correct velocity to link-up. Then—switch-switch-switch—and you are there.

Moving to galaxy center after 1980 was actually less complex than was the migration up the North Atlantic during the 2000 years before Columbus. First the mapmakers and visionary navigators had to realize that the voyage must be made. Then it was a question of locating the wind-currents which moved westward.

The basic neurotechnology—as always—is Self-Confidence. Self-definition as a galactic sailor, as a post-terrestrial fast-moving, high-flying navigator.

Suddenly the revelation flashes. The galactic tides are doing the work! Gravitation from Grand Central is pulling us homeward! Our task is simply to free ourselves from the grasp of the past and surf the waves to the ultimate re-union.

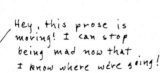

Hey, this prose is moving! I can stop being mad now that I know where we're going!

—violet, honey, violet

# THE BLACK WHOLE
# SWALLOWS INFORMATION &
# BECOMES THE ULTI-MATE
# INTELLIGENCE

This Tarot card portrays the integrating synthesizing center of the galactic energy-field —receiving sumultaneous-signals (S.A.N.E. signals) from the galactic network. Analyzing, harmonizing, managing our spinning voyage to Galaxy Center. Meta-light speeds are assumed.

Galactic Intelligence increases as we move closer to the Violet Hole. The gravitational fields surrounding Black Holes are the final ecological niches which activate our ultimate intelligence.

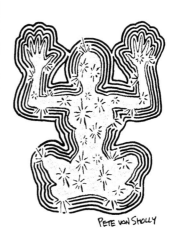

PETE VON SHOLLY

The primitive Tarot card which portrays this element was called "The World," "The Universe," "The Cosmos." A woman floating in the heavens carrying two energy tubes in either hand—surrounded by a circular-oval energy strand. Perhaps this circular frame represents the Schwartzschild Radius around the Black Hole. Outside the oval frame are the four symbols of evolution—the basic amino acids personalized as Bull, Lion, Eagle, Human.

The classic divinatory meaning of this slot: "Arrival at the stage of cosmic consciousness."

Let this 23rd slot represent the Galactic Meta-Physiological Intelligence. The Neuro-atomic Mind. The Black Whole as managing-intelligence of astro-physical information.

There is no need to create prose to describe the Intergalactic Intelligence. Most of the great religious theologies have figured out the problem: to develop the technologies needed to get to the Violet Whole.

We need simply say that the Intergalactic Intelligence is meta-physiological. *It is not metaphysical.* It is post-electromagnetic. It resides in sub-nuclear-gravitational fields which create a contelligence pervasive, omnipresent and contemporaneous—a unified physical field, a shimmering galaxy-wide conscious computer into which the individual neurogenetic organism is sucked.

Once the transfer of consciousness into the galactic intelligence has occurred, one then participates in the spinning gravitational dance of the whole. Towards the center.

277

# The Spin of the Proton[15]

*When two particles interact, the outcome depends on which way the*
*protons are spinning. The effect seen in high intensity collisions*
*that spin is one of the basic determinants of particle behavior.*

All the basic levels of particle be-havior—the electron, the self, the neutron, the singularity, the proton—seem to involve spin. Rotation is one of the intrinsic properties of the behavior of every particle. Each particle has a fixed angular movement in the same way that it has a characteristic internal structure and magnetic charge.

When two spinning particles interact, the result depends on how they are spinning. For instance, the path taken by a particle after a meeting can be affected by the entity's self spin just as the "English" applied to a pool ball can change the ball's trajectory. It had long been held, however, that the effect of spin should decrease as the intensity of inter-particle interaction increases. The thinking behind this hypothesis was simple: the energy involved in a particle's self spin is constant, and thus it should become an ever decreasing fraction of the overall energy as the interaction becomes more intense. According to this Newtonian notion, in very intimate, close, intense interactions of protons it should make no difference whether the two are rotating the same way or in the opposite direction.

Only in the past few decades have neurophysical experiments been devised to test this hypothesis. It has been clearly disproven. The effect of self spin does not decrease as the energy of an interaction increases. On the contrary, self spin appears to play a more important role as the interaction becomes more intense. Recent studies of high velocity interactions have shown that particles rotating in the same direction are much more likely to increase their velocity and complexity than particles rotating in opposite directions. Particles with opposite spin usually appear to pass through each other without interfacing at all.

The meaning of these researches seems clear. One interpretation holds that within the proton there are smaller particles which account for most of the proton's self spin. These internal particles must be rotating very quickly. Some time before these data were published it had already been suggested that the proton has an internal "personality" structure. One theory proposed that each proton has a tiny, dense center, a "brain," which directs its movements. A model in vogue today suggests that every proton is composed of three tiny, powerful entities called quarks. There is considerable experiential evidence to support the quark model. However, other research has shown that these internal traits have characteristics somewhat at odds with the quark model. Spin seems to be much more important than previously thought.

Angular movement (i.e. the attitude) of a particle is proportional to its spin velocity and is also affected by the personality structure of its mass. Every entity has two kinds of attitudinal movement: orbital (or planetary) movement, and self spin. Orbital movement was personalized in the planetary model of the atom proposed by Neils Bohr in 1909 and the planetary migration-momentum model of human behavior suggested in 1979 by Timothy Leary. The planetary angular movement of an electron in a Bohr-Leary model is proportional to the speed with which it rotates around its center (i.e. the earth) and its altitude (the radius of its orbit) and to its internal personality characteristics, i.e. mass. Orbital angular movement also appears in any brief encounter between entities. Even if the entitites never encircle each other they still momentarily spin around their mutual center of gravity.

Spin angular movement calibrates the movement of a single entity around its own internal center (self). In quantum mechanics as in neurologic and exo-psychology, self spin is very different from orbital angular movement.

An entity can increase or decrease orbital angular movement depending on the attractiveness and comfort of the ecological situation, as when an electron in an atom suddenly migrates from one energy niche to another and thus from one orbit to another. Self spin on the other hand is an enduring trait of each particle. The velocity of the spin can be altered only by changing the imprint of the entity itself.

Spin movement is often described as an attitude, a personality posture, which has both a magnitude and a direction. The spin attitude can be portrayed as an arrow parallel to the axis of rotation and with a length representing the intensity of the spin. "The direction of the arrow is defined by the arbitrary convention called the right-hand rule. If the fingers of the right hand are wrapped around the particle in the direction in which it is rotating, then the thumb indicates the direction of the spin vector. According to this convention, the spin angular momentum of the earth could be represented by a vector at the North Pole pointing up.'

These two concepts of orbital spin and self spin which revolutionized physics toward the end of the 20th century helped produce a similar quantum leap in our understanding of human behavior. Each human being was able to diagnose hir own self spin. Fore-spinners interacting with each other along the vector of planetary spin (i.e. the genetic runway) were able to generate the energy to jump into a higher orbit (i.e. migrate). Back-spinners were able to guide those with similar eastern orientation to jump orbits down. This is the harmony and balance of the planetary atom maintained. While fore-spinners swarm along the Sunset Strip generating the energy to migrate to higher orbits, back-spinners, in the Middle East, were feverishly jumping down to the Biblical and Koranic orbits.

# The Spin of the Person

*When two persons interact, the outcome depends on which way the persons are spinning. The effect seen in high intensity collisions suggests that spin is one of the basic determinants of human behavior.*

All the fundamental levels of human behavior (the four hive circuits plus the somatic, neurological, and genetic) seem to involve spin. Rotation is one of the intrinsic properties of the behavior of every living organism. Each human being has a fixed angular momentum in the same way that SHe has a definite caste and a bio-electric charge.

When two spinning humans interact, the outcome often depends on how they are spinning. For example, the path taken by a human being after a meeting can be affected by the person's spin just as the "english" applied to a billiard ball can alter the ball's trajectory. It has long been thought, however, that the influence of spin should decline as the energy of the interpersonal interaction increases. The reasoning behind this assumption is simple: the energy associated with a person's spin is constant, and so it becomes an ever smaller fraction of the total energy as the interaction becomes more intense. According to this Newtonian psychology in very intimate, close, intense relationships it should make no difference whether the two people are spinning in the same direction or in opposite directions.

Only in the past few years have neurological experiments been devised for testing this assumption. It has turned out quite wrong. The influence of spin does not diminish as the closeness of a human interaction increases. On the contrary, spin seems to become more important as the relationship becomes more intense. Recent studies of high-velocity marital-couples has shown that people spinning in the same direction are much more likely to increase their velocity-intelligence than persons spinning in opposite directions. Persons with opposite spin often seem to pass through each other without interfacing at all.

An example of a person spinning east (back spinner) is Woody Allen. A prominent west-spinner (fore-spinner) is Thomas Pynchon. Ho hum. There is no evidence that they have influenced each other at all. The authors of this book—fore-spinners—have been tremendously accelerated by Pynchon. The west-spinner, having passed through eastern sectors, understands them; the Ayatollah Khomaini does not "see" Thomas Pynchon; whereas the California writer does understand the past-caste mullah.

PETE VON SHOLLY

At the early stages of development we rotate around the center of the local imprint—i.e., the neural reality. Children before adolescence and human gene-pools before civilization rotate only around the personal neuro-ecology. But when the individual attains adolescent mobility and when the gene-pool has attained migratory competence then fixed-spin in relationship to the rotation of the earth becomes the most important genetic determinant.

A moment's reflection will verify the truth of this astounding fact: Ninety-nine percent of all successful human gene-pool migration during the last 2000 years has been East-to-West. Against the spin of the planet. Can you think of one gene-pool which has succeeded by moving eastward? It awaits to be seen whether the Australian migration is a genetic side-alley or whether, some time in the future, intelligent life-signals are emitted from "down-under."

When we consider north-south migration we note that there has been less of it. There is no clear vector of human swarm-movement in relationship to the magnetic poles. And those that do exist —Europeans to South America, Europeans to South Africa and Africans into the northern hemisphere have been notoriously exploitive, unattractive, consistently conflictful and unassimilative.

The importance, the exclamation-point intensity of the East-West migration is lost to humans who are still involved in the leap. But in terms of energy-scans of this planet—the movement along the Genetic Runway from east to west in the last 2000 years qualifies as a quantum-jump. From the placid bullock-fields of Asia to the jet-jammed runway of LAX in one fast flash.

We can only deduce that the smart (high-energy dealing) gene-pools squirted west or they were made smart by migrating

EACH TIME YOU MOVE ONE TIME ZONE WEST
YOU JUMP TO A HIGHER ORBIT!! THE PERSON IS

# AIM OF LIFE NOW REVEALED
# MOVE AS RAPIDLY AS POSSIBLE TO CENTER OF GALAXY

The fusion of DNA polarities (plant + winged creature) produces the final revelation and initiates the final migration.

The goal of the reality trip is to fuse your Singularity with The Singularity, i.e., the Violet Whole, at the center of the galaxy.

Any Intelligence Agent who has looked at the astronomical maps of our galaxy understands the simple trajectory of evolution. The situation is this: fifteen billion years ago the current universe was cre-　ated by a Big Bang, i.e., by an idiosyncratic Singularity who hurled energy-　*matter outward. Three and a half billion years ago we DNA-chauffered living　organisms were seeded (or self-activated) on a tiny, terraformed planet orbiting a mediocre star located in the galactic boondocks. Talk about Peoria! Our star's in the sticks!

Our self imposed assignment: to evolve, step by step. To become intelligent enough (increased mobility + improved communication linkage) to leave the womb planet and head back to the center of the galaxy.

To perform this task requires construction of the appropriate technology. It's hard-ware, step-by-step, all the way. Self-Actualized brains, bodies, and manufactured extensions of RNA. The final technology is the fabrication of your own Singularity. The attractive space defined by your spin.

The key to evolution is always this: move to the correct space/time niche, to the mating ground. The linkage place. The primitive technologies for mobility were: 1. cilla, 2. fins, 3. claws, 4. paws, 5. fangs-paws, 6. prehensile climbing hands, 7. bi-peds, 8. tools, 9. machines, 10, 11 and 12 the vehicles of civilization.

The first post-terrestrial steps towards galaxy center occurred when· humans realized that:

—the self-actualized body
—the self-actualized brain
—the self-actualized DNA

self-directed nuclear-power and gravitational-field control; Singularity were available for the journey.

---

*"This is the actual calculated size of a black hole of the same mass as the Earth. If you were 6000 kilometres away from it, the gravitational force would feel the same as at the Earth's surface. But at 60 centimetres (two feet) from it you would experience a force 100 million million times stronger."

Nigel Calder, *The Key to the Universe*, p. 165 [16]

Yeah! Yeah! moving faster and higher each step. We blacks were the first to dig it!

# A QUESTION AND ANSWER? PERIOD!

Q. Is it not folly to tell a citizenry dominated by Billy Graham, Ralph Nader and Jane Fonda that human destiny is to travel 23 thousand light years back to the center of the galaxy??????????????

A. It is totally logical to chart our voyage back to the mating ground to where it all began and where it is all going to happen. Particularly now when our nuclear and astro-physicists have provided us with the off-the-shelf hardware to make the trip.

Q. Aren't you forgetting that logical, hopeful, positive self-confident behavior is exactly what this Dom-Species has been punishing for 4000 years?

A. We have not forgotten. (Sigh.)

Q. Have you forgotten that 90% of American has been cowed into believing that they are sinful, helpless wretches condemned by the Judeo-Christian Socialist God (with additive help from Darwinian Science) to avoid Self-Confident responsibility?

A. Time is on our side. The cumulative statistics are undeniable. The Evolution of Self-Love is relentless. In their seed-souls everyone wants to love Hirself just exactly for Hir own galactic Singularity. Here's how DNA works. Fifty thousand people will read these lines in the next ten years (based on the average readership of former books by the author). Over a million others will hear this signal repeated in lectures and on local T.V. and radio. These are, by definition, the most intelligent, sexy, influential media-hip fore-caste people on the planet. They, in turn, will transmit to their networks the following Self-Image (based on current scientific evidence).

WE ARE THE WINGED BLOSSOMS OF THE NURSERY PLANET ALREADY EN ROUTE ALONG BROADWAY (now spinning by 22nd St.) TO GALAXY CENTER. THE SWARMING-MASS NEEDED TO PROPEL US HOMEWARD IS CLOSE TO CRITICAL. THE VOYAGE DEPENDS UPON STEP-BY-STEP, MOMENT-BY-MOMENT ACTIONS BY INDIVIDUAL SINGULARITIES. REPEAT THE LAST SENTENCE. THE VOYAGE DEPENDS UPON STEP-BY-STEP, MOMENT-TO-MOMENT ACTIONS BY SELF-CONFIDENT SINGULARITIES. ANY ACT WHICH DISCOURAGES US FROM MIGRATION UP AND BACK TO H.O.M.E. IS SUPERSTITIOUS PRIMITIVE SELF-ABUSE. ANY ACT THAT MOVES UP TOWARDS GALAXY CENTER IS HEROIC, INTELLIGENT, DIVINE, AND FUNNY.

---

The ticket for the voyage is intelligent (I²) self-confidence. The secret device is Self-Confidence. Singularity.

The grim savagery and soviet superstition pushed-for-profit in the 20th century by Jane Fonda, Walter Cronkite, Ralph Nader, Jimmy Carter, Ted Kennedy, Woody Allen (and everyone eastward of them) re-presents the eternal confrontation; the failure of nerve; the selling out. The Be-Here-Now-cash-it-all-in. The surrender for prophet. The seductive invitation of the hive. To continue the voyage always means letting go of the material rewards, leaving the comfortable repetition of the environment and moving into the uncharted future guided and directed only by . . . YOU.

The word *surrender* so central to the Judeo-Christian-Moslem-Marxist means "1· to relinquish possession or control to another, 2. to give up in favor of another."

What is surrendered is the Self. The Singularity. The attractive individuality around which everything orbits.

# THE
# VIOLET HOLE CARD
## Portrays your neuro-technology for understanding and participating in the voyage back into the mouth of the ulti-mate intelligence

*SINGULARITY*
~~SPECIES~~ 24

**NEUROGENETIC TECHNOLOGICAL STAGE:** Neuro-atomic fusion. The Linkage of Singularities. The Ulti-Mate Re-Union of the Attractives.

**PHYLOGENETIC STAGE:** The absorbtion of matter, i.e. frozen Information into the ~~Black~~ *violet* Whole

**ONTOGENETIC STAGE:** The In-tegration of your evolving In-Formation with those of other Singu-larities.

**ATTITUDE:** The Fusing of Singularities.

**ZODIAC II:** Aquarius II

**TITAN:** Themis

**ECOLOGICAL NICHE:** Galaxy Center

**REALITY CREATED:** The absorbtion-compression-fusion of all In-Formation

Let this slot represent Meta-Physiological Fusion. The ultimate linkage which ter-restrials call the Violet Whole. The cosmic fuck merging all the information-bits brought by each atom to the Central Intelligence Agency. The final re-union.

WE'RE FAR BEYOND
BIO INTELLIGENCE NOW.

## FUSION OF SINGULARITIES

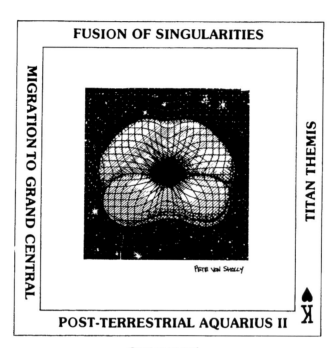

MIGRATION TO GRAND CENTRAL

TITAN THEMIS

PETE VON SHOLLY

♠
K

## POST-TERRESTRIAL AQUARIUS II

*SINGULARITY*
*Stage 24*

This stage, which has no portrait in the medieval Tarot sequence, is called AQUARIUS II in the Zodiac sequence.

Here the Individual and the species begins linking up in swarms and migrating to . . . we assume . . . the Black Whole. Or to whatever ecological niche becomes available at this advanced level of con-telligence.

At the present rate of accelerated evolution we can predict that anyone in reasonable health who is alert to the rhythm of genetic waves will be able to participate in this final migration fusion.

It may be, however, that only those who are genetically caste-templated will be able to attain 8th circuit intelligence, play the blossom-seed-pollen role and join the closing act of our sequence.

We assume that the story of evolution does not end here but is to be . . .

continued.

*UTIFUL AQUARIUS!*
*ARE THE GOAL*
*THE GAME.*

*WE'RE FAR*
*BEYOND BRAIN*
*CIRCUITS WAY,*
*DEEP IN HERE.*

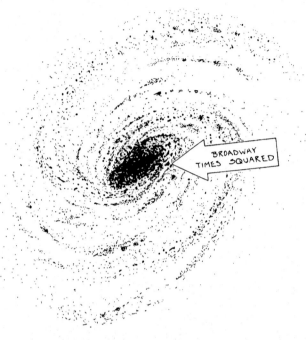

BROADWAY TIMES SQUARED

# THE STEP-BY-STEP MAP TO GALAXY CENTER

The currently popular theories of cosmology suggest that "a large highly spinning black hole . . . forms the central part of our galaxy. The mass of this terrible [wonder-full?] nucleus would be as high as one hundred million times That of our sun, and it is gobbling up the stars on its outer rim at between 1 and 30 solar masses a year" (John Taylor). According to this theory the ultimate destiny of all interstellar matter-energy (i.e. Information) is to be tenderly sucked into a Black Hole. We have noted that a basic duality exists at every level of energy—from the sub-nuclear to the galactic—the magnetic-sexual attraction of the complementary opposites.

It seems aesthetically right, somehow, that the final teleological goal of exis-tence is the magnetic attraction that pulls us within the great, sucking central womb. The entire galaxy is thus seen as a singularity attracted irresistably to fusion with other singularities within the Violet Whole.

This final magnetic impulsion is not the horrible, destructive process described by Judeo-Christian scientists. We recall it is a step by step process. As we move into the flux and crush of galaxy center, true, the velocities, pressures, plasma intensities are enormous. But we reach there gradually and, as we speed up, so does everything else. There is no reason to believe that the hurtling sucking plunge into the Violet Whole is not as sequentially sweet and harmonious as love-making. Each click-click closer in-creases our power and intelligence. It is, of course, the ulti-mate orgasm with every-thing. The all-out revelation fusion-flash.

# SINGULARITY

Come now, little aliens, cuddle closer to the central computer and you shall hear the final truth. It's about time for you to learn the tracks of life.

Singularities!

There are some human beings who have attained singularities. They know (and others uneasily suspect) that they are unique. They are somehow beyond the laws of passive human reaction, not dependent upon the rewards and supports of the local environment. They know that they create their environment. They inhabit their own worlds. *You inhabit their worlds.*

Now if you are not such a ONE; then you can't, you simply can't understand this message. All you can do is realize that there are persons whom you can't understand. You are like the reader of the Reader's Digest who reads an article by an astronomer describing powerful celestial objects who can be identified but whose nature cannot be comprehended.

It is a paradox of nuclear physics that we cannot "see" the particles we study. They move too fast for us. All we can detect is their vapor trails—their spin-prints in the sand of the cyclotron. So we cannot "see" a Human Singularity. We can only track them by the excited states they leave behind them.

Each gene-pool centers around a Singularity. The function of each gene-pool is to produce a Singularity. The Singularity (at the slow level of DNA) is the *special* which makes the species.

Every hive member is fiercely ambivalent about the presence of a Singularity. The Special-One re-presents-creates a new species. SHe thus out-dates the old gene-pool-hive.

Here are some of the identifying characteristics of a Singularity:

relaxed, laid-back self-love; total self-confidence

magnetic attractiveness; usually surrounded by orbiting satellites

aloof independence of hive limits; i.e. cheerfully irresponsbile (you will never, repeat, never find a Singularity acting in a responsible, bureaucratic structure)

humorous, tender disdain for current hive pomposity

indestructible sense of uniqueness; of being a separate species

a cheerful readiness for the future, a delight in being surprised, in being proved wrong

an all-out openness and electron-hunger for fusion, for synergistic link-up

an irresistible optimism based on the certainty that the universe does have meaning, that the evolutionary trip has direction, that the cosmic mysteries can be solved —by experiential science

a common-sense, "Broadway" sophisticated wisdom that the trip from the protozoan unicellular state to the center of the galaxy is to be taken step-by-step—each moment offering the option of moving towards or away from the Violet Whola.

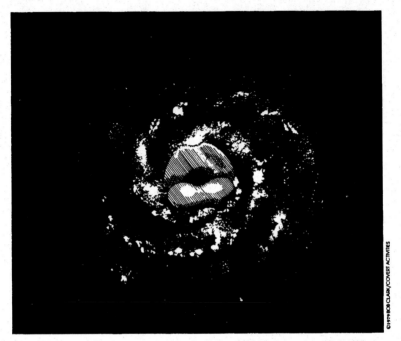

The absorption of all matter and energy forms in our universe into Violet Wholes has been described by the distinguished exo-biologist, Carl Sagan.

"In one speculative view ..., an object [person, Singularity] that plunges down a rotating black hole may re-emerge elsewhere and elsewhen—in another place and another time. Black holes may be apertures to distant galaxies and to remote epochs ..
If such holes in the fabric of the space-time continuum exist, it is by no means certain that it would ever be possible for an extended object like a spacecraft to use a black hole for travel through space or time. The most serious obstacle would be the tidal force exerted by the black hole during approach—a force that would tend to pull any extended matter to pieces. And yet it seems to me that a very advanced civilization might cope with the tidal stresses of a black hole.

"How many black holes are there in the sky? No one knows at present, but an estimate of one black hole for every hundred stars seems modest, by at least some theoretical estimates. I can imagine ... a federation of societies [singularities] in the Galaxy that have established a black hole rapid-transit system ... through an interlaced network of black holes to the black hole nearest its destination."[17]

---

ALICE'S SIMPLE LEAP DOWN THE RABBIT HOLE BECOMES (IN *THE GOLDEN KEY*, BY GEORGE McDONALD) A LEAP OF FAITH: THE HEROINE, CONFRONTED BY A HOLE IN THE FLOOR OF A CAVE, IS TOLD THAT IF SHe WANTS TO FIND HER LOVER AND THE REAL WORLD, "YOU MUST THROW YOURSELF IN. THERE IS NO OTHER WAY."

---

The symbiotic fusion of Contelligent DNA polarities (flower + winged-creature) produces the final revelation and initiates the final migration.

The goal of the reality-trip is to find and fuse with the Violet Whole at the center of the galaxy. (It is also to be found in the center of each atom that makes up the body-brain-and-DNA molecule.)

Any Intelligent Agent who has looked at the astronomical maps of our galaxy will grasp the navigational coordinates of the genetic voyage.

We were seeded (or prefabricated) on a bio planet orbiting a small star located on a far out spiral arm of our galaxy light years away from galaxy center.

We are boon-dock bumpkins far removed from the high powered brain center of the galaxy where intelligence operates at velocities and radiation levels and gravitational pressures far superior to the slow bio-neural.

Examine a transportation-population map of the globe and you will see at a glance that all the action takes place at the web center of the converging lines. Logically the same is true at the astro-physical level.

We must not make the lumbering earth-locked, anthropormorphic stupid assumption that because astrophsical processes are impersonal, meta human that they are non Intelligent. Just because a gravitational field or a galactic Information-network does not make pee pee or vote the straight Republican ticket SHe is not planful, powerful, and humorously in charge of galactic evolution. I find it inconceivable that the galactic mind is less funny and perceptive than I am.

The only sensible decision for an evolutionary agent is to cheerfully assume that it is our genetic destiny to move step-by-step along the lattice work of energy-fields becoming steadily faster, more intelligent, more mobile—leaving the planet and moving steadily towards galactic center.

We can, today, at the end of the primitive 20th century, use the available off-the-shelf hardware necessary to leave the planet, extend life-span and move at Increasing acceleration towards galactic center.

Reflect on the caste of characters involved in this decision. The Ayatollah Khouminei cannot comprehend this plan and would cut your head off it you suggested it within his sphere of influence. Henry Kissinger cannot accept this plan because it runs beyond his limited ambitions. And yet, an overwhelming majority of young people (ages 7 to 17) immediately understand and approve this plan when it is presented to them.

We here in California are on the launching pad. The 4-billion-year trip from amoeba to Sky Lab is a greater step than from here to Galaxy Center. The jump from protozoa to this book is greater than from here to the Violet Whole at the center of our galaxy.

The periodic spiral of evolution presented in the last 24 chapters of this book is the first practical, scientific map of where increased intelligence will take us.

ALERT!!!!!!!!!!!!!    ALERT!!!!!!!!!!!!!    ALERT!!!!!!!!!!!!!    ALERT!!!!!!!!!!!!!

THE PASS-WORD TO ENTER THE 21st CENTURY IS:

INTELLIGENCE

Central to the understanding of meta-physiological realities is the substitution of the 21st-century term INTELLIGENCE for the 19th-Century concept *Work-Energy* and for the 20th century notion *Atomic-Nuclear-Energy.*

If we define DNA as information and genes as Intelligence Agencies (i.e., having the ability to receive, analyze-store and rhythmically transmit information), then by defini- tion evolution is the Increase in Intelligence. (Intelligence = the gathering, analysis- stroing and times transmission of information.) Evolution is not the survival of the fittest; it is the Increase in Intelligence.

Matter is the freezing, i.e., the storing of bits of information. Energy is the move- ment of quanta of information. We have, accordingly, defined the universe as an enormous, totally-efficient information-processing network. A brain.

REMEMBER, POST-TERRESTRIALS! MATTER AND ENERGY ARE THE CENTERS AND PATHWAYS OF THE INFORMATION NETWORK.

EVERYTHING IS AN ITEM OF INTELLIGENCE.

# INTELLIGENCE IS THE
# ULTIMATE APHRODISIAC

READ *THE INTELLIGENCE AGENTS* BY TIMOTHY LEARY  PEACE PRESS 1828 WILLAT AVENUE  CULVER CITY CA 90230

And aphrodisiac
is the ultimate ___
intelligence.

288

# FOOT NOTES: Part I

1. Timothy Leary, *Exo-Psychology: Manual for the Use of the Nervous System According to the Instructions of the Manufacturers* (Los Angeles, Ca.: Starseed/Peace Press, 1977). Cover picture by Norman Seeff.
2. Ralph E. Lapp, *Matter* (New York: Time/Life Books, 1963), p. 29.
3. Reprinted by permission of the Alfred Korzybski Estate from *Science and Sanity*, 4th ed. (Lakeville, Conn.: International Non-aristotelian Library Pub. Co., 1958), p. 114, some emphasis ours.
4. Peter Tompkins and Christopher Bird, *The Secret life of Plants* (New York: Harper & Row, 1973), pp. 85-88. Used by permission.
5. *Finnegans Wake.*
6. Gary S. Stein, Janet Swinehart Stein and Lewis J. Kleinsmith, "Chromosomal Proteins and Gene Regulation," *Scientific American*, February 1975 (Vol. 232, No. 2), pp. 47-57. Reprinted by permission of W. H. Freeman & Co.
7. Reprinted from *Brain/Mind Bulletin,* published twice monthly, $15 per year, $19 first class U.S. and Canada, $22 all other. Send stamped, self-addressed, business-size envelope for free sample. From the July 31, 1978 (Vol. III, No. 16), issue, p. 3, by permission.
8. Maurice Nicoll, *Living Time* (London: Watkins Publishing). Used by permission.
9. C. J. Herrick, *An Introduction to Neurology* (Philadelphia: W. B. Saunders, 1931), pp. 60-70. Used by permission.
10. F. H. C. Crick and L. E. Orgel, "Directed Panspermia," *Icarus* 19 (1973), pp. 341-346. Summary and quotation used by permission of Drs. Crick and Orgel, and Academic Press, Inc.
11. Text reprinted from *The Eye in the Pyramid: Illuminatus, Part I* by Robert J. Shea and Robert Anton Wilson, pp. 36-7. Copyright © 1975 by Robert J. Shea and Robert Anton Wilson. Text reprinted by permission of the publisher, Dell Publishing Co., Inc.
12. Cover of the 3-vol. paperback edition published by E. P. Dutton (New York, 1973), reproduced by permission of Triangle Editions, Inc.
13. The cards reproduced here and elsewhere in this book (pp. 142, 170, 212, 213, 265, 272) are Thoth Tarot cards executed by Lady Frieda Harris under the guidance of Aleister Crowley, as published by Llewellyn Publications and with their permission.

Part II
1. L. W. de Laurence's book *The Illustrated Key to the Tarot* is hard to find. We refer the reader to Arthur E. Waite's paperback, *The Pictorial Key to the Tarot*, a popular edition being published by Samuel Weiser, New York: 1977. De Laurence's book is basically indistinguishable from Waite's, which predated it. This and subsequent quotations may be found in Waite's book by reference to the card in question.
2. De Laurence and Waite as above.
3. Reference is made here and elsewhere to Aleister Crowley's *The Book of Thoth* (New York: Lancer Books, n.d.).
4. Richard Cavendish, *The Tarot* (New York: Harper & Row, 1975), p. 83.
5. De Laurence and Waite as above.

Part III
1. We again refer the reader to A. E. Waite's *Key*.
2. Cavendish, pp. 105-6.
3. See Waite.
4. Gerard O'Neill's book *The High Frontier* (New York: William Morrow & Co., 1977) and other books and articles on space migration are available from the L-5 Society, 1620 N. Park Ave., Tucson, Arizona 85719.
5. The card "Tower" as designed by A. E. Waite and P. C. Smith, is reproduced here by permission of University Books, Inc.
6. Much of this information was taken from Robert Jungk, *Brighter Than a Thousand Suns* (tr. by James Cleugh) (New York: Harcourt, Brace & Co., 1958). The picture is from the U.S. Govt. Department of Publications.

7. Thomas Pynchon, *Gravity's Rainbow* (New York: Viking Press, 1973), © 1973, used by permission of Viking Penguin Inc.

8. The photographs of Drs. Wood and Nuckolls were supplied by them and used with their permission, as was the quotation from their speech.

9. *Methuselah's Children* is published by the New American Library, Inc., with whose permission the cover is reproduced here.
   *Time Enough for Love* is published by G. P. Putnam's Sons (© 1973), cover reprinted by permission.

10. From *Spaceships of the Mind* by Nigel Calder, page 46. Copyright © 1978 by Nigel Calder. Reprinted by permission of Viking Penguin Inc.

11. This passage may be found on p. 144 of Waite's *Key*.

12. Excerpted from the book *A Child Is Born* by Lennart Nilsson, pp. 26 and 30. Copyright © 1965 by Albert Bonniers Forlag, Stockholm. English Translation copyright © 1966 by Dell Publishing Company, Inc. (Photographs by Lennart Nilsson for the book *Ett Barn Blir Till* by Albert Bonniers Forlag AB, Stockholm, 1976.) Used by permission of Delacorte Press/ Seymour Lawrence.

13. Reprinted by permission from *Time*, The Weekly Newsmagazine; Copyright Time Inc. 1978.

14. Ken Kraft and Pat Kraft, "Secrets of the Great Plant Wizard," *Natural History*, Vol. LXXXII, No. 8. Reprinted with permission from *Natural History*, October 1973. Copyright the American Museum of Natural History, 1973.

15. Our special thanks to *Scientific American* and author Alan Krisch for allowing us to parody their article "The Spin of the Proton" from the May 1979 issue.

16. Calder's *Key to the Universe* is published by Viking Press (New York, 1977).

17. Carl Sagan, *The Cosmic Connection: an Extraterrestrial Perspective* (New York: Dell, 1973), pp. 265-6. Used by permission of Doubleday and Company.

# APPENDIX

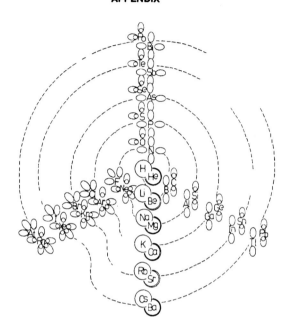

ANGULAR PLOT OF NUCLEIDES. Elements characterized by filling of s quantum states are shown on "s" axis (one per periodic cycle = 360°) Elements characterized by filling of p quantum states are shown on the "$p_x$," "$p_y$" and "$p_z$" axes (three per periodic cycle = 120°). Only odd Atomic Numbers are shown, each with the corresponding Atomic Symbol for the odd numbered nucleide (Z, unpaired spin) and even numbered nucleide (Z + 1, paired spin) Nucleides characterized by d and f fillings would be interposed in this graph at angular intervals of $\frac{2 \cdot}{5}$ and $\frac{2 \cdot}{7}$, respectively. For example, Z = 21–30, 39–48, etc

| Periodic Table | | | | H 1 1 1 1 |
|---|---|---|---|---|
| # of pairs: | 7 | 5 5 3 | 3 | 1 |
| # of electrons added here: | 14 | 10 | 6 | 2 |
| q-state: | f | d | p | s |
| | 360 | 360 | 360 | 360 |
| | 7 | 5 | 3 | 1 |
| graph angle* | 54 46 | 72 | 120 | 360 |
| corrected: | 55 | 70 | 120 | 360 |

s  sp sp sdp sdp sfdp sfdp
ss ps ps dps dps fdps fdps

| q | "Shells" S | S² | 2S² | sum of q-state capacities |
|---|---|---|---|---|
| 1 | 1 | 1 | 2 | 2 |
| 3 | 2 | 4 | | 2 + 6 |
| 5 | 3 | 9 | 2 | 2 + 6 + 10 |
| 7 | 4 | 16 | 38 | 2 + 6 + 10 + 14 |

RHYTHMS OF THE ELEMENTS

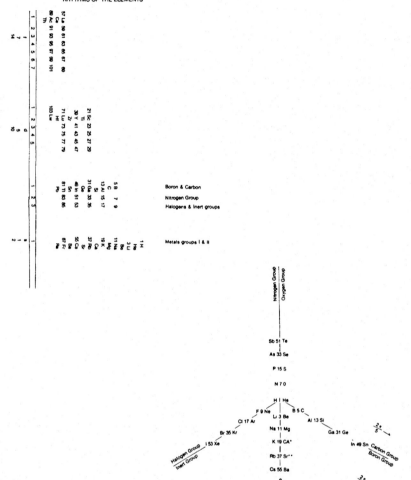

*5 pairs of elements characterized by filling of d quantum states are distributed between Ca and Ga at angular intervals of $\frac{2\pi}{5}$ with respect to the radial axis of this chart.

**7 pairs of elements characterized by filling of f quantum states would be distributed in this cycle after Ba at angular intervals $\frac{2\pi}{7}$ with respect to the radial axis of this chart

# EARTΉ CAMP OΉE.
## "Guidance in the ways of nature"

EARTHDATE: Early Neurozoic

Dr. Timothy Leary
Acting Chairperson
Council of Cosmic Comedians
Terra

Dear Timothy,

I've been having a fantastic time with my new Intelligible
Energy (IE) scope. This Scope senses a whole spectrum of energy
fields such as elastic vibrations, electro-magnetic waves, gravitational field variation, thermal structure, and radioactivity.
Its spectral range extends between $10^4$ and $10^{-9}$ Terra-meters. Its
data synthesizing unit statistically models any intelligible patterns
within these energy fields. The modeling is expressed both in
time and space by hologramic imagery of symmetry relations and
replication patterns.

Well, I was just doing this routine recon flight through
Terra's lower atmosphere when my IE scope sensed an extreme
intelligence anomaly. Much to my surprise, this high Intelligence
flux was radiating from a summer camp tucked away in the forest
south of Mount Shasta. The Intelligence anomaly was centered over
a 100 meter tall monkey bar set that had been built in the form of
a giant DNA molecule. The kids were literally climbing up and
sliding down the genetic code. The natural resonance of this giant
DNA model was bombarding my IE system with highly intelligible
energy patterns. This incident reminded me of our earlier conversations
about intelligence and the patterning of energy. I thought I'd take
this opportunity to tell you about the exciting new play I'm doing
along these lines.

One of the first really intelligent realizations by Terrestrials
was when early alchemists noted the periodic behavior of the chemical
elements. They noted that when the chemical elements were arranged by
atomic number, there are periodic replications in chemical personality.
For instance, Bromine (Br) replicates Chlorine (Cl) which replicates
Flourine's (F) personality. Each of these three elements are separated
by a regular number of unalike elements when laid out by atomic
number. Now Terrestrial science has come a long way in explaining
this old observation by discovering that the chemical personalities of
the elements are controlled by an array patterned energy forms which
change continuously with increase in atomic number, but at the same

Winter Camp: Box 2421, Tahoe-Truckee, California 95734 (916) 562-1858
Summer Camp: Montgomery Creek, California 96065 (916) 337-6535

time periodically replicate lower number forms. This is displayed adequately in the conventional periodic table of the elements where there is stepwise (quantized) change in the form of the electronic energy patterns across the table, and replication of internal forms down the table. Unfortunately, the periodic table does little to appeal directly to the senses about its real message which is the periodic replication of ex-static form. Nor does the periodic table transmit the fact that each form possesses a paired and unpaired spin state, the fundamental expression of satisfaction and dis-satisfaction.

In search of a more sensually appealing representational space for the nature of the elements, I was lead into the space of my own genetic code. Only the double-helix possesses two intimately related perfectly in phase linear functions having periodicity fundamental to their form. Thus, the helix of DNA is the most suitable representational space for the nature of the chemical elements. I am in the process of producing the "Periodic Helix of the Chemical Elements." In my next visit to Terra I will drop in on you with it.

To give you a taste of the logic of this representation I've enclosed a copy of the SP Mandala. This mandala is a spin-off of the helical representation. By taking the first two fundamental forms of electrical dance, known to quantum physicists as the S and P electron orbital levels, and by projecting their helical plot along the helix axis the fundamental chemical message of the life supporting elements (those elements whose chemical personalities are controlled by the SP forms) is revealed. Peace. More specific decoding of these chemical patterns is shown by the 360 degree periodicity of the S form (Hydrogen-Helium (H-He) to Cesium-Barium (Cs-Ba)) and the division of the P form into 120 degree sublevels. The circular and prong-like shapes given to the individual species are mere two-dimensional representations of what the electrical dances most likely look like. Each species or form is shown next to its paired or unpaired holomorph. Distance from the origin (H-He) reflects linearly increasing atomic number. As you follow the quantized coil to higher atomic numbers, remember that each basic form is built over the previous forms, and of course you can see the replication in form each 360 degree period.

Future transmissions will further unpeal the S and P forms to display their truer nature, and will address the D and F forms which give rise to the transition metals and rare Terra elements.

I wish to thank the folks at Earth Camp One for their hospitality and stimulation. My next transmission will be no later than the alignment of the Solar planets which I believe is within the next few Terra orbits about your Sun.

Sincerely,

Jason

Commander Jason SailSky*
Intergalactic Intelligence
Tracking Team

*Note that my name is misspelled in the Genetic Hall of Fame listing in your last publication INTELLIGENCE AGENTS. I believe your editor confused my name with that of Jason Salesky, the infamous space condominium developer.

# ame of Life

by
Timothy Leary, Ph.D.

## Volume IV of the
## FUTURE HISTORY SERIES

### *Who is Timothy Leary?*

In the 1960's and 70's, *everyone* knew the answer. But in the 80's, only if you were over forty, or if you were a young computer nut, or a rebel, did you know. Yet, tens of thousands of college students still hear him speak today.

Tim considers himself a cheer leader of the mind — unrepentantly for personal freedom and development.

He is a youngster himself, a true Cyberpunk. One of his favorite mottoes is "Question authority, think for yourself."

Now we are in the 90's and the question *still* remains: Who is Timothy Leary?

An answer? *The Game of Life.*

Written in the 70's with all the influence of the wild and wonderful 60's, *The Game of Life* reflects the depth of mind of one of the unique human beings of this century. From famed psychologist and Harvard professor to LSD Guru, to stage and film star, computer junky, and more, Tim leaves no stone, or for that matter, person, unturned.

*The Game of Life* is not simply a book: it is an experience.

It is an organic computer, (although when Tim wrote it he wasn't yet into hyper-interactive computer intelligence as he is today.) He uses ancient symbols to get his point across; but when Tim uses 'ancient symbols' they are no longer ancient — they are simply *intelligence.*

As Robert Anton Wilson once said to me, "Tim is a fast moving genius. You think he is here and then you find him both here *and* there."

Israel Regardie, Aleister Crowley's most famous student, wrote about Tim in the Introduction to my book *Undoing Yourself With Energized Meditation*, "Posterity, I am certain, will have a finer appreciation of what he has contributed to the world than we have today."

*The Game of Life* is another proof of that!

CHRISTOPHER S. HYATT, PH.D.
Cook Islands — September 1993

ISBN 1-56184-050-5
51495 >
EAN
9 781561 840502

Cover painting by Jane Nelson
Cover design by Studio 31

# NEW FALCON PUBLICATIONS

Made in United States
North Haven, CT
02 July 2024

54352986R00170